Rituals for Living and Dying

Also by David Feinstein

Personal Mythology: The Psychology of Your Evolving Self
(with Stanley Krippner)

Rituals for LIVING & DYING

From Life's Wounds to Spiritual Awakening

David Feinstein
and
Peg Elliott Mayo

 HarperSanFrancisco

A Division of HarperCollins*Publishers*

Supplemental Programs and Materials

An optional cassette tape that contains the guided imagery instructions presented in the second section of this book, "Cultivating an Empowering Mythology for Confronting Death," with meditative background music, is offered by Innersource for $9.95 plus $1 shipping ($2 for overseas airmail). Send check or money order to Innersource, P. O. B. 213, Ashland, OR 97520, for the tape and a brochure of other available books, tapes, and programs, or simply write for a free brochure.

Lines from "FOR A DANCER" by Jackson Browne on page 35, © 1974 SWALLOW TURN MUSIC. All rights reserved. Used by permission.

FIRST EDITION

Library of Congress Cataloging-in-Publication Data

Feinstein, David.
    Rituals for living and dying: from life's wounds to spiritual awakening.
David Feinstein and Peg Elliott Mayo.—1st ed.
        p. cm.
    Includes bibliographical references.
    ISBN 0-06-250329-4
    1. Death—Psychological aspects. 2. Mythology—Psychological
aspects. 3. Rites and ceremonies. 4. Spiritual life. I. Mayo,
Peg Elliott.   II. Title.
BF789.D4F456   1990
155.9'37—dc20   89-46454
                                                                                        CIP

90 91 92 93 94 HAD 10 9 8 7 6 5 4 3 2 1

This edition is printed on acid-free paper that meets the American National Standards Institute Z39.48 Standard.

For Patrick—he'd be so amazed!

And in loving memory of Fred—Garnet's husband and Donna's father—who taught us so much about courage, laughter, and learning how to see.

The individual dying in an ancient or pre-industrial culture is equipped with a religious or philosophical system that transcends death, and is likely to have had considerable experiential training and altered states of consciousness, including symbolic confrontations with death. The approach of death is faced in the nourishing context of the extended family, clan, or tribe, and with its support—sometimes even with specific and expert guidance through the successive stages of dying.

The situation of an average Westerner facing death is in sharp contrast to the above in every respect. . . .

—Stanislav and Christina Grof,
Beyond Death: The Gates of Consciousness

Sacred psychology [begins] with the wounding of the psyche by the Larger Story. In this wounding, the psyche is opened up and new questions begin to be asked about who we are in our depths. . . . The anguish is enormous and the suffering cracks the boundaries of what you thought you could bear. And yet, the wounding . . . may contain the seeds of healing and transformation. The recognition of this truth is not new. In the Greek tragedies, the gods force themselves into human consciousness at the time of pathos. It is only at this time of wounding that the protagonist grows into a larger sense of what life is all about and is able to act accordingly.

If we would only look far enough and deep enough, we would find that our woundings have archetypal power. In uncovering their mythic base, we are challenged to a deeper life. . . . Wounding involves the *breaking* or *penetrating* or *opening* into the human flesh or soul by a force or power or energy coming from beyond our ordinary recognized boundaries. The violation of these boundaries makes us vulnerable to be reached by larger forces. . . .

In times of suffering, when you feel abandoned, perhaps even annihilated, there is occurring—at levels deeper than your pain—the entry of the sacred, the possibility of redemption. Wounding opens the doors of our sensibility to a larger reality . . . Pathos gives us eyes and ears to see and hear what our normal eyes and ears cannot.

—Jean Houston
The Search for the Beloved: A Journey in Sacred Psychology

Contents

Part Three
The Alchemy of Transmuting
Grief to Creativity   119
Peg Elliott Mayo

Foreword

In 1961, I attended a provocative symposium at the annual meeting of the American Psychological Association titled "Taboo Topics." At that time, dialogue about death, hypnosis, or sexual behavior was suspect, even at psychology conferences. Herman Feifel, the panelist who discussed the psychology of death, recalled being admonished, "Isn't it cruel, sadistic, and traumatic to discuss death with seriously ill and terminally ill people?" His experience, in contrast, had been that most such patients appreciated these discussions, welcoming the chance to voice their doubts, affirm their faith, and communicate what their impending demise meant to them.[1] Up until that time, however, Western culture's denial of death was rarely challenged in professional circles or in the larger society.

A shift began to occur a few years later when the Swiss-American physician Elisabeth Kübler-Ross launched a series of books that courageously confronted the issues faced by dying patients.[2] Her work opened the way for a more realistic approach to the fearful mystery of death. She went so far as to suggest that it is out of pondering and coping with the reality of death that "the highest spiritual values can originate."[3]

Following in her ground-breaking footsteps, Peg Elliott Mayo and David Feinstein have drawn upon a wealth of personal and professional experience in writing *Rituals for Living and Dying*. Building upon the fact that facing death frequently leads to a deepened connection with one's spiritual foundations, the authors offer a series of brilliantly crafted exercises for imaginatively grappling with the facts of life and death. The power, ingenuity, and depth of these structured experiences distinguish the work as unique in its field. The book is also wise and humorous, sad and uplifting, captivating and helpful.

The authors are realistic as they acknowledge that Western culture still tends to deny death. Just as there was a silence about sex in the Victorian era, there is still silence about death in many segments of today's society. Despite the efforts of Kübler-Ross, Stephen Levine, the hospice movement, and the many individuals who have brought greater awareness to the issues involved with death and dying, we still see terminally ill patients being offered false assurance by relatives who conspire with physicians to keep from mentioning death. Mary Chadwick, a psychoanalyst, has described the fear of death as the Western individual's most fundamental anxiety.[4] The culture tenaciously shields us against aging and death by constructing defenses such as wrinkle removers, hair transplants, nursing homes that keep dying people out of sight, and elaborate ceremonies in which the "loved one" awaits burial in a "slumber room" after elaborate cosmetic treatment. Feinstein and Mayo provide an al-

xiii

ternative to these desperate psychological palliatives that is based upon mobilizing inner resources through a creatively conceived set of private experiences they refer to as "personal rituals."

These personal rituals challenge you to square off and face your mortality, confront your fears, and begin to contact deep sources of inner wisdom that provide empowering alternatives to your culture's images about death. Western images portray life as a straight line extending through time. Death is the point at the end of the line. The longer the line, the higher the achievement; longevity is equated with success. A young person's death is seen as a tragic event that shakes one's religious faith or demands elaborate rationalizations—the youth was "called by God," "needed in heaven," or "paying a karmic debt." Many Eastern and tribal traditions, by contrast, do not view life as a straight line but as a circle. One cycle is completed when a young person reaches puberty; another cycle is completed when he or she has brought children into the world. After puberty, the individual expands outward, serving the community, the earth, and the Creator. Wherever on this expanding circle a person is when death arrives, he or she dies in wholeness. As the Oglala Sioux leader Crazy Horse commented, "Today is a good day to die, for all the things of my life are present."[5]

In many Native American traditions, the puberty ritual included a solitary journey into the wilderness, desert, or mountains for several days of fasting and prayer. These and other practices were geared to assist young people to receive a vision-inspired death chant they could use throughout their lives to maintain contact with the Great Spirit during times of stress and danger.[6] When a person was being attacked or was deathly ill, this death chant was a constant companion. It was available in times of need, creating a familiarity with the unfamiliar. As a result, it prepared a person for death. Many Native Americans died with great clarity, deeply immersed in a mythology that integrated living and dying.

Receiving a death chant is one of the personal rituals described in this book. It bears witness to the understanding that few experiences bring us in closer touch with what it means to be alive than encounters with dying. Yet Western culture has developed few rituals of this nature. Organized religions offer some pallid death-bed ceremonies that attempt to comfort. Lacking, however, is a lifelong preparation for death that, at the same time, can affirm the meaning found in day-by-day activities. This meaning is essentially spiritual in that it helps people to make conscious connections with the values and ideals that spring from the deepest (or, if you like, the highest) parts of their psyche, those parts that seem to join them with God, the Tao, the Cosmos, or the Ground of Being.

This book offers concepts, case studies, and a program for creating private as well as shared rituals for constructively encountering death.

Interacting with a book will be a new concept for some readers, but the Egyptian and Tibetan "books of the dead" are venerable prototypes in preparing people to encounter the final mystery of their lives. The Egyptian *Rev Nu Pert Em Hru* (*Chapters of Coming Forth by Day*) dates back to about 1600 B.C. and is a collection of texts that contain formulae, prayers, hymns, and descriptions of the "Fields of Peace" in the afterlife. The eighth-century B.C. Buddhist *Bardo Thödal* (the *Tibetan Book of the Dead*) offers guidance at the time of death and in the after-death state. To follow its precepts is said to foster understanding by enabling the practitioner to transcend what is transitory. Dying is seen as containing the potential of initiation and the power to consciously control the process of death and regeneration. The *Bardo Thödal* teaches the dying to face death calmly and with a clear mind, able to transcend bodily suffering and infirmities with a trained intellect directed toward transcendence.

Similar books exist in the Hindu, Islamic, and Mesoamerican literature, each reflecting a different mythology concerning death. The European parallel to these works is a medieval collection of literature known as *Ars Moriendi*, or *The Art of Dying*. In some of these books, the reader is advised that the states of consciousness associated with dying can be experienced during life; hence, certain parts of these texts can also be used as manuals for meditation or initiation.[7] A manual for working with drug-induced altered states of consciousness,[8] for instance, is based on the *Bardo Thödal,* and *The American Book of the Dead* presents certain esoteric teachings about death for an American audience.[9]

The current work can be placed in the tradition of these modern "books of the dead." It begins by taking you on an intimate journey with a family whose young, dynamic husband and father has been diagnosed with a progressive and incurable form of cancer. Peg Elliott Mayo orchestrated a series of family meetings, discussions, back-home assignments, and individually tailored ceremonies for the patient, his wife, and his children. You are provided diary excerpts, poetry, conversations, and even the results of a vision quest that poignantly demonstrate the way that these ritualistic activities enriched the final months of the patient's life and gave his family a way of coming to terms with unspeakably painful emotions. It is deeply moving to watch each family member find a way to grasp the personally horrifying reality that is unfolding, and it is inspiring to read of the series of rituals that individually and collectively evoke their courage, their collaboration, their most creative and humane responses. In the process, you will be learning how you may draw upon an understanding of ritual to help you in situations where your own terrors, grief, and anger may seem raw and untamable. Witnessing this family's experience leaves you with a blueprint—a sophisticated model for using rituals invented for the occasion—to bring family members closer to one another and enable them to constructively confront their impending loss.

Having seen the organic manner by which rituals may be constructively introduced into tragic circumstances, you are next provided with step-by-step techniques that can help you face the issues involved with your own mortality. In this second section of the book, David Feinstein, a pioneer in teaching people to understand and transform their personal mythologies, presents a sequence of eighteen "personal rituals" designed for cultivating a more empowering mythology for living and dying. Early in the program, you are invited to explore your beliefs and attitudes regarding death. One of the rituals in this stage, also derived from Native American custom, involves creating a sacred shield to serve as an ally in living well and in facing death. The eighteen rituals are lucidly organized within a five-stage program designed to enhance your power in dealing with life and death. You will examine your system of death denial, find ways of transcending death anxiety, and bring both your fear of death and your hopes for its transcendence into a confrontation. The narrative promises that you will emerge from the process with a renewed and more inspiring mythology about death. The final stage of the program offers guidance for translating this renewed mythology about death into daily life.

The book ends with Peg Elliott Mayo's "The Alchemy of Transmuting Grief to Creativity." This final section guides you through a set of concepts and personal rituals that offer substantive help for people experiencing grief and bereavement. The writing is decidedly personal and potent; the author is not only an outstanding clinician but also is someone who has lost to suicide a biochemically depressed husband and later a son. She knows the territory. The powerful inwardly focused rituals she offers for coming to terms with loss and sorrow involve meditation and movement, mantras and song, journal work and "auditory drawing," visualization and dream analysis. A poignant and effective approach is offered for ritualistically saying good-bye to one who is no longer physically present, whether because of death, divorce, or other permanent separation. Mayo describes "spiritual awakening" as a coming into awareness of an inner power and a sense of direction beyond that of ordinary consciousness. She observes that the crises of life strip us of our platitudes, challenging us to confront areas of spiritual poverty and to establish a deeper sense of connection with all of creation. With this perspective permeating the book, combined with the "personal rituals" that are woven into the text, the work lives up to its ambitious subtitle, *From Life's Wounds to Spiritual Awakening*.

Rituals for Living and Dying provides a broad-spectrum approach to facing your own mortality, facing the death of treasured companions, and learning to live more fully. Rituals that effectively lead you through the outrage, confusion, desolation, and terror associated with death and bereavement also pave the way toward peaceably and creatively embracing your life path and your inevitable date with death. The book makes a noteworthy contribution for anyone wishing to confront the issues deeply and directly — it stimulates thought, confidence, and hope.

STANLEY KRIPPNER

Author's Preface

Rituals for Living and Dying has been gestating for more than two decades. When we met in 1968, David was beginning his graduate studies in psychology. Peg served as his first clinical supervisor. Together we started Lifeline, one of the country's first large-scale hotline/drop-in counseling services, operating out of the Downtown San Diego YMCA. The creation of Lifeline was one of those synchronistic events in which improbable ingredients combine to form a recklessly innovative enterprise, and it still counts among the most exciting professional ventures in which either of us has ever participated. In our collaborations together on the Lifeline project, we became fast friends and confidants, and now have seen each other through over twenty years of life development, broken and successful relationships, career changes, dark nights of the soul, disagreements so intense that the reverberations shook everything else in our lives, and considerable play—all the while comforting, instructing, laughing, cajoling, and more than once bailing the other out of a seemingly insoluble mess.

In the year prior to our meeting, Peg's husband, the father of their four adolescents, suffering from a lifelong battle with biochemical depression, walked into the empty master bedroom one Sunday morning and fatally shot himself. That tragic moment marked a profound turning point in Peg's professional as well as personal life. Grief changed her. Her understanding of others' suffering matured exponentially, along with her determination to facilitate in her clients the ability to exercise their intelligence, goodness, and humanity to touch and transform their own deepest pain. However much psychotherapy is about fostering hope and empowerment, human distress is its fuel. The suicide four years later of Peg's gentle, erudite eldest son, Patrick, kept her on this rugged path where unspeakable grief shows the way toward compassion and creative transformation. David, though sometimes living as far as a continent away, offered stable and trustworthy counsel and companionship as Peg wrestled her way along this path. Every inch she traveled altered and deepened her work. She has consistently drawn into her clinical practice souls whose struggles with their own dying, bereavement, or suicidal despair were horrendous. Over the years, her work has taken on an increasingly optimistic and spiritual, perhaps shamanic, character.

As a community psychologist as well as clinician, David has throughout his career emphasized the profoundly practical implications of understanding the relationship between the social construction of reality and the way individuals create and maintain their personal realities. He has long advocated the term "personal mythology" for describing the underlying themes—cultural myths in microcosm—that, for better or worse, guide each individual's life.[1] He has been particularly interested in the parallels that sometimes exist between physical illness and the individual's personal mythology. By working with the individual's guiding myths, energies can often be mobilized that maximize the body's capacity for self-healing.[2] This intimate association with illness, often of a life-threatening nature, led him to an active involvement in the "conscious living/conscious dying" area. One of his proudest works is his collaboration with the singer Ann Mortifee on the album "Serenade at the Doorway," which takes the listener through the emotional stages of facing a life-threatening illness, and places the issues surrounding death into a larger spiritual context. David's work with serious disease as well as his own bout with mid-life angst led to his concern with "Cultivating an Empowering Mythology for Confronting Death," which is the title of his primary contribution to this volume.

Writing *Rituals for Living and Dying* together has been a surprise and a privilege. During our long years of friendship, we painfully learned that there are certain activities we do not do well together, writing— because we are both writers—being one of the most conspicuous. As much as our careers had independently brought us each to work with the issues involved with death and grief, it never occurred to us to attempt a book together on the topic. Then Peg had a series of dreamlike experiences that instructed her to collaborate with David on such a book. At first we just laughed, having once barely escaped with our friendship after another co-authorship attempt. But the vision was persistent and tied in with David's own inner sense, and once we were finally committed to the project, the task became deeply gratifying.

Working together proved to us that bone-deep temperamental differences (David is more methodical; Peg, more spontaneous) and disparate personal mythologies can be harmoniously melded. The process was sometimes onerous, sometimes exhilarating, and always educational. We wrote our separate sections independently and then exchanged drafts, commented, fought, adjusted, compromised, thanked, and finally got together face-to-face to polish off the remaining rough spots. There are passages where neither of us is certain who wrote what, and the influence of each of us on the other's writing is keenly felt throughout the book.

Our appreciations with respect to this project are many. First, we are indebted to the hundreds of clients who have opened their souls to us during a combined half century of clinical practice and whose struggles, insights, and achievements have afforded us a privileged view of the human journey. Names and details regarding those who serve as our case examples have, unless otherwise noted, been carefully disguised to conceal identities. Second, our gratitude for Stanley Krippner's wise counsel and generous support cannot be overstated. We are also deeply appreciative of the literally hundreds of constructive suggestions Ana Trelstad offered in her meticulous readings of the evolving manuscript. The institutional support of Innersource in the development of this book is gratefully acknowledged. And it is a great joy to express our gratitude to our spouses—Donna and Don—who are not only friends with each other in their own right, but who are marvelously tolerant of us; we thank them for their powerful support in birthing *Rituals for Living and Dying.*

Rituals for
Living and Dying

Part One

Rituals for Living and Dying: One Family's Experience

Peg Elliott Mayo

Rituals build community, creating a meeting-ground where people can share deep feelings, positive and negative ... a place where they can sing or scream, howl ecstatically or furiously, play, or keep a solemn silence.

—STARHAWK

I loved red-haired Dan Bennett. And I love his family—Sylvia, Michael, and Teddy. As a colleague—we were both psychotherapists and writers, and we both loved crafts—he gave me an unusual, perhaps unique, vantage on a man's dying and his family's response. Every resource I had—personal, professional, and spiritual—was tested. The Bennetts invited me into the most profound experience of their lives. What follows is a requiem for Dan.

This account demonstrates the stages of incredulity, outrage, searching, reconciliation, and transcendence we all experienced. I offer it in thanks for the privilege of participation and with the hope that others will find a map through their dark places.

The Bennett family lived in San Diego. Dan Bennett, forty-one, was a child psychologist specializing in treating abused children. He was a writer of refreshingly sensible professional papers and wry, wise essays on everyday life in a busy family. He was an avid sailor who loved racing and kept his boat, *Good Times,* in spit-and-polish condition. His woodworking, particularly his wooden clocks with inlaid marquetry and exquisitely detailed carvings, was fine enough for a museum. Dan was six feet three inches tall, red-haired, and strongly built. He'd experienced few illnesses.

Sylvia Bennett, thirty-nine, was a pediatric nurse-practitioner, poet, equally avid sailor, and gourmet cook specializing in Asian food. Her great passion was gardening, and she was an activist in environmental causes, particularly the defense of endangered plant species. Of average height, she was strong and attractive with brown, curly hair and green eyes. Sylvia worked half time in a pediatrician's office, more to keep her hand in her profession than from financial need.

Dan and Sylvia's sixteen-year marriage was solid. Sailing the family's boat, a forty-one-foot Ericson, was a common bond, as was writing. Both had published professional and popular works. They owned a comfortably lived-in old house on the edge of a large bay with a view overlooking Shelter Island's pleasure boat anchorage. The Bennetts were too busy with careers, kids, and creative interests to do much entertaining. When they did, it was usually an impromptu neighborhood potluck picnic where they would jam with other "garage musicians"—Dan on mandolin and Sylvia on drums. They rejected social relationships with their professional colleagues and with other members of the yacht club as "too dull." Their dream was to ultimately retire to a large boat and sail around the world. The only major emotional crisis they had experienced was the death of Sylvia's father of colon cancer six years before this account begins.

Michael Tyrone Bennett, twelve, was interested in geography, history, sailing, and serving as crew on the *Good Times.* He was a Sea

3

Scout and an adequate though not outstanding student. Mike and his father had a somewhat strained relationship. Dan vacillated between taut acceptance of Michael's lack of interest in excelling academically and irritable pressure on the boy to "do better." Michael's relationship with Sylvia was warm, but the onset of adolescence was driving a wedge. He felt most affinity for his younger brother, Teddy, and his maternal grandmother, Rose Johnson. He spent considerable time reading "anything I can get my hands on." Red-haired, slender Mike was awkward with his outsized hands, perennially too-short jeans, and big jaw.

Theodore "Teddy" Marcus Bennett, three, a "surprise baby," was much loved by his parents and older brother. An amiable child just entering preschool, he had a number of allergies that required careful monitoring.

Rose Johnson, sixty-five, Sylvia's widowed mother, was slowly losing her sight and felt lonely and frightened of life alone. She had never held a job, had no interests beyond her grandchildren, and was, as Sylvia ruefully said, "a 1940s housewife." She lived three blocks from the Bennett home.

Arthur Evans Bennett, Dan's father, seventy-six, was a retired Methodist minister. He lived in another state and was primarily interested in evangelical work. Dan, an only child, felt distant from his father. Arthur's health was good, except for arthritis in his knees, which Dan attributed to "too much praying and not enough playing." A pillar of his community, tall and white-haired, he was a commanding pulpit figure.

Myrna Myers Bennett, Dan's mother, was seventy and herself the daughter of a Methodist minister. She had married Arthur at nineteen and played a traditional role, carrying out the multitude of unpaid, highly visible chores that fall on a minister's wife. Her only private interest was raising tropical birds; she was an expert on toucans.

The following narrative is a collage of my journal, two taped sessions, and the writings of the family. I have corrected spelling and punctuation, determined the sequence of statements, made judgments about emphasis, and disguised identities. Much has necessarily been deleted, but nothing, I think, that distorts the truth. Material in brackets is mine, added for clarification.

As a neighbor, friend, fellow writer, and clinical social worker, I had been an intimate of the Bennett family for nine years at the time Dan's illness manifested.

From Peg's Journal—Late September, Friday, 10:30 P.M.

I'm sitting here at my desk, feeling unreal—almost disembodied. A minute ago I spilled hot tea across my hand and could hardly feel it. Dan Bennett has cancer. I might as well write "the moon is made of green cheese" or "water runs uphill" for all the sense that makes to me. Even stranger, what he wants from me is almost too much of an honor—or maybe it's a burden. I've got to sort it all out, and I feel completely inadequate.

In order, this is what happened. I saw on my office appointment book that Dan had reserved my last slot of the day. This puzzled me—he could have caught me at home an hour later if he needed to see me. I said as much when he settled in the client chair. Without any real preliminaries, Dan told me that he needed a therapist, probably one who could work with his whole family, and that I was his first choice, but he had alternatives if I didn't want to be involved. He said he'd understand.

I jumped to the conclusion that he was thinking of a divorce—even though I had never seen a hint of any serious trouble between him and Sylvia—but I kept a nice professional silence as he laid out his business. He didn't take long. I don't think I'll ever forget his words: "Doctor macAlbee has just told me I should plan on winding things up in the next four months—it seems I've got the 'Big C.' " His voice was as flat as Kansas, and only the strange glitter in his eyes showed any emotion.

I told him of my disbelief; all the while, I was searching his face and body for clues. I had noticed he was losing weight, but anyone who works and plays as hard as Dan is entitled to get a little gaunt once in a while. Now I could see he looked sallow, holding his mouth stiffly as if he didn't trust his self-control. It took me a minute to realize how awful it must be for him to have to persuade *me* he was dying.

We talked awhile. He filled in the details of weird symptoms (it's his liver that's involved), Sylvia's insistence on the medical workup, and what it might mean financially and practically for the family. It was as if he had totally mobilized his intellect for dealing with the crisis—like all his emotions, intuition and spontaneity were turned off. We sat there talking like mechanical people.

Then he came up with his mind-boggling idea. I want to record what he said as accurately as I can remember: "Look, Peg, I've been a therapist for seventeen years. I *know* what this kind of thing does to a family. It brings out the weaknesses; it sometimes breaks people—not that I think that'll happen here, but who knows? Anyhow, Teddy is just a baby, and Mike is at a pretty critical stage in his development. I don't want to mess up these last few months I've got left. Sylvia is going to take it hard, but will stiff-upper-lip it. What I want you to do is hang around, be our friend *and* therapist."

I made some sort of noise—disbelief, disclaimer—something awkward. He gave me a look and then the clincher. "I want my sons to understand whatever there is to understand, and I don't think that's possible now. I'm asking you as therapist and writer—as well as friend—to keep a record so that when they're older, they'll know I didn't just go off and abandon them." It was then his eyes welled up with tears and I knew he wasn't mechanical at all, nor was I. We both wept, strangely comforting each other with smooth professional words like "that's good—let it out" and "take a deep breath—let your feelings flow." Kind of peculiar, two therapists crying like scared little kids and coaxing each other along.

Now I have to make a decision. It can't wait. Am I to be the attendant of the Bennett family in the next months? Can I do what he asked? Part of me says "No!" Part of me doesn't *want* to be so intimate with anybody again. Isn't it enough that I've buried Joe [first husband], Dad, and Patrick [twenty-three-year-old son], all in the last five years? Isn't it enough challenge working with the psychotics and sufferers built into this damn profession, anyway? Why pick on me? I don't know enough— may not be strong enough—don't *want* to move into this particular maelstrom. I even resent his trust—feels intrusive—he's asking too much.

The rest of me is—what's the word?—flattered. Truth is, I feel important and honored. Like, how could anyone trust me any more than Dan? And I think of his kindness when Pat died. How "there" for me he was, sending me to the right therapists, listening to me howl out my complaints to the world and God. He took the risk of blowing it and came close. Can I do differently? Of course not.

I am in a privileged position. Sylvia and I are pretty close—sharing our poetry and environmental concerns. Mike's a good kid—a little too laid back, but not a problem. Rose is another cup of tea—I really don't like her—she seems so *flabby*, emotionally and intellectually. Although always complaining and never initiating, she's part of it as Sylvia's mother. The older Bennetts are a blank book to me—how they'll react is hard to figure. Probably with sanctimonious virtue and complete denial of emotion. The Lord's will be done.

I told Dan I'd think it over and tell him in the morning, but I think he knows it's yes. God, but I'm scared! I've got to wrap my head around the magnitude of this thing and then come up with a plan—and I don't know what the hell I'm *doing!*

I'll ask for a dream to give direction—provided I can sleep.

From Peg's Journal—The Next Evening

I had my dream, worked on it, ate a very slow breakfast, walked over to the cliffs [a favored place overlooking the ocean] to meditate—but failed, since I couldn't turn my head off. Finally faced up to things and walked over to the Bennetts'.

I'd better record the dream and what I made of it before I go on. Dream: I'm in the basement or dungeon of a stone building that I somehow know is very large. It is dark and dank—water running down the walls, only a little light coming through high window slots, my footsteps echoing. I desperately want to get out to where I can hear people laughing and talking as if at a party or something. I'm shackled to the wall by a heavy chain. Even though I have a lot of slack, I still can't get to the stairs I see far off in the gloom. I'm desperate and scared and confused. I feel as though I'm being unjustly punished. I can just make out a big, black iron key hanging on a peg near the stairs. I can't reach it. I wake up, sobbing. [When I got my wits about me, I scratched down the main points of the dream, still feeling disorganized and frightened. Decided to work on main elements (key, dungeon, stairs, chain) with free association. I took about an hour.]

> DUNGEON: Dank—dark—horrible—spiders—toads—gray
> blood—clammy—cold as death—Dan in his coffin—
> intolerable!—grave—earth—worms—decay—rot—flesh—
> human flesh—brief life—long death—resurrection—only for
> Christ—wrong—seeds—plants—life from death—cycle of
> seasons—too pat—not facing facts—reality—Dan's death—
> soon—everyone's death—my death—anytime—nuclear war—
> vulnerable—threat—built—mistakes—lost chances—sorrow—
> make it up—how?—do the best I can—*unequipped!*—
> cowardly—want *out!*—no way out—whine—repulsive—brace
> up—behave as-if—dignity—pretend—no!—dignity.

I don't feel all that satisfied—maybe I just didn't come to grips with it all. I'll do a CP [creative projection]:

I'm a dungeon. I'm subterranean, unlighted, dank, mysterious, sinister. There is much suffering and bondage in me. People can cry out in me, and all I do is echo their sounds. Help never comes. There are creepy things in me, ugly and dangerous. I'm very old and deep, the lowest part of a castle. A woman is chained to my wall with iron rings around her ankles. She's making a lot of noise, but I can muffle all her sound and no one will ever hear her. She can die in me—lots of people have already. I'm a grave without grace. No flowers adorn me—no one preaches inspirational sermons in me—there is no grace in me—I'm purely the dark shadow of death and everyone, sooner or later, has to spend time in me. I don't do much. I'm passive. I'm just a nasty dark place that gets used for torture and confinement. I've been here for thousands of years and I'll go on for thousands more *because nothing ever changes in me.*

Wow. That is heavy—*am* I being passive? This is clearly a shadow part of me—I feel trapped by Dan's need—chained. That stuff about echoes and not being heard—hell of a thing for a therapist to find out about herself. I've got to take charge of myself—I can't be passive and just rot here. He's better than that, and so am I. I need a change of attitude.

> STAIRS: Escape—upward—outta trouble—release—climb—
> one by one—out of reach—unobtainable—need—help—help
> me!—selfish—help Dan—help Sylvia—don't know enough—
> chickenhearted answer—face up—try harder—give more—
> *care* more—love Dan—friend—companion—lonely—human
> condition—rise to the occasion.

That's it. I have to rise to the occasion. Something is settling down in me as I do this.

> CHAIN: Heavy—merciless—chafing—stronger than me—
> limiting—undignified—shame—exposure—guilt—weight—
> sorrow—deep—anchor—stable—pun—horse barn—
> frivolous—playful—laughter—tragedy—untimely death—who
> chooses time?—God or Whomever—anger—mad at God—
> stupid—abandoning belief—ultimate goodness—confusion—
> don't understand—accept.

That's it (me). Accept. Not an easy assignment, given the players.

> KEY: Lock—trap—leg crusher—animal—coyote—maverick—
> abused—misunderstood—unfair—Dan—cancer—terror—
> death—horrible—pity—fear—children—damaged—Sylvia—
> unprepared—me unprepared—not fair—no justice—victim—
> pain—drugs—poison—hopeless—lost faith—faith in what?—
> order—divine order—calm—Something else is in charge.

It comes to me that the key is hanging on a peg. I'm Peg. I've responded to Dan's request as if everything hangs on me. I feel sudden release—as though I've found another key. *I'm not in charge!* That's a real relief. *I* don't have to control—I *can't* control—what's happening. Don't be grandiose. The key is to remember I'm not in charge and that God, or some Greater Power, *is*. I feel lighter.

So, what did I learn? Simple—accept that I'm not in charge, and that if I get grandiose it'll be the worse for me *and* Dan. That there's nothing, really, to do but accept the situation. And, hang onto dignity. More subtly, this dream felt "directed"—as if it were coming from the Source. There is a lot of difference between passivity—flat immobility—and acceptance. To me acceptance suggests I'm an active part of what's happening but not the whole tamale. I'll be mulling this awhile.

I walked over to the Bennetts' about eleven. Dan was cleaning out the garage, looking normal. We b.s.ed a few minutes, not looking in each other's eyes. Finally I told him I was "in for the duration." He nodded. Just as I expected, he knew I would do as he asked. I went in, looking for Sylvia.

She was drinking coffee—something she rarely does, and arranging flowers—something she does a lot. She had big, gray bags under her eyes and looked like she'd been doing the flowers all night. I got myself a cup of coffee and sat down, watching. Finally, I asked, "You know what Dan asked me to do?" She just nodded. So I pushed it a little. "I think we need a plan." Finally, we agreed to get together about five to talk. I went home.

Poem by Sylvia Bennett—Early October

Buttons missing off Mike's shirt
Pickets falling off the fence
Hornworms in the tomatoes
Dan's side of the bed, empty.

Sound of vomiting
Trying not to hear
Trying not to know.
Be a brave wife
Be a good nurse
Howling, inside.

Gray hair at my temple
Mold on the cottage cheese
In the dirty refrigerator
Dust insidiously intrudes
Under our king-size bed.

Things incompleted
Work not finished
Loopholes in the contract
Holes in my sweater sleeve
Everything is unraveling.

From Dan's Journal—Early October

It's going okay. Felt pretty good today, except for sore liver and some early morning nausea. Got together with Sylvia and Peg this afternoon. Pretty solemn, all of us. Hope we can get some laughs going; the heaviness is weighing me down, affecting decisions. We decided that I should tell Mom Johnson first, since Mike is likely to run to her when he finds out. Will do that tomorrow, at her place. Will take next week off from work to get my head together, see Doc macAlbee regarding treatment alternatives (with Sylvia), and talk to Ken about my will and the investments. There's a hell of a lot to do to get ready to die. And I haven't really taken time to think how I *feel* about it.

From Peg's Journal—Early October

Hard day. Had a full client load—not a free minute. Ate at my desk. Got home, looking forward to a long soak and a trashy novel. Had water in the tub when the phone rang at eight-thirty. It was Dan. All he said was something like, "Better come over if you can, Peg. Looks like we've got us a little crisis."

When I got there it was dark, but Mike was throwing a basketball over and over as hard as he could against the garage door. He acted as if he didn't see me, but I'm pretty sure he did. Dan and Sylvia were sitting in the living room across from each other, both clutching drinks and looking stricken. I was extra concerned because I know Dan isn't supposed to drink, and Sylvia, frankly, has a tendency to go too far. When she does, she usually does too much talking. Neither of them was drunk, though, just tense and clearly angry.

It seems that Doc macAlbee has recommended that Dan have chemotherapy and radiation, under the care of an oncologist he knows. Dan is dead set against it, and Sylvia is pushing, a little too hard. When I got my bearings and saw what was happening, I pulled on my therapist hat. What follows is my best recollection of the essence of their dialogue.

DAN: I'm not going to do it. There's no way I'm going to let myself be tortured like that.

SYLVIA: You're just closing your mind and reacting. A lot been done since Dad died. [Her father had died of colon cancer about six years earlier after surgery, chemotherapy, radiation, the works. It took almost a year from diagnosis to death, and it wasn't pretty.]

DAN: Not enough. Look, like the man said, "Whose life is it, anyway?"

Sylvia took a big slug of her drink and stared down into the glass. Finally, she said, "I want you to live, Dan. I want my husband alive."

Dan looked stricken, but stubborn. "Puking my guts out, constant diarrhea—hair falling out—tubes in my arms and cock. I don't call that living."

Sylvia replied (weakly), "A lot can be done—buy some time. Maybe some of the research will find a cure . . ."

Dan just looked at her, and I stepped in. I defined what I thought the surface issue was—whether the strenuous course of traditional treatment was worth the physical and emotional price. I suggested that Dan talk to Doc macAlbee about alternatives and compromises. He agreed, and Sylvia seemed to let down a little. Then I suggested that we all come to grips with the feelings that were so evident. A long, emotional session followed.

Dan is burned up at fate and is taking an if-I-can't-have-my-way-I-quit attitude. He *says* he's making a rational decision—I've got my doubts. I gave him two assignments: try on Sylvia's position *and* make a month-by-month plan for himself. I leaned on him to do it in the next twenty-four hours. I'm going back to their place tomorrow night.

Sylvia is terrified and desperate. For an independent, capable person, she is remarkably uncreative at the moment. All her nurse-practitioner training is telling her to "mind the doctor," and she's not doing much empathizing. I told her I wanted her to make a list—a free association—of her fears and *not* to share it with Dan. I don't see any advantage to his dealing with all her clutter before I can help her discharge the worst of it. We're getting together at my office before the evening at-home session.

I asked about Mike and Teddy. So far, Teddy is basically okay as far as any of us can tell, though he had an asthma attack the night before. Sylvia blames it on the sitter giving him milk. Dan told Rose [his mother-in-law] a week ago, and she behaved pretty well. Cried, and she wished it were her not him, and begged him to do as Doc macAlbee told him. Dan told Mike the day before yesterday. Took him out on the *Good Times*, ostensibly to polish some brightwork, paint, and do other maintenance.

Dan is one of the best child psychologists I know of. He told me, later, that he applied everything he knew. Talked about his own feelings and sense of incompletion with Mike. Talked about his regrets for being inconsistent and too busy some of the time. Told him he loved him and was ready to answer any questions. Apparently did it right, but the kid didn't react as he'd hoped. Now, Mike has clammed up, won't talk to anybody, just keeps throwing that damn basketball against the garage door and refusing to look at anyone or talk. I went outside, after we were done, to talk to him, but he'd gone to bed. Kind of worried what Rose will say to him. The two are pretty thick.

From Sylvia's Homework Assignment—Mid-October

I'm supposed to free associate on my fears. They seem obvious enough. My husband is dying at forty-one and won't take the medical treatment indicated. I'm scared to be alone. I've never been alone. First I lived at home, then I went to school, got my R.N., got married, had Michael. I've never been alone in my life. I'm scared Dan will suffer, and I won't be able to help. I'm scared Teddy and Mike will be damaged. I'm scared about money. How can I work with all this going on at home? I'm scared Mom will go to pieces and I'll have to take care of her, too.

Scared of living
Scared of dying
Scared of the kids
Scared of myself
Scared of pain
Scared of winter
Scared of everything.

Scared of Dan
Scared *for* Dan
Scared God got lost in the smog
Scared I'll wake up
And another day'll be gone.

From Dan's Journal — Mid-October

Peg said, "Be Sylvia. Climb in her skin, think and feel like her, and write it all down." Okay, but first I gotta record that this is tougher than I expected. I thought she'd be a brick, a regular tower of strength. Maybe she's more like Rose than I figured. I resent that.

"Okay. I'm Sylvia, and I resent having my life torn up like this. I resent Dan's getting sick. Everything I value is in danger: my calm home, professionalism, security, sense of myself. All of a sudden, the rules have changed, and I'm being *forced* to deal with stuff I don't like. And Dan won't do what Doc macAlbee says needs to be done. He isn't putting up a good fight, the way my Dad did. He's just caving in and saying to the cancer, "Come and get me." I feel helpless, uninfluential, as if everything is going to come down on me without me having any say about it at all. And I'm pissed off about it all. Dan should put up a fight. He *might* win and he *owes* it to the kids and me to try as hard as he can. I don't like being married to a quitter."

I wonder if she really does feel like that, or if it's all my projection? How come she doesn't remember the hell her dad went through to wring an extra couple of lousy months out of life? That's a nurse for you — life at any price. I don't like being seen as a quitter. Dammit, I never quit anything in my life! Except my life? *Am* I giving in too easily? Partly, it doesn't seem real — kind of as though I'm looking at things through the wrong end of a telescope or on a TV screen. I'm not really involved or in touch. Have I passed into Kübler-Ross's denial stage? But there's no denying the pain under my rib and the yellow color in my skin. Better get on to the next assignment, or Peg'll get me good.

MONTH BY MONTH PLAN FOR THE REST OF MY LIFE

OCTOBER: Business, new will. Put money into trust for kids. Transfer title of house and boat to Sylvia. Talk to accountant. Make decision about practice — keep on? Quit while I'm ahead? Make decision on medical stuff. How? Talk to Peg and Doc macAlbee about alternatives. No chemotherapy. No radiation. No compromise. No surrender! Spend time with kids, Sylvia. Sail to Catalina.

NOVEMBER: Thanksgiving! Probably tell Dad and Mom. Before holiday? After? Maybe level with them about how I feel about organized religion. See if I can get one human, honest statement out of the old man—one shred of acceptance of *me,* the man. Put my writing and papers in order. Hike (?) out in the desert with Mike. Give him a chance to speak his piece. Enjoy ourselves.

DECEMBER: Christmas. Last Christmas. Make it good. Look into cost of horse and stabling for Mike. What can I do for Teddy that he'll remember? Big family blowout—build in a lot of good stuff—make it count. Will Doc give me pain medication without a fight? Don't want to be remembered hurting or sniveling.

JANUARY: Who knows? Probably weaker. Teddy's fourth birthday. Maybe take him to a circus if there's one anywhere within reasonable distance. Listen to Bach. Try to make some sense out of my life. Did I accomplish anything? Who'll remember in five years? In ten?

Can't think any further. The future, as Dad would say, is in the hands of the Lord. Maybe I ought to talk to someone about God. Who? *Not Dad!*

Pretty short future. Not much fight showing. I feel like crying like a little kid. It's so hard to understand.

Family Counseling Session—Early November

The following are edited excerpts from a tape of a family session, in my office, with Dan, Sylvia, Mike, and Rose.

PEG: Dan, what did you have in mind when you called for this session?

DAN: So much has happened in the last six weeks that I want to say some things, clear the air, and make sure that Mike and Teddy will have it straight and clear how things are for me. I want to know how things are for my family, too, and this just seemed the best way to do it.

PEG: Okay. How do you want to do this, Dan?

DAN: I figured you'd have some ideas, and beyond that—just an open mike, I guess.

PEG: All right, I'm going to start with how I feel right now. That might work out as a good idea for each of us. Agreed?

SYLVIA: Sure. I feel stagy, though, with the machine on.

MIKE: Me, too. Can we turn it off?

DAN: I really want it on, son. I'm asking you to trust me that someday it'll be valuable to you.

MIKE: I think it's weird. Nobody else does stuff like this.

DAN: I feel pretty weird, too, son, but do you remember the film they took of the boats at the yacht club at the start of the Ensenada race? How when we looked at it later, you said you learned a lot about how to get away by studying the other skippers' techniques?

MIKE: Yeah.

DAN: This is a time for a lot of learning for all of us. I'd like to ask you to let the tape machine stay on—feels like it really could be valuable.

PEG: Besides, your Dad wants . . .

MIKE: Sure! Anything Dad wants, Dad gets! Just because he's sick everyone has to do everything *his* way. Leave the old tape on, but don't expect me to like it.

PEG: Okay. Agreed. It stays on, and nobody expects you to like it. Anyone disagree?

SYLVIA: Is this going to accomplish anything?

DAN: If we let it. Look, like it or not . . .

ROSE: For heaven's sake, will someone tell me why . . .

PEG: I'd like to be the person who kind of directs things until we begin to feel a little easier with each other. It's what I agreed to do, and I ask your cooperation. Now, everyone, just close your eyes a minute, and take a couple of long, deep, smooth breaths. Calm yourself. Pull your energy inside; take charge of yourself. Spend a minute realizing that we're here to make things better for each other—and we *can!* [Silence, except for sound of breathing and sighing.] That's good.

Now I'm going to describe how I feel—both my body and my emotions. I suggest we just go around the room and everyone do this first, then we can go on. Okay. I'm really very alert. I feel as if all my attention is focused here. I hear the fish tank bubbling. I'm taking my shoes off. My feet feel better. My voice is getting calmer. I want a deep breath. Inside, I feel a longing to be useful to my friends—particularly Dan. I feel complicated when I think of Dan—sad, angry, a little scared, even a skosch of hope. That's me for now. Who's next?

[Lengthy silence.]

DAN: My turn. My butt is sore from those damn vitamin shots yesterday. It's hard to get a deep breath in, but it feels good when I do. I'm uptight thinking that this won't work, and I can't let go of the idea. I want to feel us all *together.*

[Sound of crying.]

PEG: Put some words with that, Rose.

ROSE: [wailing]: I feel so *helpless!* This is all so sad and pointless and wasteful, and I can't do anything about it and I just feel *awful!*

SYLVIA: Mom—

PEG: Let her speak. That's what this is all about.

MIKE: God—

PEG: Hang in, kid. Things are going all right, you'll see. Rose, begin some sentences with "I feel," and then fill in with a few words.

ROSE: I feel out of place. I feel . . . I don't know . . . led around and disregarded. I feel old and thrown away. Is that enough?

PEG: I don't think that's all you have to say or all you're feeling, Rose.

ROSE: No. It's not, but . . . what good is this doing?

PEG: Trust the process a little. Go on with your list of "I feels."

ROSE: I feel terrible. I feel for Sylvia and all you're going through. I feel terrible for Mike. I feel *sick* when I look at Dan. Life is just so unfair, so lonely.

PEG: Lonely. Anyone else besides Rose and me feel that way?

DAN: Damn right! I'm the one with the cancer. I feel pretty damn lonely right now. How about you, honey? You haven't said much . . .

SYLVIA: What's to say? All it seems to me we've done is make arrangements—for the house, for the taxes, for your practice. Arrangements and fights about your treatment. I've never been so alone in my life. [Sobs.]

DAN: Are you mad at me, honey? I wouldn't blame you if you—

SYLVIA: What's the point?

DAN: What's the point of letting me know how you feel? Same as ever—makes us closer. That's the only cure for loneliness I know.

SYLVIA: You said you have some stuff to say . . .

MIKE: Do I have to stay? This is weird.

DAN: I want you to stay, Mike. Okay, honey, I guess it's time for me to speak my piece. That seem right to you, Peg?

PEG: Sure.

DAN: It's not like I have a speech or anything. Just some stuff I want you all to know. First, I'm not a quitter. I got the idea that because I turned down Doc macAlbee's grand plan, you thought I was. For the last two weeks I've been going to the Horton Clinic—

SYLVIA: Quacks!

DAN: No. Nutritional therapists and holistic types who are using a whole raft of nontraditional techniques—visualization, acupuncture—I'm learning meditation, and I'm feeling better. No pain pills for two days. That's progress.

SYLVIA: I'm sorry. I feel raw, frazzled. I'm *glad* you're going—getting some relief—some hope—

ROSE: But doesn't Doctor macAlbee know bett—

PEG: That's not the issue here, Rose. Dan's making a point I want to help him get across. Say it again, Dan.

DAN: I'm not quitting. I'm living as much as I can for as long as I can, for myself and for my family. I need you to recognize that. What I *am* doing is deciding for myself how I'm doing it.

ROSE: Does that mean that you're right?

DAN: I don't know how to answer that . . .

PEG: Rose, put what you're feeling out in a simple sentence that begins with the word "I."

ROSE: I resent being told how to talk!

PEG: Good. You followed the instructions perfectly. Now do you have something else to say following those rules?

ROSE: No.

PEG: Your pain and concern for the family is clear, Rose. I'm sorry this is so strange and difficult for you. The most important thing we can each do for ourselves and for the others, I think, is to be gentle and honest.

DAN: What's important to me is that the next few months—whatever I've got—be good. That nobody gets hurt any more than I can help. I'm still the dad here . . .

SYLVIA: Oh, Dan . . . [cries].

PEG: Put out what you feel, Sylvia.

SYLVIA: I'm confused. I love you, Dan. I'm scared. Like, I don't know what to do or how to think about this. It's too much.

PEG: Overwhelming.

SYLVIA: Yes. Overwhelming.
[Next half-hour not transcribed here. Each person, with the exception of Mike, spoke of a sense of helplessness, outrage, and need for understanding.]

PEG: Dan's asked something very specific. Does anyone remember what it is?

MIKE: I do. Dad, you said you weren't a quitter, and you wanted us to know it.

DAN: Yes! Thank you, son.

MIKE: Well, then, how come you've got this, this . . .

DAN: Cancer.

MIKE: Yeah. Cancer. You must have done *something* . . .

DAN: I don't know. I honestly don't know. I ask myself that. I asked Doc. There doesn't seem to be any good answer.

SYLVIA: That's what I hate! No answer. No why. It's not fair. A good man like you . . .

DAN: Maybe the answer is somewhere else—like karma or fate or something. I don't know.

ROSE: It made more sense with Bill. He was almost seventy . . .

DAN: I don't think we're going to come up with a definitive answer.

PEG: What do you need now, Dan?

DAN: A sense that my family's with me. Hope. To laugh. Have a good Thanksgiving and Christmas. To know it's okay for me to . . . I don't know . . . do what feels right.

MIKE: Weird, Dad.

DAN: Yeah, son, for me too.

SYLVIA: I'm with you, Dan. What do you think would give you a laugh? I could use one myself.

DAN: Let's get some Laurel and Hardy films. And I'd like to go away with you for a weekend, honey. Maybe to Agua Caliente and soak in the hot springs?

SYLVIA: I'm taking a leave from the office—my attention is just too split for being good at home or work—so there'll be time for that good stuff . . .

PEG: Sounds like a plan. Before we wind up I want to set up another session, if you're willing, and give everyone some homework.

DAN: I'm in. You guys? Good!

PEG: Okay. Let's meet here next week, same time, same station. I'm suggesting that each of you write a couple of paragraphs about how you feel about death. Death is the word we've all avoided, and it's too important to hide from.

MIKE: What do you mean?

PEG: We've been all wrapped up in personal feelings and arrangements, as your mom said. But your dad has a serious disease and is facing the end of his life, sooner than anyone would have expected. If we're to be with him—in

our hearts and minds—we have to face up to death. All
of us. The best way I know is to *decide* to do that. So,
I'm suggesting that each of us put down on paper what
we think death is, how we feel about it, and what we
think comes next—if anything. Clear?

MIKE: I guess so.

ROSE: I don't want to do this anymore. No insult, Peg, but I
don't want to participate.

SYLVIA: I feel better, Mom, don't you? Just getting stuff *out* helps
. . .

ROSE: I don't. I feel terrible. Some things are better kept to
yourself. I'm sorry, Dan, but . . .

DAN: It's okay, Mom. I just didn't want anyone left out.

PEG: Rose, I recognize that this may not be the best way for
you to deal with all the hurt, but I do think that it is important that you face up to it. Before you leave, I'll give
you the name of a therapist I know, a late middle-aged
man who is both gentle and capable. My guess is that he
could be very helpful to you right now. Okay?

ROSE: I don't know . . .

PEG: Think about it. I think there really is comfort for you if
you'll just reach out for it, Rose. Now, are the rest of
you willing to take on that assignment of writing your
views of death? Good. Let's quit after one round of appreciations.

DAN: I appreciate all of you. Thanks for doing this; I know it's
tough.

SYLVIA: I appreciate *you,* Dan—for being steady and knowing
what's right. And Peg. Thanks.

ROSE: I don't know what to appreciate, but I *am* grateful that
God gave us the time we've had with Dan.

MIKE: I appreciate that it's over.

PEG: I appreciate the privilege of your trust. I'm grateful for
this learning time.

Mike's Definition of Death

Death is when everything stops and they put you in the ground.
I don't really know what it means. I was only six when Granddad died,
but I remember how everyone was saying it was better than living like
he was. When Bosco died, Dad and me dug a hole for him under the
loquat tree, and that was that. Dad's got cancer, and he's going to die.
I don't want to think about it because I get scared and mad. That is
what I think of death.

Sylvia's Definition of Death

Sinister black shadow in the night
Snatching
Babies and old people and my other half
Dan.

Hospital death with machines and
Science.
Cold compresses, emesis basins, and
Monitors.

Waxy skin, pinched nose, and
Pallor
Brain death and no vital
Signs.

The Old Man's Friend is
Coming
To take Dan who is a young
Man.

Death is a blank door
Closing
Off loved from beloved
Permanently.

Death is good-bye and no
Seeyalater
Unless, of course, I'm
Wrong.

Dan's Definition of Death

Death is personal. It was always sort of academic or remote before. Maybe it's the start of a great adventure. Maybe there is a long tunnel and a white light and bliss. Dad would say it's the end of life as we know it until the Savior comes again. Makes no sense to me. Death of an animal or a plant seems different from *my* death. They have short cycles—well, maybe I do too. A dead plant disintegrates into the soil and makes it rich. Maybe I will too. Maybe I'll have a rosebush or mango tree planted over me. Something to grow out of what's left of me.

Death is a hell of a lot of giving up. Giving up this life: Sylvia, kids, future. Letting go.

Death isn't as frightening as dying. Choosing my own death begins to seem reasonable, since I can't seem to stop it. Why suffer?

Death is the end of suffering (I hope). Dad would say it's just the beginning if I don't *believe* as he believes. What if he's right? He's not. Makes no sense.

Death is coming. I'd better get it together. Death is almost here. I'll never have another birthday, win another race, counsel another mixed-up kid, flirt with another woman, see my sons grow a beard. I have made my arrangements, and now I had better look after my soul. The idea gives me strange peace.

Definition of Death from Peg's Journal

Death is. Life is. Bodies are the least of us—everything else goes on after our bodies die. Essence—life energy—goes on. There is some purpose and reason to this cycle. Whether "Peg energy" goes on forever I don't know—but the carbon and phosphorus and hydrogen that is my body will be part of something else, eventually, so why not my essence?

Death is a doorway between realities. I only fear it because I haven't seen for myself what's on the other side. Death is the great test of how we've lived. "As ye sow, so shall ye reap." Karma. Paying off debts, reaping rewards, laying the groundwork for next time. Rising on the spiral.

Death separates us from all that is familiar, and that is what I fear— the loss of those things and people I love. That and being out of control.

From Sylvia's Journal—Mid-November

Have finished up at work for the foreseeable future. Not easy to take the step, but Teddy was very sick three nights ago, almost as if he picked up the vibes around here. Not from Dan. He's better than Mike or me. Teddy's allergies flared up, and I know he hasn't had milk and there's no pollen this time of year. How much does a baby know? Almost four. I gave him a shot and a cuddle. Now he seems better.

Had a scare two nights ago. Mike disappeared. It wasn't like he ran away; he just disappeared. All his stuff was in his room, including his basketball and the book he was reading. I went in to kiss him good night, and he wasn't there. Didn't want to wake Dan, who went to bed early. Called Peg, who came over. We called around to the neighbors' and Wally's houses, but no one had seen him. I was frantic and wanted to call the police, but Peg said to wait awhile. Finally, at nearly midnight, he came in the back door still wearing his p.j.'s. He'd walked down to the club and sat looking at the *Good Times* and crying. Then he came home.

He finally told me that he was confused because he thought I was mad at Dan for getting sick, and he also felt Dan was treating him like a patient. I held him on my lap for a long time, big as he is, and we talked about how we felt. Finally decided that loving each other is the best thing we can do for Dan and ourselves. I've never felt closer to anyone in my life. Peg had tears in her eyes through the whole thing, but we all ended up planning a picnic for next Sunday. Dan can ride in comfort in the back of Peg's van on a mattress. We're going to Mount Laguna to see the new snow. It will be Teddy's first trip when he's big enough to ride a sled. Mike's looking forward to teaching him, and I think Dan'll like seeing him do that—looking out for his little brother. It ought to be fun. I want it to be, for all our sakes.

From Peg's Journal—The Week Before Thanksgiving

Dan's had a setback. He was in the hospital for tests when he got worse. Seems the original tumor has spread to his lungs. He's going to need a nurse and a breathing machine from here on in. Sylvia decided to bring him home, and I've supported that. He has a kind of transparency to him now—you can look right down into his eyes and feel you're in another reality. He's lost a lot of weight.

I've been working with him on pain control. He wants to take as little medication as possible, so as to participate in life to the best of his ability. He doesn't get up much any more; it's too hard on his lungs. We've been working on visualizing the pain as a bear's claw and then picturing it lifting off his body. He is learning good breath control and now concentrates better than anyone I've ever seen. We have also been doing some trance-induction, wherein he puts on a silk shirt, very soft and comfortable. The shirt has ten buttons, and as he buttons each one, he feels less and less discomfort. It's working very well for late-night trouble.

He's given up on the Horton Clinic. The strange medicines were hard on his veins, and the vitamin therapy gave him some subcutaneous ulcers without seeming to help much. He's stood fast in his determination not to accept chemotherapy or radiation, and Sylvia has finally stopped leaning on him. Doctor macAlbee has been willing to provide pain medication in increasingly strong dosages as needed. We all talked and decided that since they could afford in-house nursing care, Dan will die at home. Strange, six months ago he was sailing competitively and building a wooden-works clock for his parents' golden wedding anniversary.

Dan's spirit seems stronger than his body, which is wasted and emaciated. He laughs easily at old movies and still reads a good deal—mostly Mark Twain, Kazantzakis, and, oddly, the Bible. Says he's preparing himself for the grand debate with his father. Teddy hangs out with him, playing with blocks and crawling into bed for stories. I think for Dan the physical pain of being jostled and crowded is well worth the closeness to Teddy.

Mike is still withdrawn, almost sullen. He avoids Dan's room and says very little when the family gathers in the living room to watch old comedies, as they do almost every evening. He is closer to Sylvia now and avoids Rose, who is keeping up her litany of misery, no matter who says what to her.

Sylvia is different. That night when Mike broke down changed everything. She's calm, even smiles some. Teddy's allergies quieted down when she did. Rose is a problem—keeps calling up and telling whoever answers how upset she is and how she wishes it were she who is dying instead of Dan. Frankly, so do I. I've recommended another counselor for her—I'm just too out of sympathy to do her any good. She really is pathetic—old, dependent, out of it.

Dan has decided he can't conceal his condition from his parents any longer. They are coming in from Denver for Thanksgiving, and all they know is that he's been sick on and off for the last few months. I spent some time with him concerning his feelings about his father. The old man has always been righteous, bland, and intellectual—won't deal with feelings at all. He wanted Dan to be a preacher and hasn't forgiven him for the disappointment, but he never *says* anything Dan can get hold of. Dan wants desperately to make contact—feel the old man loves and understands him. I'm pessimistic. Doubt if under stress the old dog will learn new tricks—I'm afraid he'll just be more like he's always been. I've been trying to prepare Dan for that eventuality while encouraging him to express his feelings to his projected father in our therapy sessions.

Dan's plan is to be up in the living room when Sylvia brings them back from the airport. He hopes to have a good evening with them without mentioning his situation. He's out of his mind if he thinks anyone couldn't tell he's dying by looking at him. Hope springs eternal. Plans to tell them the whole story the next day. I'm working on his reality testing without wanting to dampen his hope in his plan.

From Sylvia's Journal—Late November

Just back from my vision quest. Peg suggested that since so much depends on me and greater challenges are certainly ahead, I needed to take some time out and regroup. She had to talk me into it. Taking time for myself just seemed too selfish, and besides, it meant losing some of the little time I have left with Dan. Finally she gave me a book that shows how modern people can do something similar to tribal custom. That is, go apart, fast, and do a ritual, seeking guidance. The idea caught my imagination, and God knows, I need *something* to sustain me. The kids' needs, Mom falling to pieces, Dan's folks coming, and watching Dan fade are overwhelming. So I did it.

Took my tent, sleeping bag, ground cloth, water supply, warm clothes, and first aid kit. That's all. Thankful for all the primitive camping experience I've had with Dan, I drove out into the Anza-Borrego Desert looking for the right spot.

I was pretty scared. I've never been really alone, and there is a whole lot of stuff stirred up in me now. Took a dirt side road that seemed lonely. Found a box canyon after a short hike and decided to set up camp. The plan was for me to fast for three days [Sylvia also had food in the car for the trip back and had preselected a likely area with Peg, which were important for safety] and just spend time alone in nature. I was to make up a ritual that would help me feel part of the place and remain open to any guidance that came my way. Pretty radical. No books, no journal, no writing material. Just me and the desert. I was my own resource. Part of a vision quest is the presence of real—genuine—danger. Meeting the challenge.

I was hungry only the first day. Then I got fascinated with all the detail around me: rocks, sand, skyline, creosote bushes. Saw a tarantula loping along looking for bugs or whatever they eat. Was surprised at its beauty—not threatening at all. As luck would have it, the canyon faced east, so the sun woke me. I slept out on the ground, even though I knew it wasn't smart what with snakes and scorpions around. I couldn't resist the wide-open, star-spangled sky. I could feel the weight of the sickroom falling off me with every breath of the cool, clean air.

Things began to feel different about the middle of the second day. The sky is so big! The landscape so dramatic! I felt small, yet part of it. I was surviving—probably because it was November, not August. I began to really feel part of it. Like if I died, I'd dry out. The ants and maybe buzzards would eat me, and it would be all right. I can't really explain. The desert is so harsh, so beautiful, so clean that dying just seems part of it, but so does life. I noticed some little, tiny leaves on the underside of the mesquite. Gray, oily little guys, but alive and keeping the plant going. I sort of felt like one of those little leaves.

Made a ring out of stones I dug up and hauled. It was about eight feet across and took (I counted) 379 rocks, rough white stones with veins of quartz (I think). Found four extra big ones and almost ruptured myself getting them into position at (I think) the four cardinal points. Wished I'd brought matches so I could have a little fire in the middle. Found a piece of broken glass and tried to focus a ray on some dry twigs, but no luck. Fire eluded me. Wasn't satisfied with just the stone ring, so I hunted around until I found part of a skeleton of a rabbit, the skull and some long leg bones. I made a little quartz rock altar in the middle of the ring with the skull on top. I put the leg bones in my hair, but I don't have a rational reason why. I found some colored dirt, a rusty red and a yellow ochre. It took me awhile, but I dug enough from the wall of a wash to make a couple of piles the size of basketballs. I looked down at my stained hands and broken nails. As if I were re-enacting a tribal memory, I carefully smoothed the coarse sand around the altar and made three concentric rings, alternating the red and ochre dirt. The contrast was beautiful, at least to my eye. For a while I sat and couldn't think what else to do. I was plenty tired and had probably been working on my ritual circle for four or five hours. I drank some water, which tasted delicious. I didn't want food.

Finally, remembered what Peg told me about chanting. Seems that primitive people used it to achieve altered states of consciousness. Something about the rhythm, sustained effort, maybe hyperventilation is hypnotic and leads to changes in metabolism and thus consciousness. Kind of self-conscious at first (though there probably wasn't anyone within fifty miles of my camp), I began. Somehow the traditional "om" seemed too Oriental for the place, so I just made some weird wavering sounds, experimenting. Felt *really* odd at first. Then I began to move around the colored circles, inside the stone ring, in a clockwise direction. I decided my clothes were in my way, so I took them off even though the air was probably about forty degrees. I even took off my shoes, taking my chances with thorns and creatures. This seemed to help, and I really got into it and went on and on. Round and round the circle I went, sometimes bending low, other times prancing and lifting my arms. My breasts swayed, and I could feel my hips jouncing as I danced. I liked how strong my thighs and calves felt and I danced with my shadow for a long time, almost mesmerized. The air on my skin was like menthol, and even though it was pretty cold, I soon had sweat running down my ribs. I almost never sweat and usually think of it as unpleasant, but there in the desert, it felt good. I even liked the smell of it, something new for me.

The exercise felt good, and I set up such a rhythm that I was, somehow, transported and actually forgot I was the one making the sound. Felt exhilarated for a while, then dizzy, disoriented, then finally I think I tranced out. It was then I had the vision or the dream or hallucination, whatever it was. When I woke up, at first I couldn't remember where I was or when I stopped dancing or chanting. My legs ached, and I was chilled through, lying there on the sand in front of my little altar. But most important was the vision.

It was as if the rabbit skull got bigger and bigger until it filled the whole sky. It was shiny white and light went in through the eye sockets so I could see the skull sutures and the pores in the bone. I was afraid and crouched down, trying to be small, but I could tell it wasn't doing any good, so I stood up and walked toward it. I went inside the skull throughout the open area under the cheek sinus and found I was in a room lit with translucent light and filled with a strange booming, whistling sound. It took me awhile to realize that the sound was my own heartbeat and breathing. I was filled with wonder and said, out loud, "What am I to do?" I didn't think about it. I just said it.

In the next moment, I was filled with the most wonderful sense of, I don't know the right word, *safety*, maybe, or *rightness*. Like I was absolutely protected, and I was *right* in what I was doing. No cares, no bad anticipations, no fear, no questions. What was, was, and that was proper. The words don't describe the feeling. I stayed in the skull a long time, and it was like a womb or heaven or something like that. I just *knew* that things were as they should be and that I was as I should be, and there wasn't any conflict or problem. I wish I could describe it better, but the feeling was so strong that I can bring it back anytime I just quiet myself by taking deep breaths and focusing inward. This probably sounds—or is—crazy, but I know it is real. Awful as objective reality is, with Dan dying and the world turning upside down, the paradox is that deep within, all is as it should be.

From Tape Made at the End of November

PEG: Dan, how is it working out for you to have these interviews recorded? Is it comforting?

DAN: It just seems I'm down to bedrock and what I'm going through might mean something to the boys later. Maybe it will mean something to you or someone else. Maybe I'm grandiose . . .

PEG: When you called me, you said you'd had your talk with your father.

DAN: I should have said, I *tried* to have a talk with him. He can't talk. All he can do is *preach*.

PEG: Unsatisfactory, huh?

DAN: Worse, I feel it was our last chance to make contact. I wanted to make *contact* with my father.

PEG: What happened?

DAN: Well, I did what you said. After I told both of them— Mom and Dad—about my cancer and the lousy prognosis, we had a pretty emotional time, and I was worn out. So I went to bed after telling Dad I wanted to have a heart-to-heart before they left. He seemed to say okay. The next couple of days were bad with Mom. She didn't say a lot, but I could tell she was torn up. I told her that I loved her a lot and that she'd been a good mom. She didn't say much, but she rubbed my back between the shoulder blades the way she did when I was a little kid and hurting. It was pretty clean between us. She was never complicated, she just went along with Dad's program, but slipped in some pretty good mothering on the way. I've always known she loved me even though there isn't much to talk about except the past and the kids.

PEG: And your dad?

DAN: You know, he really is a Methodist minister—at all times of the day and night. That and just that. Sees it as his business to preach and, as he says, "do the work of the Lord." No feelings—at least not many—just righteousness and distance. I've never heard him say what he feels about much of anything, outside of the church and its politics. But sometimes he just *exudes* disapproval . . .

PEG: Tell him. Put him in that chair. Take the time to make him real for yourself. Attend to how he'd sit, his expression, what he'd wear.

[Lengthy silence.]

DAN: I'm so damned disappointed—I wanted to do it with the real him . . .

PEG: Make him real for yourself—this is critical work, as you know, Dan.

DAN: I know. Okay. Give me a minute. [Silence.]
Goddammit, Dad, I want you to *hear* me. No, I want you to *talk* to me. Tell me what you feel . . . Dad, I'm going to die pretty soon. I've got the "Big C" in my chest and liver and probably everywhere else. What do you *feel* about that?
It's no good, Peg. He's just sitting there, looking professionally sorrowful because I'm not saved the way he thinks I should be.

PEG: Tell him.

DAN: Goddammit, Dad, *care about me!* Tell me so! Cry, even. You goddamn son-of-a-bitch bastard! Why can't you show me? Touch me? I don't want to belong to your goddamn exclusive Christian club! I believe something else, and it's none of your business! I want you to tune in to me! Christ, I'm your only son, your only kid. Can't you feel how much this means to me? [Sobbing.]

PEG: Keep it coming, and recognize that you're emptying out a lot of bitterness—years of it. Begin some sentences with "Dad, I resent . . ." or "Dad, you should have . . ."

DAN: Yeah. Dad, you should have lightened up. Dad, you should have come down out of the pulpit once in a while. Dad, you should stop being such a goddammed *robot*, all logic and coolness. Did you ever feel your balls? Did you ever give a thought to anything except your goddamn message?

PEG: "Dad, I resent . . ." "Dad, you should have . . ."

DAN: Right. Dad, I resent growing up not knowing anything about feelings from you. Dad, I resent the narrow, bigoted, stupid way of thinking you inherited from your father. Dad, I resent your lack of thinking. Dad, I resent your lack of feeling. That's what I really resent—your lack of feeling. Talking to you is like talking to a cardboard cutout. *Nothing* comes back. I resent your *nothingness,* your hollowness, your stupid, pious talk of eternity and hell and salvation. Why the hell didn't you save out a little for your kid? For me? Dad, I resent being lonely for you all my life ... [sobbing, gradually quieting].

PEG: Was that it?

DAN: Yeah. That's what I feel, felt. Christ, I'm tired.

PEG: I know. You're not done, though—there's more.

DAN: More?

PEG: Can you find anything to appreciate in him? Anything you like or admire? Have you any good memories?

[Silence.]

DAN: I don't know.

PEG: Let's see. Begin some sentences to that father there in the chair with "Dad, I appreciate ..." or "Dad, I remember ..."

DAN: This is hard.

PEG: I believe you. Do it anyway.

DAN: You're a tough woman, Peg. Okay. Dad, I appreciate your financial help in getting my degree even though you disapproved of psychology, particularly for a living. Dad, I appreciate that you always provided for us first, before yourself. Dad, I appreciate that you worked hard and set a good example. I appreciate your teaching me woodwork and giving me that set of Swedish chisels for my sixteenth birthday. I wanted a car, but I've still got the chisels. Dad, I remember the tree house you built in the old maple. Dad, I appreciate the time you got me down from the top of that tree when I'd gotten myself stranded. Just climbed up and talked me down move by move and never told anyone about it. Dad, I remember *and* appreciate your telling me that Sylvia was a fine woman when I told you I was getting married. Dad, I remember singing "Amazing Grace" in the car going to Cincinnati—singing it over and over until my ears were ringing. I thought it was the best song in the world. I still do, as a matter of fact. Dad, I remember watching you swim across the lake that summer in Wisconsin. You were strong, and I remember how straight you went for the island. I wanted to grow up just like you. Dad, I appreciate my life ... [sobs].

PEG: Any more?

DAN: I don't think so—that covers it. Covers me.
PEG: Time to say good-bye, Dan. Time to let go of that Dad
      so you've got a chance to get the contact you need from
      those of us who can give it. He can't give what he hasn't
      got or doesn't understand.
DAN: Good-bye, huh? This hurts. All right. How?
PEG: You need to say the word and use his name, "Dad." Say
      it to him with whatever last words you've got, and *let
      him go.* He'll fade out of that chair, and you'll be in a
      different place—much more open to the love you need
      from the rest of us. Say the words, Dan.
DAN: Oh. All right. Dad, it's time to let you go. You did the
      best you could—same as me. You didn't do what I
      wanted, but you did your best. I've got to get closer to
      my family—make more contact, and I can't while I'm still
      looking to you for it. So, good-bye, Dad. Good-bye. Best
      of everything. Good-bye. [Sobbing.]
PEG: Can I hold you? I don't want to hurt you with . . .
DAN: Please . . .

From Peg's Journal—Mid-December

Medically, Dan is losing the fight. It's absolutely unbelievable to
me that six months ago his biggest concerns were getting a good crew
for the Ensenada race and deciding whether to invest in condos or mu-
nicipal bonds.

Something critical and wonderful happened after Sylvia's vision quest
and Dan's letting go of his father. They both seem to be quieter inside
and, at the same time, much more demonstrative with their affection
to each other and the boys. And me. I feel included in their love. In
fact, that increased love and demonstrativeness might be the most significant thing that's happened. Margo and Tilly, the nurses, have both
told me that caring for Dan is a healing experience for them. And he's
hurting, physically. It's amazing to know that his body is wracked up,
yet he's resisting the pain medication. His energy feels so good to be
around.

As Dan explained to me, he stopped treating Mike like a textbook
example and got a whole lot more real with him. Cried with him. Told
him what he resented, remembered, and appreciated. He said Mike did
the same to him—with some stuff that really stung. Then Dan told me
that even when Mike's resentments hurt, he realized he was *in contact*
with his kid. The withdrawal is pretty much over on Mike's part. Dan
told me he was resisting laying any expectations on Mike—like taking
care of Teddy or trying harder in school. The way he put it, "There

shouldn't be a dead hand on the throttle." Then early one morning, before school, Mike went in to Dan. He had a notebook and pencil. He said he wanted to know what Dan wanted him to know. That unlocked the gates; Dan told him what he felt about integrity, keeping your word, working hard, having fun, loving. He told me that he hadn't even known he felt that way, himself, until his son asked him. If he'd started laying responsibility trips on Mike, he figured that the kid never would have asked. Pretty wonderful stuff happening.

Dan and I have come up with a plan. He needs a special time for just his family and me. There is some question of whether he'll be alive at Christmas. I *am* part of the family now in every respect except blood. I feel so privileged to be part of this. Anyhow, the plan is for the five of us to get together Sunday night [a week before Christmas] for our own celebration.

From Sylvia's Journal

> There is mercy in a drenching rain
> Washing the dust and dog crap away,
> Leaving trees and city freshly cleansed.
> There is mercy in a raging storm
> Ravaging the coast and removing all
> The sailors' wine bottles and Twinkie wrappers.
> There is mercy in ripping, rending pain
> In the agony of separation and unanswerable questions
> Removing all the etiquette, false smiles and
> Untried, politic assumptions about reality,
> Leaving truth and love and laughter and God in its wake.

I wish I could remember this all the time. When I do, I feel back in the giant rabbit skull, sure of the rightness of myself and what comes. When I'm weary or wake up terrified about the future, I forget.

Mike's Essay

MY DAD
by Michael Tyrone Bennett

My dad has red hair, like me. He is a good sailor and wins lots of races. When I grow up, I'll get a bigger boat than the *Good Times* and sail around the world to Fiji and Borneo, like he wants to do. My dad eats the potato chips and then says he doesn't know what happened to them. When I was little, he used to take baths with me and we'd play boats. He told me never to blow bubbles in the bathwater when Mom was around. He's lots of fun to build models with. My dad wants me to do good in school. I'm bored at school, so I don't do too much work. I'd rather play basketball.

My dad has cancer, and he has to spend a lot of time in bed. He gets shots for pain at night, and then he snores. I like to hear him snore because I know he isn't hurting.

My dad knows how to talk to kids, and he does it all day at his work. Once a kid my age was doing bad things like smoking dope and stealing. After he talked to my dad he got better, and his parents got better too. I heard Dad talking to Mom about it when they thought I was watching TV.

My dad spanked me for starting up the car without permission. I think he was scared. So was I. I'm glad I have the dad I have.

The End

From Peg's Journal—Late, After Our Christmas Farewell Celebration

I'm sitting here—it's almost two in the morning—staring at a bouquet of peacock feathers in a rich, brown stoneware vase. It was Dan's gift to me. All he said when he handed the whole thing to me, unwrapped, was, "They remind me of you." Pretty wonderful gift.

Tonight was wonderful. Sad and wonderful. Dan can get out of bed for an hour or so twice a day, with help. He's got a huge, oddly shaped swelling at the lower back of his skull, and he's dizzy a lot. Looking at him, I wonder how he is alive, but alive he is—with eyes as clear as the air after a rain. He's almost transparent—so thin and white he doesn't seem real. But he can still laugh a good guffaw, and he moves his hands around with some animation. I have no doubt he had a good evening, even though the effort probably cost him a lot. Sylvia told me he was on a very low dosage of morphine, just enough, she said, to "take the edge off." That's the sad part.

When I got back to the Bennetts', the scene was set. Fire in the fireplace, candles, silver dishes, poinsettias, and the Limoges china. It was a dessert party in the living room—everyone had chosen their favorite, and Sylvia saw that it was there. Mike chose lemon meringue pie; Teddy ordered vanilla-cherry ice cream with chocolate *and* marshmallow sauce; Sylvia had little cream puffs; and I brought a chocolate-rum torte. Dan wanted mangoes. They even had a T-bone for Bosco II, which he worked on noisily under the piano throughout the rest of the evening. Even though Dan isn't eating much nowadays, he had a spoonful of everyone's treat—except Bosco's. We all talked and laughed at the choices.

Sylvia surprised us by taking out her recorder. She used to play in college, but hadn't done much with it in the last few years. She played "Greensleeves" and one of Dan's favorites, "Danny Boy." My eyes were brimming by the time she finished the last of that plaintive air "for ye must go and I must bide." In fact, there wasn't a dry eye in the house. Then Mike said he wanted to do some magic tricks and read something he'd written [see essay pp. 29–30]. He's pretty good with the scarves and cards and had us wondering how he knew which card we each held. He looked healthy and self-confident, even when he dropped the whole deck halfway through his act.

We continued the entertainment with Sylvia and Teddy acting out all the parts of "The Three Bears." She was Goldilocks and Momma Bear—Teddy was Daddy and Baby Bear. They ended up with a big bow and Teddy saying "and that's me, Teddy Bear!" I laughed until my sides ached, and so, I saw, did Dan. When our eyes met, it was an intimate moment of pure shared pleasure. Very simple and deep.

My part of the entertainment was to read one of my stories to them—it was about a singing sheep and the effect she had on her owner, one of the "singing impaired." Everyone but Teddy was laughing at the end, and he was sound asleep, his head on Dan's arm, where they lay together on the couch.

Finally, we got to the gift exchange. I'd been in a quandary, wanting to do something very special and not coming up with it. Almost like fate, I'd wandered into a gallery during my lunch break, not at all sure of myself. In a dark corner, I came across a Chinese scroll, ink on silk. The picture showed Lao Tzu, sitting on his buffalo, smiling with amusement at the world passing before him. I knew instantly that it was what I'd been looking for. I had it mounted on a double oak frame with a fragment from Lao Tzu's *The Way of Life*, verse 67, written in ornate calligraphy:

I have three treasures, which I hold and keep safe: The first is called love;
The second is moderation;
The third is called not venturing to go ahead of the world. Being loving, one can be brave;
Being moderate, one can be ample;
Not venturing to go ahead of the world, one can be the chief of all officials.
For he who fights with love will win the battle;
He who defends with love will be secure;
Heaven will save him, and protect him with love.

I was pleased with how it looked because it seemed to have the lesson we'd all been learning the past three months. I put a little note on the back about how privileged I felt to be part of Dan's life.

Everyone had obviously given a great deal of thought to their gifts. Sylvia and Dan gave Mike a horse bridle, with the promise that after the first of the year, when Christmas was over [and Dan, most certainly, gone], Sylvia and Mike would pick out an animal at the Morgan Ranch in Pine Valley. I never saw anyone as transported with delight as that kid when he realized what was coming. You could almost see the future open up for him after Dan's death. Dan made a joke about how Mike could have the horse, but he'd only get to feed it if he did his homework. We all knew it was a joke, but I think something settled into Mike's mind at that instant. At least he won't forget it when he's faced with schoolwork.

Then Dan brought out his gifts [I've already mentioned my peacock feathers and vase]. For Sylvia and the boys, he managed to create three small wood carvings—amulets about three inches high. Teddy's was a bear—a perfect choice. Made of a tight-grained, rosy wood, it was a wonderfully detailed replica of a bear standing upright—arms raised, head up, looking alert. Not a cuddlesome *or* ferocious animal, rather one that was strong and self-assured, even noble.

Mike's carving was of a dog—perfect representation of Bosco II, down to his plumy Golden Retriever tail. Dan had gone with Mike to pick his first puppy when the boy was four. Together, they'd buried Bosco when he was run over after Mike left the yard gate open. A month later, Bosco II showed up in a basket by Mike's bed one rainy Saturday morning. He is probably the most loved animal in the Southwest.

Dan went all the way with Sylvia's carving. He'd managed to carve a hollow sphere, all lacy and intricate. When I examined it closely, I saw it was a bird cage with a miniature bird inside. The bird had a shiny eye—maybe a diamond chip. But the most remarkable thing was the *cage door stood open!*

Teddy still slept soundly, and Mike was fading, so Sylvia and I tucked them into bed. At the end the three of us talked softly and freely—not somber or solemn, but seriously. How we cared for each other and how each of us, in our own way, had glimpsed Something More. For Sylvia it was a centered certainty that what was happening was part of what *had* to happen and felt right. Then she said she wished she didn't have to learn this lesson this way.

I talked about how I see Nature offering bountifully, wasting nothing, cycling and recycling. I told them how I feel part of the natural world and that some part of my essence resonates with the water and wind and trees. I told how once or twice, in my best moments, I've lost track of my boundaries and *felt* part of everything. Once was while giving birth and another time was when I was body surfing and saw a porpoise in the same wave, doing the same thing, grinning in delight and looking right at me. I figure that's how we're supposed to be, and when we get rid of our clutter, that's how we actually *are.*

Dan was looking worn out, but his eyes glowed with a kind of intimate intensity that drew me closer. His voice sounded weak, and he talked very slowly, saying, "When I first got sick and found out how bad it was, my reaction was to be pissed off. There was so much—damn much—I wanted to do and I felt I was just hitting my stride. Travel around the world on my own boat. Publish a paper on hyperkinetic kids and television. I don't know—just *live.* I felt as though I'd been tripped by a piano wire—something invisible had been in my path, and I'd stumbled and fallen. I was really sorry for myself, sorry for Sylvia, sorry for the boys, sorry, sorry, sorry—and pissed. Wasted a lot of time. It's all honed away now—not enough energy, not enough left for complaining. So much has happened—so much incredibly good stuff—love— has happened, that I'm sort of eager, to tell the truth, for what comes next. I think Dad got part of it right—Christ—if Christ means 'love'—is the answer. Right now, I don't feel I need a thing except some music and to go to bed."

Moved beyond anything I had ever felt before, I sang "Amazing Grace" with Dan and Sylvia and then helped Sylvia get him into bed. I left for home. There isn't a hell of a lot more to say, right now.

From Peg's Journal—Last Day of December

Dan died at three-thirty this morning. Sylvia woke up from a light sleep and went in to see if he needed her. He was awake, but too weak to say anything. She asked if he needed more morphine, but he half-smiled and shook his head. She sat down by him, holding his hand. They looked into each other's eyes, and he just shut his, gave a sigh, and that was that. She called me at 4:30 and I went over.

Dan was so thin he hardly mounded the covers; he appeared as colorless as the sheets. Really, it was clear he wasn't in his body. But the feeling in the room was something else—there was an aliveness that I can't explain. Sylvia and I held each other and cried a little.

Just as dawn was breaking, we did as we had planned with Dan, weeks ago. I woke the boys, told them Dan had gone, and brought them into the room. They were a little frightened, but trusted me enough to come. Sylvia talked to them a few minutes, and they all cried together. Then she put the hem of the sheet over Dan's face—a graceful, releasing gesture. We each lit a white candle in a brass stand and put it on the windowsill between the poinsettias. No one said anything for a while, but Teddy was crying, and Mike stared straight into the flames with a grown-up expression on his face. Sylvia said, "The music Dan wanted played is on the machine. Let's stand up and listen to it." The glorious chords of Handel's *Messiah* filled the room, and when it was over, Dan was gone.

*   *   *

The following three years that I lived near them, the Bennetts and I got together each New Year's Eve to remember Dan. We had the same desserts, read our latest writings that we thought he'd have liked, sang "Amazing Grace," told funny stories from the past, lit our white candles, and closed with the "Hallelujah Chorus." I looked forward to it as a fulfilling time.

Part Two
Cultivating an Empowering Mythology for Confronting Death

David Feinstein

No matter how close to yours another's steps have
  grown
In the end there is one dance you do alone.
                                    —JACKSON BROWNE

The story of Dan Bennett's final days is a study in the rapid changes that may occur in the personal mythologies of family members when one of their number faces a life-threatening illness. As the specter of death seized their hearts and home, the Bennetts found themselves undergoing an intense reexamination of their values, priorities, hopes, and dreams.

A great irony often observed by people who have had the privilege of knowing someone like Dan Bennett, who died well, involves the way the person comes to participate more fully in living. A shift in attention occurs as the preciousness of each moment is recognized and savored. Often the change is no less than a spiritual transformation. There is both an opening to one's deeper nature and to qualities of existence that transcend one's individual identity. Whether or not traditional religious concepts are used to explain the experience, there is a deepened sense of purpose and a more profound sense of connection with other people and with the universe. One's higher passions are stimulated; love, beauty, truth, and justice are savored anew. Those who have observed the way such peace and simple dignity come upon a person confronted with imminent death may wonder why we must wait until the final season to attain such grace. Perhaps we do not need to wait.

Two years after a near-fatal heart attack, Abraham Maslow, one of this century's greatest psychologists, spoke of the intervening period as "the postmortem life." Reflecting on how these years were a kind of bonus, an extra gift, he noted that "if you're reconciled with death or even if you are pretty well assured that you will have a good death, a dignified one, then every single moment of every single day is transformed because the pervasive undercurrent—the fear of death—is removed." In the postmortem life

> everything gets doubly precious, gets piercingly important. You get stabbed by things, by flowers and by babies and by beautiful things—just the very act of living, of walking and breathing and eating and having friends and chatting. Everything seems to look more beautiful rather than less, and one gets the much-intensified sense of miracles. . . . The confrontation with death—and the reprieve from it—makes everything look so precious, so sacred, so beautiful that I feel more strongly than ever the impulse to love it, to embrace it, and to let myself be overwhelmed by it.[1]

The "personal mythology"—the deep beliefs, guiding images, and unspoken rules—you hold about how you should live and what it means to die exerts an invisible but decisive influence on the choices you make every day of your life. Your personal mythology shapes what you think, what you feel, and what you do. In this section of the book, you will

37

be touching in with your mortality, examining the mythology you have developed in attempting to come to terms with it, and challenging yourself to cultivate a personal mythology about death that is more purposeful, life-affirming, and evocative of your highest sensibilities.

A Spiritual Crisis and a Reappraisal of Life and Death

Charles Cameron was sixty-seven when his world unraveled. Within a six-month period, he discovered that he had diabetes; his company required that he retire (a step he'd wanted to postpone for another three years); and his wife of forty-four years died in a plane crash. He became despairing and suicidal.

Never a religious person, Charles had no emotional, intellectual, or spiritual framework into which he could fit his losses. His life had comprised his work, but, as he said later, "not much else." Stripped of his occupation as a sales executive for a pump manufacturing firm, of his humdrum but amicable marriage, and of what had seemed good health, he saw no reason to live. It was only at the insistence of his grown son that he grudgingly agreed to enter psychotherapy. Charles had "abandoned hope and was just going through my paces to satisfy Danny. I really *wanted* to die, but I was also afraid of dying."

His first task in therapy was to grieve his losses—professional identity, a secure and ordered marriage, and what felt like "the best years of my life—they're all behind me." It took him nearly a year of therapy to lighten his pained confusion and come to a reluctant awareness that, with proper care, he might well live another twenty years. Initially, this seemed a gloomy prospect: "All I could imagine was a life of insulin shots, waning strength, dutiful dinner invitations from the kids, and television."

At this time Charles was in a serious automobile accident. Six weeks later, we asked him to describe his experience. "I was on my way back from our mountain cabin—I was getting ready to put the place on the market—when it happened. I took a curve a little too fast—thinking about Margie and the good times we'd had up there.

"The next thing, I was airborne, and I saw the world tilt. I don't know how long it was, but when I came to, I was hanging upside down by the seat belt, and my head hurt like hell. I was cold, and it was getting dark. Everything in the car had shifted around, and I couldn't undo the buckle. The headlights were on, but I couldn't reach the horn—I was more scared than I've ever been in my life.

"I passed out, probably from all the blood rushing to my head, but I didn't pass out completely, if you know what I mean—kind of in and out. Like I knew where I was and that I was probably going to die in this grotesque way, but part of me felt sort of separated from it too. Pretty soon the separated part began to turn away, to disconnect. Then I began to look around. It was a beautiful place—deep woods, river in the canyon, and a full moon coming over the ridge. And I noticed it was sort of misty—foggy—and I was just drifting over the forest floor. I didn't seem to have any substance, and the wind was moving me.

"Then came the moment I realized—but deeper than words—that *I am part of it all!* Even though I now believe I had literally died, I knew I didn't want to leave until I made friends with the planet again. I remembered being a kid and reveling in nature, and I knew I had to touch that again before I'd be ready to die. And I knew that something was holding it all together—all the pieces. I was irresistibly drawn to finding out more about what that was.

"I came to, still upside down, but I was thinking better. I squirmed around and got the seat belt unfastened. Then I crawled out the passenger window and up the bank, and the first car along saw me.

"For a week I just basically sat and thought about what had happened. Actually, it wasn't *thought*—I sat and absorbed the experience. There never was any doubt about its reality, but what did it mean? Sally [his daughter-in-law] was a big help.

"She's interested in all that 'woo-woo' stuff like the *I Ching*, Tarot, and crystals. She told me that she was reading an article in one of her magazines that reminded her of my accident. It talked about a Tarot card called 'The Hanged Man,' and she read a passage to me:

> The card represents surrender to death and resurrection as the soul leaves the body and then returns. Personality is torn away, and a higher power takes over. In the card, a man is pictured hanging upside down, attached to the tree by a snake, a symbol of wisdom. Energy rushes to the head, stimulating greater awareness. In his limited and precarious position, his only task is that of fighting for his life. While he struggles, all of his old realities drop away. He moves into a state of non-ordinary reality where anything is possible, where freedom and enlightenment reside. The boundaries between life and death blur and, if the initiation is successful, the initiate realizes that death is part of life. He then realizes the importance of living life fully and with passion.[2]

"Blew my mind! These words described exactly my experience of hanging there in that car, and they gave form to my deepest inklings about the meaning of the experience. In the following weeks, it was as if the walls fell outward and I could explore ideas and feelings in a new way. A sense of peace came over me that I could not remember having since I was a boy hiking in the Sierra Nevada. But I also had a sense of urgency. I wanted to drink up the richness of life I saw all around me. I started hiking again, and on every hike, I've seen stunning sights I will never forget. I've also been taking much pleasure in reading John

Muir's nature journals. The greatest joy comes from my children and, particularly, I must admit, my grandchildren. I was always proud of them, but I never slowed down enough to really let myself know them. Now I can enter their world, and it is the most extraordinary privilege I've ever had. I can speak with them in their own language and begin to teach them some of the lessons I've garnered in my own life. I hope I will be around long enough to see them into their own marriages and children, but even if I'm not, I think I'm planting the best guidance I have right into their foundations."

One of the paradoxes about confronting death is that it is easier to accept its inevitability when one has lived fully. Fortunately, it seems that even if people don't come to this realization until the last few years of life (as Charles Cameron's story illustrates), or even the last few days (and clinical evidence bears this out),[3] as they do come into the process of living fully, they come to find in retrospect meaning for the lives they have lived, and they come to a sense of peace about dying. But why do we wait?

Many experiences bring us face-to-face with our own mortality, but we tend to brush them out of our minds as quickly as possible. After all, we cannot live effectively if we are endlessly focused on the precariousness of life. If, however, we can genuinely face the precariousness and come to terms with our mortality, we pass through the narrow and delicate doorway to another realm of consciousness that Charles Cameron encountered when his car veered off the main road. The instinctual terror of death may explode within us as we approach this passage, but to successfully move through it is to conquer a fair measure of the nameless anxiety that we, individually and as a culture, exert so much effort to keep out of our minds.[4] When we have effectively squared off and faced that anxiety, we see the world freshly and engage with it less encumbered by nameless fears—and with new vitality—as we reclaim our misplaced energy. But it is a challenging passage to traverse, and our culture gives us few *rites of passage* to help us through it.

Rituals and Rites of Passage

"Illness," observed Marcel Proust, "is the most heeded of doctors: to goodness and wisdom we only make promises; we obey pain."[5] And fear. The inner strength and renewed vigor that proved to be the fruits of Charles Cameron's life crisis were harvested within a field of emotional pain. Pain and the fear of pain are certainly among nature's primary ways of guiding our behavior and directing our growth. Pain is an emphatic critic and teacher, but it is not the only teacher along the way.

Education is humanity's compassionate alternative to pain as a means for providing its youth with the lessons of life. Substantial resources in every human culture are directed toward educating children and influencing their development. Most other creatures on this planet have a much simpler and in many ways more efficient system of inner guidance than ours. It is based largely on instinct. As the human species evolved, mythological thinking—the ability to symbolically address large questions—replaced instinct and genetic mutation as the primary vehicles by which individual consciousness and societal innovations were carried forward. We are compelled to follow a deep, largely unconscious, often internally inconsistent, emotionally loaded, yet largely learned complex of concepts, images, and ways of perceiving—a personal mythology. Because this inner symbolic guidance is so malleable—particularly during the prolonged dependence of children on adults—families, schools, churches, and other social institutions exert an enormous influence on how a society's members develop.

Rituals and rites of passage are traditionally among the most powerful culturally sanctioned vehicles available for exerting this influence. They are social inventions for instructing the human spirit on its journey into the world. They transmit the combined wisdom of previous generations and are built on the promise that future generations can derive the lessons of painful experiences without having to repeat them. Rituals, like myths, address (1) our urge to comprehend our existence in a meaningful way, (2) our search for a marked pathway as we move from one stage of our lives to the next, (3) our need to establish secure and fulfilling relationships within a human community, and (4) our longing to know our part in the vast wonder and mystery of the cosmos.[6] Rituals carry the mythology generated by the culture in response to these needs, and they translate that mythology into the individual's experience. The guidance the culture's mythology has to offer is etched into the mind and body of every person participating in the ritual. In this manner, rituals—family ceremonies, community celebrations, church liturgies, the sacraments of baptism, marriage, and burial—help to form the individual's personal mythology and continue to shape it with each life passage.

Historically, rituals provided unequivocal direction for regulating people's lives. The beliefs and customs held by the members of tribal cultures were relatively uniform, allowing for little question or variation. Each individual embraced the tribe's time-honored mythology, and the rituals for maintaining and deepening the mythology were powerful and unambiguous. Today, our mythology is neither uniform nor stable. It can no longer be conveyed by a single shaman or storyteller around a campfire. In contrast, we find many competing myths and fragments of myths tugging at us, delivered through the powerful and unprecedented myth-making machinery that is a product of modern electronic technology. Superficial and spiritually barren ideas and pursuits—such as the notion that you are confined to the lower echelons of personal fulfillment until you are able to own a BMW—are artificially sweetened and expertly packaged until they seem as emotionally alluring as the momentous and profound.

It is hardly surprising, amid this alienating mythic cacophony, that contemporary society is typified by a poverty of vibrant rituals— ceremonies that are connected to the deeper realms of human existence, the realms traditionally touched by mythology. This bankruptcy of meaningful ritual in American homes is seen by some anthropologists as representing cultural decay. One of the first things to occur when a primitive culture begins to deteriorate under the impact of the West is that the ceremonial systems disintegrate. This leads to internal disorganization, loss of values, and social fragmentation.[7] At the very least, our lack of ritual signals a period of massive transition in our cultural beliefs and practices.

The lack of unity and coherence in the culture's myths and rituals allows, and in fact forces, individuals to think and act for themselves in ways that were unimaginable in the past. Major mythic shifts— regarding issues as vital as what it means to be a man, a woman, a parent, a good citizen, a success—are being hammered out today on the anvil of people's lives. We make the best we can of our circumstances without, for the most part, the benefit of inspiring myths or meaningful ritual. But we are collectively starving for myths and rituals that are attuned to the unique needs of the day—able to support the emphatic individuality that so strongly characterizes the modern psyche while promoting cooperation and a stronger sense of community.[8] Is it possible to develop such animating myths and rituals? We believe that it is, and that their cultivation is, in fact, a critical agenda if the culture is to reflesh its ideals and its humanity.

Where does one start? How can we develop rituals that speak to today's individualistic spirit while furthering our desperate need for a sense of genuine community? In the opening section of the book, we watched Peg Elliott Mayo as she sensitively designed a set of family rituals—such as having each family member grapple with and share what death means to them, Dan's real and imaginary meetings with his father, and the family's "dessert" party—that paced the Bennetts through the most bitter crisis of their lives. We saw how the rituals that helped the Bennetts prepare for, face, and commemorate their loss were based on a compassionate understanding of their deepest emotions; of the importance of encouraging hidden feelings to be registered, expressed, and responded to; of the natural progression of denial, anger, hope, depression, and reconciliation; and of the resources the family members possessed for themselves and for one another. The Bennett family's experience is a case study in the invention of creative ritual. Families are certainly fertile settings for such efforts, and periodic family celebrations of successes and transitions, large and small, can provide a natural opportunity for meaningful ritual. Couples who write their own marriage vows and families who design celebrations of accomplishment or ceremonies in memory of loved ones are exercising their ability to create more relevant ritual.

New rituals can be seen emerging in various segments of our culture. Rock concerts mobilized around causes such as peace, poverty, and human rights have become powerful vehicles for ritualistic activity in modern societies. Programs such as Outward Bound and practices imported from other traditions, such as vision quests and sweat lodge ceremonies, can serve as rites of passage into greater self-reliance and inner harmony. During the 1960s and 1970s, there was an explosion of temporary intensive community experience, such as encounter groups and workshops for personal development. These events served some of the same functions that rituals and rites of passage have served in other cultures. Participants were often able to lay bare and heal early wounds, glimpse a better course for their development, find renewed meaning in their lives, and establish a deepened connection with their spiritual roots. However, these temporary communities were separated from the communities in which people lived, divorced from the structure of their lives, and disconnected from their traditions. Though they were important experiments that were in many ways attuned to the modern individual's complex path, their lessons need to be brought back home to our families, our neighborhoods, and our places of work and worship.

The approach taken here for innovating new and relevant rituals begins in the laboratory of your own being. In another book, *Personal Mythology: The Psychology of Your Evolving Self,* Stanley Krippner and I presented a series of personal rituals that guide people in identifying, examining, and systematically changing key areas of their deep mythologies. These "personal rituals" are internal rites of passage designed to modify and revitalize beliefs, attitudes, and patterns of behavior. They guide you toward fresh contact with the core of your being. Personal rituals can provide fresh meaning and purpose to your life as they serve critical functions that cultural rites and rituals are no longer able to address.

In the following pages, you will be led through a series of inward-focused rituals to help you understand and transform your distinctly personal mythology regarding death. Our hope is that by generating a series of richly meaningful inner experiences, you will develop not only a more inspiring and empowering mythology regarding life and death, but also that you will be better equipped in your home setting to apply your discoveries in a manner that, as in the Bennetts' experience, allows shared rituals to be developed as the occasion demands.

Creating an Empowering Mythology
for Living and Dying

In her introduction to *Death: The Final Stage of Growth*, Elisabeth Kübler-Ross summarizes the "one important message" she hopes the book will convey: "Death does not have to be a catastrophic, destructive thing; indeed it can be viewed as one of the most constructive, positive, and creative elements of culture and life."[9] It is our hope that the program you are about to begin will lead you toward this realization and toward a more "constructive, positive, and creative" relationship with death. The personal rituals that comprise the remainder of this book are patterned after those developed in our workshops and clinical practice.

The program presented in this chapter is designed to stimulate an inner transformation, a rite of passage of sorts, toward a more empowering mythology regarding death. For some, it will mark the conscious inauguration of a lifelong process. For others, it will provide a checkpoint along the way. It will focus on the personal myths you hold related to living and dying. It will also unearth some ideas that were forged to contain the natural anxiety about death that fueled your childhood nightmares and fears of monsters under the bed. Thus it may not always be comfortable. It is important to respect your own needs and pace as you enter the territory that the program will help you explore. Our experience has been that the people who have been drawn to this program have found it constructive and beneficial, but we also caution you not to force yourself into experiences you intuitively believe you are not ready to handle. If after reading the case examples and instructions about a particular personal ritual, you are reluctant to proceed with it, feel free to skip over it and consider the one that follows it.

There is an Oriental image called "the Guardian of the Threshold" that can be instructive regarding such reluctance. The Guardian of the Threshold is a dreadful monster that is often depicted at the gates of a temple. According to Roger Woolger, these guardians are images of our own fears and are there to prevent us from entering realms for which we are not ready. He suggests that "whether we are aware of them or not, each of us has our inner guardians of the threshold to prevent us from going too deep, too fast. There is a subtle inner economy of psychic and spiritual unfoldment in which every individual proceeds at his or her own pace, governed by these inner guardians and guides."[10] We encourage you to tune inward, respect your own guardians of the threshold if they appear, face them, and alertly discover what they have to teach you before they are ready to allow you to more directly encounter a particular area of your inner life.

If your intuition or your guardians are insisting that you are not ready to go through the program, you may nonetheless want to read this section of the book without actually performing the exercises. You will still become more attuned to the place of your mortality in your inner world; you will be exposed to a set of potent techniques for using the fact of death to make life richer; and you may participate vicariously as you read about the people who serve as case examples and their experiences using the techniques.

In assessing your readiness to devote substantial energy to confronting the issue of death, also be aware of the stresses that are currently acting upon you, your present sense of emotional stability, and any messages from your guardians of the threshold. The program, however, is not morbid. By unearthing repressed fears about death that may be invisibly draining your energies and clouding your outlook, you open yourself to greater vitality and richer meaning. The issues raised here may best be faced in the presence of an intimate or counselor. Enlisting such support when confronting the issue of death is a good idea, whether or not you choose this book as a vehicle for engaging the topic. But why wait on somehow engaging it? As Stephen Levine, the empowering teacher on matters regarding life and death, instructs: "You can open your heart to the fullness of life at any time. If you've got something better to do, do it."[11] If not, let's begin.

The eighteen personal rituals in this section of the book lead you through a five-stage program that was developed to guide people in examining their deeper mythologies.[12] Each personal ritual builds on those before it, so it is important to carry them out or at least consider them in the order given. The only materials you will need are a journal or notebook for describing and reflecting upon your experience with each ritual (some people use their personal computers), colored markers, a large paper plate, and possibly a cassette recorder with tapes.

The program may be used alone, with a friend or family member, as the focal point of a small study group, as part of the training of hospice volunteers or others who work with catastrophic illness, under the supervision of a therapist, or as the basis for clinicians or other qualified leaders to design their own classes and workshops related to mythology and death. Perhaps the biggest weakness of a book format for presenting a program of this nature is that it may be difficult to maintain the concentration and motivation needed to conduct these solitary activities, however much you believe they could be of value. Some people find it easier than others to carry out private internal practices such as meditation or keeping a journal. We all, however, have a "response set" for learning within appropriately structured settings. By simply finding one other person (or several) and making a commitment to have regular meetings as you go through the program together, you activate this "response set" by providing yourselves each with a commitment, a structured learning environment, and interpersonal support.

You may either perform the personal rituals as you come to them in the text or read this entire section of the book and return to do them later. You may wish to go through some of the rituals more than one time. Use all you know about yourself to create the conditions that honor your style of learning and experiencing. Some people do better in several two-hour sittings; others may need to get away for a weekend. Some people learn best by using their eyes, others their ears, still others by movement. In designing the rituals for this section of the book we have, of necessity, chosen only a few of the possible ways to create the intended experiences. As you read through the instructions, the intent of the ritual will become clear to you, and you can modify the suggestions to support your own natural learning style. For instance, many of the rituals involve "guided imagery" journeys. You may find that the guided imagery instructions evoke powerful experiences, or you may find it more valuable to first read the instructions and then explore the suggested issues in your own manner, perhaps drawing your thoughts and feelings or expressing them in physical movement.

If the imagery instructions, as they are presented, seem a good way for you to carry out the intent of the ritual, either have someone read them to you while you are deeply relaxed or read them yourself into a tape and then use the tape to guide you through the experience. A prerecorded tape of the guided imagery instructions, with meditative background music, is also available. (See the box at the front of the book.)

If the guided imagery instructions do not suit you, you can, with full respect for the program, design your own activities to capture the essence of each ritual. Create an inner journey that explores the ideas and feelings the ritual investigates. The instructions presented in the book can be adjusted to your own style and pace and can spontaneously be taken in unplanned directions.

Keep in mind that these are not routine issues you are addressing— they are among the most profound and potentially illuminating questions that can be asked. Take time to ready yourself. Sanctify the process by preparing a physical space that is peaceful and inspiring. Begin each ritual by mindfully bringing yourself into a state of deep relaxation. Meditate or simply calm your mind, and touch into the quiet before beginning your work with the ritual. Periodically interrupt your concentrated attention in the program with activities you find pleasurable and refreshing.

Getting Started: Your Images About Death and Its Meaning

Preliminary to the five-stage program presented here for revising your mythology about death are several personal rituals to help you understand that mythology and explore its roots. In the first of these, you will be examining the conscious beliefs and attitudes you now hold regarding death.

Personal Ritual 1: Your Philosophy of Death

Articulating your philosophy of death is a way of investigating your conscious outlook and values concerning death, the process of dying, the meaning of life and death, and the possibilities of afterlife. The rituals that comprise the remainder of the program will take you progressively deeper into an understanding of your unconscious beliefs and attitudes about these topics. For this first exercise, however, the focus will be on ideas and feelings that are more readily accessible.

Freud observed that the conscious ego cannot conceive of *not* existing. Perhaps the most enigmatic question about death is, What happens after we die? "Perchance to dream," is the prospect that prevents Hamlet from taking his own life, though "in my soul, 'tis bitter cold and I am sick at heart":

> But that the dread of something after death,
> The undiscovered country from whose bourn
> No traveler returns, puzzles the will,
> And makes us rather bear those ills we have,
> Than fly to others that we know not of.

The nature of that "undiscovered country" from which no traveler returns is an ultimate concern of most spiritual and religious systems, but until recently, with the documentation of various puzzling "near-death" phenomena,[13] science has not attempted to address it. Stanislav and Christina Grof summarize the range of accounts of the world's religious, philosophical, and spiritual systems, ancient and modern, on the topic:

> Dying is sometimes seen as a step up in the spiritual or cosmological hierarchy, a promotion into the world of revered ancestors, powerful spirits or demigods, or as a transition from the complicated earthly life fraught with suffering and problems to a blissful existence in the solar region or the realms of gods. More frequently the concept of afterlife involves dichotomies and polarities; there are hells and purgatories as well as celestial realms and paradisiacal states. The posthumous journey of the soul is understood as a complex and difficult one. It is therefore essential to be well prepared when death comes. At the very least, it is necessary to acquire a knowledge of the cartography and laws of the afterlife existence.[14]

In beginning to verbalize your philosophy of death, you will be reflecting upon your own stance regarding these concerns. Your deepest beliefs about afterlife—whether your life choices are oriented toward avoiding a fate of fire and brimstone, are focused on the material world with no concern about the hereafter, or are made within a secure sense of a better world to come—exert a subtle and often potent influence on the way you live.[15] Your philosophy of death will touch upon many issues, such as the way you have made sense of the deaths of those you have loved, the way you handle your own fears of death, and the meaning that your knowledge of your own mortality adds to your life.

Place the heading "My Philosophy of Death" at the top of a page of your journal. You will be recording thoughts from your stream of consciousness as you reflect upon your beliefs, attitudes, and feelings about death. Place the following questions where you can glance at them easily, and begin to ponder them. Then, for at least ten uninterrupted minutes, write nonstop in your journal, producing an uncensored flow of thoughts and feelings:

What is death?

Why do people die?

What happens when they die?

How do I feel about my own death?

It is not necessary to address all of the questions or to limit yourself to only these questions. The list is provided solely to stimulate your thoughts and feelings about death. An alternative approach is to *speak*, for at least ten minutes, ideas from your stream of consciousness regarding these questions to another person or into a tape recorder, and then to record your feelings and ideas in your journal.

When you have finished, further develop any of the thoughts you wish. Rework the material into a well-organized statement of your philosophy of death. You may restate your ideas, making them more succinct or coherent, or draw pictures that express particular feelings or dilemmas. Organize your stream of consciousness writing into a meaningful essay. Then underline the most important ideas you have expressed. You will be using these underlined phrases in the following ritual.

After each of the personal rituals, you will find descriptions of the experiences of two individuals as they used the program to work with their own mythologies regarding death. Though space does not allow their entire journal accounts to be presented, and their journal entries have been edited for clarity as well as brevity, the portions that are excerpted or summarized after each personal ritual will demonstrate how that ritual may be carried out. You may want to read of their experiences with each ritual before you perform it. Besides providing a preview of the ritual, these reports show how two individuals deeply encounter and begin to transform their guiding myths regarding death.

The first case illustration is that of the book's other author, Peg Elliott Mayo, who served as one of the test cases as the program was being developed into its current form. The other is Robert, a successful architectural engineer who had, over the past decade, attended numerous self-development seminars and workshops. He was forty-four when he went through the program. These two accounts were chosen because they are particularly articulate, sophisticated, and sometimes poetic. They are not presented as standards for comparison. Do, however, invite yourself to allow the rituals to evoke your own most creative, aesthetically pleasing, and insightful journal work. Once you have read Peg's and Robert's accounts, reflect on the four questions posed above, begin your stream of consciousness writing, and finally rework it into a meaningful statement of your personal philosophy of death.

From Peg's Philosophy of Death.   "Death closes the circle. It means immobility. Coldness. Stillness. Peace. Silence. Gone. Missing. Dissolving. Non-being. A doorway to another consciousness. Loss of self. Loss of body. Loss. Unknown. Forgetfulness. Being forgotten. Loss of control. Loss of influence. Giving up all that is familiar. Being stripped of all that is known. Theoretically, it is all right, even good. Gutwise, it is frightening.

"People die to make room for more people. To escape intolerable conditions. To fertilize the lilies. To make compost. Because their lessons are learned. Because they refuse to learn their lessons. Because their lessons are incomprehensible. Because other people don't cherish them. For hopelessness. For loneliness. For love. For fatigue. Because it's time. Because God "calls them home." Because we are biological entities with a limited potential for self-repair and an intolerance for pain. Because we are cyclical/seasonal and there is no holding back time.

"How do I feel about my own death? Rude question. On one level I want to control it. I had no conscious choice about life. Seems only fair. Suicide is a distant possibility for me; an inevitable part of my autonomy and self-determination. What other authority is there? I wouldn't do it spitefully, out of anger or immediate panic. That's a promise. I wouldn't do it ugly. But I reserve the right to do it. I fear pain, dependency, ugliness, and loss of control. Pity from others. Being tolerated. Doctors with tubes and shots and knives and drugs. I want my dignity! I don't want to crap my bed as my last act and be remembered wasted and helpless. I don't trust others to let me die in good season; I'm afraid they'll keep me alive as a semblance out of misguided love or duty. Spare me duty.

"On another level, I want to avoid death at all costs. No matter how long I live it, it won't be long enough to learn all the crafts I want, take all the river walks I love, laugh with my friends, write stories, eat ripe persimmons, caress my man, play with my dog, live! What could be better than this world? I can see stars and anemones, taste spring water and hot chocolate, hear the river's song and my husband's laugh, touch alder bark and a grandchild's round head, smell musky humus in the forest and a man's sweat after splitting wood. I am alive in my senses: I can dance and weep, hunger and stretch, learn and do. What do I think of my own death? That it is premature, whenever it happens. I've been a laggard scholar; too many lessons of appreciation, patience, generosity, honor, mercy, humility left to learn. I need more time. I need more time.

"Something is eluding me. I'm somehow not coming to grips with the questions. Let's boil it down. I'm terrified to *die*—something in me is *terrified* of how I'll behave during the process. Will I wipe out all good memories in the minds of those who know me to the end? Will I snivel? Or scream? Will I be a toothless hag? Who will wipe my ass? Do I have to learn this hideous lesson—please, please no! Can't I avoid it? I don't trust my strength not to be disgusting.

"I'm worried about the process of dying—but death itself is not frightening in the same way. It is almost intriguing, like a journey to a foreign place that I've studied a good deal. I feel better when I tell myself hopeful, visionary stories about what will be. Maybe I will have a nice passing—something natural. Get weak, want to rest, feel a 'rightness' in dying. I don't know. I hope so."

From Robert's Philosophy of Death. "I don't usually experience a fear of death, but I get very frightened at the thought of something taking me prematurely. The fear is most strongly focused on my fear of things that would rip up my body. That's a thought that really terrifies me. I have visions of something crushing my head, of a knife going into my belly, of unbearable pain and the terrible moment of realizing I'm about to be forcefully yanked out of this world—no preparation, no good-byes. An instant death would not be my choice as compared with the thought of dying of ripe old age, but if the other choice were seeing my body getting wracked up, feeling the pain, dealing with the horror, I'd rather have it be instant. Lights out.

"I never think of myself as being afraid of death—my spiritual beliefs give me comfort on that score—but I guess the fear of getting physically mangled masks any other fear of death that may be there. I feel that fear every time I read newspaper and magazine stories about others' tragedies, and I have my share of nightmarish daydreams as well. Perhaps I also have fears of death that I keep out of my mind just because death seems so far off in the future that it isn't a looming concern. So maybe if I do have some underlying fear of death, I just never allow it to surface. Maybe death is too far off to be a concern right now. Or if death is going to come sooner, it will take such violence to cut me off from life at this point that my focus is on the gore involved in dying instead of the fact of death.

"But I also think I'm not consciously afraid of death because I find peace in my belief that living here in the world is the hardest part of existence—that on the other side it's all about love and peace. I think of life as a great experiment in which the realm of spirit is trying to manifest itself in this denser physical world, where spirit takes on flesh and sensation. I don't think of death as an end, but as a change of scenery, a new stage and form for the spirit in an eternally evolving drama. And a blissful one. That vision offers comfort!

"But what if it isn't all that black-and-white—harsh here, glorious there. Nothing else seems to be. I don't like thoughts that upset my notion of death as a continuation of conscious being in perfect peace and harmony. I guess I could accept something in-between, but I feel myself wanting to bargain for a vision of death that isn't too bad. I can certainly think of much scarier versions of death than anything I want to consider. I'm not sure where my faith comes that the nicer vision is the truer one, but everything in me wants to hang onto it."

Personal Ritual 2:
Exploration of a Personal Concern About Death

Reread the phrases you underlined in your "Philosophy of Death" statement. Choose the one that evokes the strongest unsettling feeling in you or the one that you would most like to explore. Peg chose "I need more time." Robert thought about choosing the statement "I don't like thoughts that upset my notion of death as a continuation of conscious being in perfect peace and harmony." But the concern seemed somewhat remote to him. The underlined statement he chose to explore was "seeing my body getting wracked up."

In carrying out these guided imagery instructions, it is important to realize that many people do not actually *see* clear pictures in their minds. They may know what they know through what they call intuition, by hearing an inner narration, by seeing abstract images, or by directly sensing the thought or memory. Thinking usually involves some combination of these modes, and when we use terms like *visualization* or *imagery,* we are referring to whatever blend occurs within you.

We will also remind you that in this and each subsequent personal ritual that uses guided imagery, you will need to decide which method you will use for leading yourself through the experience (reading the instructions into a tape, asking someone to read them to you, or becoming familiar enough with the instructions that you can create an experience that accomplishes the intent of the ritual). Robert used a prerecorded tape that led him through the guided imagery instructions; Peg, after reading the text until she understood the essence of each ritual, innovated a personalized version of it. She would think about the question raised, meditate, and set time aside to create an inner experience based on the idea of the ritual.

.

If you tape the instructions or have someone read them to you, they should be read slowly and deliberately. Pause for about ten seconds each time you come to the word "pause" and each time you come to the end of a paragraph. At any point during a guided visualization where you need more time to allow a particular image to develop or to carry out an instruction, simply signal to your partner or turn off the tape (a "remote" switch, such as those often found on the microphones that accompany cassette recorders or those that control the electricity at the wall outlet, is recommended). After reviewing the statement from your "Philosophy of Death" that you would like to explore further, find a comfortable position, close your eyes, and begin to relax.

As you settle into this safe, secure spot, focus on your breathing. Release any tension in your body. [Pause.] Listen for and feel each in-breath and each out-breath. [Pause.] Notice how your stomach and chest fill . . . and empty. [Pause.] As you continue to breathe and relax, you are better able to concentrate on my voice and on the suggestions I will offer. If outside sounds or passing thoughts cross your mind, they fade quietly into the background just as they occur, like autumn leaves being carried away by the wind. Your breathing is slow and deep as you relax more completely with each of your next five breaths. One [pause]; two [pause]; three [pause]; four [pause]; five [pause].

Bring to mind the key statement you chose from your "Philosophy of Death." [Pause.] Notice the feelings evoked in you as you recall this thought. [Pause.] Focus on the part of your body in which these feelings are the strongest. [Pause.] Bring your attention to this part of your body. [Pause.] Experience this part of your body through your breathing, your muscles, and your inner imagery. [Pause.] Find a word or a phrase that describes the way this part of your body feels.

In a moment, you will imagine yourself expressing this feeling in some new ways. First you will see yourself expressing the feeling through movement. If you were to dance this feeling, how would you dance? [Pause.] Imagine yourself expressing your feeling through movement. [Pause.] Do your movements seem free or constricted? [Pause.] Does your dance accurately portray the feeling it is expressing? [Pause.] Continue the dance in your mind and let it evolve. [20-second pause.]

Allow the dance to come to a close now, and imagine yourself settling into a relaxed, centered, calm position. [Pause.] You are about to create a clay sculpture of your feeling. Imagine that you are holding soft clay. You begin to work the clay with your hands. You are creating a sculpture that represents your feeling. Your sculpture may look like something that you recognize, or it may be abstract. [Pause.] Soon, your sculpture is complete. [Pause.] Experience it with your eyes and hands. [Pause.]

Has its color changed from that of the original clay? [Pause.] How does it feel in your hands? [Pause.] What does it show you about your original feeling? [Pause.] Get to know this sculpture. [Pause.] If your sculpture could come to life and speak to you, what would it say? [Pause.] In the following pause, sense what it has to tell you about the underlined phrase from your "Philosophy of Death." [60-second pause.]

It is nearly time now to come back to your normal waking consciousness. You can slowly begin to return to the present moment. Counting from five back to one, you will be able to recall all you need of this experience. When you hear the number one, you will feel alert, relaxed, and refreshed, as if returning from a wonderful nap. Five, moving your fingers and your toes. [Pause.] Four, stretching your shoulders, neck, and face muscles. [Pause.] Three, taking a deep breath. [Pause.] Two, bringing your attention back into the room. [Pause.] And one, opening your eyes, feeling refreshed, confident, and able to effectively and creatively meet the requirements of your day.

Summarize this experience in your journal by reflecting on the following questions. On which thought from your "Philosophy of Death" did you focus? What feeling did it evoke in you? How did you experience that feeling in your body? How did you express that feeling in movement? What did the sculpture look like? What did the sculpture have to tell you?

Peg's Exploration.　Starting with her statement "I need more time," Peg identified her most prominent feeling as an eagerness to get on with her life. "It centers on my face, which is the locus of my senses (eyes, ears, nose, mouth, skin). My dance is a wild one, around a blazing campfire on the banks of the river. I am fluid, uninhibited, and firelike in my movements. The light reflects on the water with great beauty. I form a flowing, abstract shape with the clay—it has the appearance of a flame. It doesn't speak to me, but there is a 'knowingness' that seems part mind, part intuition that says this flame is primal, that its existence is dependent on fuel and oxygen (as mine is), and that it is without morality, sentiment, or thought—it simply *is*. That for it to do work, do harm, or to be controlled takes a sort of intelligence that is not implicit to the fire. Same as me. The burning flame represents an inevitability about life and, therefore, about death. Even my very important death. *I need more time*—I will live with the gusto of a campfire, but I know—eager or not, reluctant or not—when the fuel is gone, so am I."

Robert's Exploration.　"I started by focusing on my fear of a violent death. In my body, I could feel a tenseness in my throat and a hardness in my stomach when I thought of dying that way. As I imagined dancing the tenseness, I only saw myself crouching up in a fetal position with my hands protecting my head. I didn't make a sculpture, because my little crouched version of myself just became the sculpture. When it could talk with me, it said 'You are much more afraid of death than you know, and the fear has something to teach you. First, while much is out of your control regarding the dreadful things that could happen to you, there is also much you can do to prevent or not invite such things. Still, no matter what you do, tragic possibilities remain. But that is the lot of all of humanity.' Then the little sculpture scolded me for not taking greater enjoyment in the life I have. 'If there is anything the threat of sudden loss ought to teach you,' he said, 'it is that the failure to savor the life you are living is a loss of the greatest magnitude.' His words hit hard. They cause me to think."

Personal Ritual 3: Creation of Your Death Shield

The next ritual involves the construction of a Death Shield. Many Native American cultures used sacred shields for spiritual protection, healing, and reverence. An image received in a powerful dream or during a vision quest or other purification ceremony might be interpreted by the tribal shaman and painted on a circular hide, hung with feathers, fur, tassels, or shells. The symbols on the shield might tell of the person's ritual identity, history, or aspirations. We would like you to think of your Death Shield as an ally in living, there to help you face your fears of death and to support you in maintaining a proper attitude about living and dying.

Your Death Shield should be about a foot in diameter or larger, and you should be able to draw or paint on it. Some people have created their Death Shields out of rawhide stretched over a rim made of willow. Others have made a shield by putting unbleached muslin in an embroidery hoop and using textile paints. A simpler method, which we suggest unless you are particularly drawn to one of the others, is to use the back of a large paper plate or to cut a piece of white construction paper into a circle. You will also need crayons, colored markers, or a paint palette.

Draw a line through the center of your shield, dividing it in half. Draw a second line so that your shield is divided like a pie cut into four equal pieces. On the outer rim, label the sections with the words: "First Memories About Death," "Death Fears," "Transcending Death Anxiety," and "A Renewed Mythology About Death."

Once you have constructed your Death Shield, use the following instructions to evoke the imagery that you will draw onto the section labeled "First Memories About Death." Later, you will be drawing images on the other three sections of your shield to symbolize your experiences as you perform subsequent personal rituals. When you have completed your Death Shield, it will serve as a succinct overview of your work in this program. In the following guided imagery journey, you will be taken back in your memory and helped to find a symbol that you will draw on this first section of your shield. When people mentally return to earlier times in their lives, they may not be sure if their memories are accurate. Know that whatever your psyche produces in response to these instructions, even if it arises totally out of your imagination, is, if not a memory, at least a metaphor and will be adequate for the purposes of this exercise.

Make the preparations for another guided visualization experience. Tape-record the instructions, arrange to have someone read them to you, or familiarize yourself with them well enough so that you can create an experience that accomplishes the intent of the ritual. Look at the section of your Death Shield labeled "First Memories About Death." With your journal, shield, and drawing implements nearby, find a comfortable position, close your eyes, and begin to relax.

As you settle into this safe, secure spot, focus on your breathing. Release any tension in your body. [Pause.] Listen for and feel each in-breath and each out-breath. [Pause.] Notice how your stomach and chest fill . . . and empty. [Pause.] As you continue to breathe and relax, you are better able to concentrate on my voice and on the suggestions I will offer. If outside sounds or passing thoughts cross your mind, they fade quietly into the background just as they occur. Your breathing is slow and deep as you relax more completely with each of your next five breaths. One [pause]; two [pause]; three [pause]; four [pause]; five [pause].

You are about to come to a memory from early in your life. You will slide backward in time, safely and securely allowing yourself to recall the sensation of being very young and naive. You will come upon a scene from your past that involved one of your earliest encounters with the reality of death. Perhaps you saw something in a movie or on television that brought this awareness to you. It might have been the death of a pet, a neighbor, a relative, or a friend. [Pause.] If more than one memory comes to you, select one you would like to examine in greater detail.

Breathing deeply now, feel yourself, with your next three breaths, going back to this earlier scene. One, know that you are well protected. Two, smoothly and surely, you are moving back in time toward the earlier scene. Three, you are in the scene, and you begin to survey it.

You can see yourself more clearly now. You understand your feelings and have great insight into their basis. Recall the details—place, time, circumstances. [Pause.] Notice who is with you. [Pause.] Sense what they are feeling. [Pause.] How did they involve you? [Pause.] Did they offer comfort? [Pause.] Observe how the attitudes held by your parents or other adults were conveyed to you. [Pause.] Recognize the attitudes you came to hold regarding death. [Pause.] Spend a few more moments examining this scene. [20-second pause.]

Focus on a sensation in your body that relates to this experience. Identify the part of your body where this sensation is the most intense. [Pause.] Find the shape of the sensation—notice its borders. [Pause.] See its color. [Pause.] Explore its texture. [Pause.] In a moment, you will recognize a symbol emerging out of these shapes and colors.

Watch as a symbol that you associate with this earlier experience appears. [Pause.] You may actually see the symbol take form, or you may simply sense what it is. It will further evolve over the next few moments. Relax as it becomes increasingly clear. [20-second pause.]

As a fitting symbol emerges from your memory, prepare to draw it on your shield. [Pause.] Return to the present moment, and take several deep breaths. [Pause.] Begin to stretch your body. [20-second pause.] Gently open your eyes, and draw the symbol on the portion of your shield labeled "First Memories About Death." As you draw this symbol, you may find that it is changing even as you are creating it, or that you have more than one image to draw. Draw whatever comes. Do not be concerned about what may be "aesthetic" or "correct." As long as the drawing is meaningful to you, it will serve its purpose. When you have completed your drawing, you will find that you have returned to full waking consciousness, feeling refreshed, confident, and able to effectively and creatively meet the requirements of your day.

If you wish, you may examine other scenes as well. Return to the paragraph that beings: "You are about to find a memory from early in your life." Carry out the instructions from there. You may repeat this sequence one or more times. When you have completed the "First Memories" portion of your Death Shield to your satisfaction, consciously breathe out, and physically shake out any unpleasant sensations in your body.

In your journal, under a heading called "My First Memories About Death," describe your experiences with this exercise. Focus particularly on the attitudes you came to hold regarding death as a result of this experience. Did the experience make death more mysterious or less mysterious; more fearful or less fearful; more accessible for discussion with others or less accessible?

Finally, use the "creative projection" technique first illustrated on page 7. "Become" the symbol (or one of the symbols) drawn on the first portion of your Death Shield. Describe yourself as the symbol—first person, present tense, "I am . . ." If the symbol on your shield was a whale, you might begin: "I am a big blue whale. I can disappear under the water for a long, long time, but I always come up again. Sometimes when I go under the water it seems . . ." Continue to write, or speak into a tape or to your partner, for several minutes while "staying in character" and allowing a story to develop as you describe—in the voice of your symbol—yourself, your needs, and your purpose for being. This process will enrich your understanding of the personal significance of the symbol.

Peg's Early Memory and First Death Shield Symbol. "I was four when my Grandma Lampkin died. My Irish grandmother. With the brogue and the lemon meringue pie. I didn't know about dying or that she was sick. She was eighty-seven, but that meant nothing. They told me she'd 'gone to Heaven.' I wanted to go with her, and I was mad she'd gone without telling me. I thought going to Heaven was like going to town or someplace 'real.' Everyone crying made me cry. I can remember them telling me she was 'happy now' (I never thought of her as anything else) and that I could see her 'someday.' It was then I got really upset—I knew I needed more time with her *now*. I felt something important was missing, and I still do.

"What I learned was that I was excluded from the important parts of dying and that there were a lot of promises that didn't comfort my loss. I learned death was for grown-ups to deal with, but that since it was 'just like going to sleep' it could happen to anyone at any time. Even little me.

"An image of Grandma Lampkin's brass bed with the red-and-white quilt she'd made to cover it came to me. I saw the huge down pillows, their lace-edged cases embroidered with strawberries and violets. There was the smell of lavender. The bed is empty. Neat. Cold. I'm never again going to climb in with her, cuddle up, feel her soft breasts under the flannel nightie against my back. I'm never again going to hear, in that lilting whisper in the dark, stories of 'the Faery' or what the trip to America was like. Never. Never. Never.

"I feel very young and abandoned. I can remember no psychic pain that precedes this memory. I realize that 'young and abandoned' is the root of my feelings about bereavement. I feel vulnerable regarding my own death. I question, 'Where did she go?' and, more urgently, 'Why did she go? Was I bad? Is she mad at me? Is that why she went? Will she come back if I am very, very good? What if Daddy dies? What will happen to me? *What will happen to me?*'

"The beautiful empty bed is my Death Shield symbol. 'I am a big brass bed. I'm a place for cuddles and stories. I'm safe and warm. People have made love—made babies—in me. I've heard the whispers in the dark. I'm a place for touching and resting. I'm strong, and I've been around a long time. My mattress has a hollow where two people have lain, spoon style, for many the long hour. Sometimes it was the man and woman, other times the woman and children. I'm marked with menstrual blood and the blood of giving birth. There are transparent yellow rings of spent semen. I have a stain from spilled tea, taken by a sick child seeking comfort. And no one uses me anymore. I'm some sort of shrine. Everything is too neat. My pillowcases don't show the dent of resting heads, no bodies mound up my linen sheets and bright quilt. People look at me and sigh or weep. They remember me as I was for them and never notice that I could still be used. I am very sad.' "

Robert's Early Memory and First Death Shield Symbol. "I was about twelve. My parents went to a play with friends. One of them had a heart attack and died. I had never seen my mother cry before. This was not something adults did. I saw her struggle not to cry. I saw her cry. I didn't know what to do. We never talked about the death. My questions evoked discomfort, and I quickly dropped the subject. But I learned that my mother thought death was too terrible to talk about. I learned it was something that even the great and wise world of adults could not control. And I learned that it made you have awful emotions that you also could not control.

"I drew a face on my Death Shield. It was a face because I didn't know how to draw a scream. When I remembered the scene with my mother, I felt she needed more than the few tears that fought their way through. She needed to scream. I felt in my body how unable she was to express the depths of her feelings. And I felt in my body how unable I became to scream my screams and cry my tears. So on my shield I drew a face that was screaming. It was my mother's scream, the scream she never screamed for the death of her friend. Okay, 'I am the face that needs to scream. I am tense. I'm in agony, so I shut off my feelings. All my feelings. I'm very sad, though I feel only my deadness. I need to scream. I must scream. A scream starts from my belly, rises in my throat, and escapes as a haunting wail.'

"Having this unuttered scream make itself heard some thirty years hence releases something in me. It opens my inhibitions, opens my flow of energy, opens my ability to embrace life in both its horrors and its joys."

The First Stage: Rattling Your System of Death Denial

Beneath the level of daily activity, beneath the level of your unspoken mythology, lies the raw, primal, undiluted terror of death. This terror is easily activated by the approaching sound of skidding tires on a slick roadway, the abrupt appearance of an ominous figure on a dark street, or the surreal perils of a nightmare. Such terror is a reflex, an inborn response, so that a threat to your survival instantly mobilizes you for action. No other order of business even begins to compete. As Samuel Johnson once put it, "When a man knows he is to be hanged in a fortnight, it concentrates his mind wonderfully."

The terror that arises when you believe your life is in danger, even if it is a fleeting terror, usually leaves a lingering impression. Children, who are particularly vulnerable to becoming ensnared in a tangle of overwhelming fears, generally give such experiences a prominent spot in their evolving cosmologies. As Ernest Becker describes it, children have

> their recurrent nightmares, their universal phobias of insects and mean dogs. In their tortured interiors radiate complex symbols of many in-admissible realities — terror of the world, the horror of one's own wishes, the fear of vengeance by the parents, the disappearance of things, one's lack of control over anything, really. It is too much for any animal to take, but the child has to take it, and so he wakes up screaming with almost punctual regularity during the period where his weak ego is in the process of consolidating things.[16]

As the child's ego engages "in the process of consolidating things," a mythology about death is being formed. What cannot be denied or repressed is woven into the emerging personal mythology by which life and the human condition will be understood. In addition to the terror of death that has been catalyzed in moments of perceived physical threat, a more pervasive fear of simply ceasing to be also plagues the child and begs to be addressed. In developing an emerging sense of self, the child is fully engaged in the establishment of a separate identity, and the prospect of ceasing to be runs so intensely counter to this mission that it is an ongoing source of existential anxiety. The term *existential* means, most basically, having to do with the bedrock issues of human existence, such as freedom, destiny, responsibility, isolation, loneliness, the quest for meaning, and the awareness of one's mortality.[17] With the prospect of death, the hard-earned sense of self, the psychological identity one has spent one's entire lifetime developing, faces the threat of dissolving into oblivion. The existential task is to find meaning along the way. The child's first primitive attempts at this lifelong project establish the foundations of an evolving mythology about death.

Irvin Yalom describes the stages by which the child comes to terms with death.[18] Although the parents' explanations about death and the feelings they model give some structure to the toddler's emerging awareness of death, they hardly provide adequate comfort for the primary anxiety that grows out of this awareness. Gradually, with the budding psychological defenses of preadolescence, the child develops "efficient and sophisticated forms of denial, awareness glides into the unconscious," and the overwhelming fear of death is contained. But the awareness of fear will break through again: "During adolescence, childhood denial systems are no longer effective. The introspective tendencies and the greater resources of the adolescent permit him or her to face, once again, the inevitability of death, to bear the anxiety, and to search for an alternate mode of coping with the facts of life."[19]

Psychological defense mechanisms such as repression, displacement, rationalization, and "personal efforts to overcome death through a wide variety of strategies that aim at achieving symbolic immortality" allow us to emotionally manage the fear of death.[20] Some of these defenses may lead to highly constructive activities, such as Charles Cameron's passion to teach his grandchildren all that he could. Others may involve a broad array of foolish pursuits. Ernest Becker's book *The Denial of Death,* which was awarded a Pulitzer Prize two months after Becker's own death, persuasively implicates the fear of death as a major accomplice in the motivation for a wanton accumulation of wealth, fame, or power. *Successful coping with life requires that effective means be found for coming to terms with the eventuality of death.* In fact, psychopathology has been linked directly to inadequate attempts to transcend the fear of dying.[21]

Later, in the second stage of the program, you will be examining the means you have developed for transcending the fear of death, and you will also be exploring new modes that may ultimately prove more constructive. In this first stage, however, the focus will be on the fear of death itself. In advising psychotherapists to uncover their clients' repressed anxieties about death, Yalom emphasizes that this is not a call to a morbid preoccupation with death but rather a reminder that when one is able to become more conscious about the nature of being, including the certainty of death, life becomes richer. He quotes Santayana: "The dark background which death supplies brings out the tender colors of life in all their purity."[22] And he points out that the therapist does not have to create the experience of death anxiety but rather help the person recognize what is already there: "Ordinarily we deny, or selectively inattend to, reminders of our existential situation; the task of the therapist is to reverse the process, to pursue these reminders, for they are not ... enemies but powerful allies in the pursuit of integration and maturity."[23] The following three personal rituals are tools to help you gently touch into your own anxieties regarding death, recognized and repressed, and to begin to place them into a meaningful framework.

Personal Ritual 4:
Opening Your Heart to Your Deeper Fears

This fourth personal ritual calls upon you to participate in an activity that might not normally occur to you. It requires some effort and some courage, but we believe it will lead to a valuable experience. Arrange to visit a nursing home or other setting where you will be able to find someone who is very old or is for other reasons facing his or her mortality. You may select either an acquaintance or someone you have never met. Find a person whose faculties are intact and who seems eager to talk. Your local hospice may be willing to arrange such a meeting, or if you go to a nursing home, the staff will probably be happy to introduce you to someone. Sensitive human contact from outside the institution is a scarce and precious resource for many people in such settings. If it would provide a useful structure for your visit, or simply make you more comfortable, you may accurately represent the visit as part of an educational program that suggests you expose yourself to individuals who are in the final stages of life.

Prepare for your visit by cultivating your curiosity about what it is like to be living wherever you plan to visit and to be approaching death. When you are with the person, engage in conversation that encourages discussion about whatever he or she feels is important. Particularly open your heart to the fears or frustrations this person may be experiencing. Sensitively, and with respect for the other's feelings, convey your curiosity about his or her experience at this point in life. Ask about the person's hopes and fears. Deepen the conversation by listening with both compassion and a strong intent to discover what you can learn from this person. If he or she brings up the topic of death, do not be afraid to pursue it, but neither should you push your way into sensitive areas the person seems to be avoiding. Your only job is to be a good listener. You are not trying to influence the other person's attitudes or beliefs in any way. Notice primarily the feelings the discussion generates in you. Listen, observe, and learn.

If this assignment seems too uncomfortable, or if you really don't think it would be worth the effort and you decide against carrying it out, at least set aside half an hour and role-play a conversation between yourself and the person you imagine you would have found at the nursing home. Take both roles described above. With two chairs facing one another, literally switch positions as you go from being yourself to being the other person. If you yourself are in the final season of your life, place in the other chair a naive interviewer, someone who is puzzled about feelings of impending death and wants to understand your experience. Continue the dialogue until you have reached a satisfactory level of depth.

In your journal, record your experience and your feelings. Focus particularly on this question: In what ways was this visit and interview [whether it was an actual visit or play-acted] a catalyst that opened me to fears about death that are usually outside my awareness?

The Fears Opened by Peg's Visit.   "Being old and abandoned. Weak. Confused. Subject to. Dependent. Unloved. Wasted. All the years wasted. But my fears are about dying, not death. Death, if I were Hilda [the woman she visited], would be water in the desert. It's living sick and old that seems grotesque, intolerable, a humiliation. The dying part. She has pain, and they give her pills and a pat on the head. No one holds her. No one meets her questioning eyes. No one comes to see her, but she has an institutional aluminum Christmas tree on her windowsill. She remembers snow on Christmas, 'up to your belly.' She knows she's out-lived her usefulness. She knows it's time to go, but *they won't let her.* The IV unit runs four hours every day, and the hiss of oxygen never stops. She can't leave her bed except as a burden to someone stronger. She sits on a sheepskin to keep down the bedsores. And this woman used to dig field lilies for a living. She raised seven children; she lived through the depression; and was a World War II widow. She was capable and tough. Now look at her."

The Fears Opened by Robert's Visit.   "I visited John Parnelli [a neighbor who was dying of cancer]. He's going to leave the boys and Johanna behind him. He is mad and miserable. He can't quite believe it's hap-pening. Neither can I. I certainly can't understand why. He is so young. Here death seems senseless and cruel. It tries my faith that justice has anything to do with the Big Plan. When I put myself in John's place, I can feel a lot of fear. Besides the unthinkable losses—delightful wife, wonderful kids, promising future—and the pain, there is that impending date to go over the edge and into the unknown. The prospect seems chillingly unpredictable and desperately lonely."

Personal Ritual 5: The Fear of Death at Its Foundation

Head a new page of your journal "My Fears About Death." Review your experiences with the first four personal rituals. Remain particularly alert for areas where fear is evident. Describe these in your journal. Were some of these fears previously outside your awareness? What are the effects of first recognizing them? Take the time to consider these questions carefully in your journal. Among the fears Peg identified were those of "pain, dependency, ugliness, and loss of control. Pity from others. Being tolerated. Doctors with tubes and shots and knives and drugs." Robert focused on the feeling he attributed to his neighbor, that death seemed "chillingly unpredictable and desperately lonely."

When you have written as much as you have to say, reread your words. With your Death Shield and colored markers nearby, find a com-fortable position, close your eyes, and begin to relax.

As you settle into this safe, secure spot, focus on your breathing. Release any tension in your body. [Pause.] Listen for and feel each in-breath and out-breath. [Pause.] Notice how your stomach and chest fill

... and empty. [Pause.] As you continue to breathe and relax, you are better able to concentrate on my voice and on the suggestions I will offer. If outside sounds or passing thoughts cross your mind, they fade quietly into the background just as they occur. Your breathing is slow and deep as you relax more completely with each of your next five breaths. One [pause]; two [pause]; three [pause]; four [pause]; five [pause].

You have been giving much thought to your fear of death. [Pause.] The fear of death is not new to you. When you were a child, you had many fears about death. You may remember the terror of a nightmare or of a monster that you imagined had crawled under your bed or into your closet. You may have feared for your own life or the life of a parent or other loved one. You are about to focus on one of these fears from your childhood. You may return to the same experience you identified in one of the previous personal rituals or to a different one. Pull yourself back to being very young and feeling your fear. [Pause.] Feel yourself moving back in time now to this early experience of your fear of death. [Pause.] Where are you? What is occurring? Who is there? [30-second pause.]

You are about to find a symbol of these fears. Focus on a sensation in your body that relates to this early experience. Identify the part of your body where this sensation is the most intense. [Pause.] Find the shape of the sensation—notice its borders. [Pause.] See its color. [Pause.] Explore its texture. [Pause.] In a moment, you will recognize a symbol emerging out of these shapes and colors.

Watch as the symbol appears. [Pause.] You may actually see the symbol take form, or you may simply sense what it is. It will further evolve over the next few moments. Relax as it becomes increasingly clear. [20-second pause.] This symbol represents your fear of death, and you will be able to remember it so you can, in a little while, draw it on your shield.

First bring your attention back to your early experience. Again, see yourself as a child who knows the fear of death. [Pause.] Now imagine an adult entering the scene. The adult is you at your current age. You have traveled back in time to give support to this young, frightened child. As an adult, you are not afraid of the fear and vulnerability you see in the child. You may even feel touched by the child's innocence. From your compassion for this child, you are able to provide the comfort or affection that you sincerely needed when you were young and frightened. Imagine yourself providing that comfort and affection now. [30-second pause.] In addition to comfort and affection, you have some advice and information about the path that lies ahead. Allow a conversation to develop between your current self and this younger self. Hear the words, see the expressions, feel the contact. [60-second pause.]

Now gently place your adult hands upon the child and lovingly communicate peaceful, curative energies to the small body. Your hands are able to bring about a healing of old emotional wounds left over from this period of your life. [30-second pause.]

It is time to say good-bye for now to this inner child. Allow yourself to embrace this young person. [Pause.] Take a few last moments together, and then say a heartfelt good-bye. [20-second pause.]

Again recall the symbol representing your fear of death. Does it feel different now? Prepare to draw this symbol on your shield. [Pause.] Take several deep breaths, and begin to stretch your body. [20-second pause.] Open your eyes, and draw the symbol on the portion of your shield that is labeled "Death Fears." As you draw this symbol, you may find that it is changing even as you are creating it, or that you have more than one image to draw. Draw whatever comes. When you have completed your drawing, you will find that you have returned to full waking consciousness, feeling refreshed, confident, and able to effectively and creatively meet the requirements of your day.

In your journal, describe the scene you remembered and what occurred when you went back there as an adult. Also, reflect on the meaning of the symbol(s) you drew on your shield. Consider using the "creative projection" technique for further examining its personal significance. You would "become" the symbol as you did earlier and describe yourself as that symbol, using first person, present tense.

Peg's Journey Back in Time and Her Death Fear Symbol. "Throughout my childhood, my mother was very sick. She spent much of her time at home in a hospital bed. I can vividly remember, every few weeks, overhearing as she told my father, in terror, that she was about to die. When I went back in time, I told the little girl that it means her mother is afraid and in pain. I was as eloquent as I know how in making the point that she was not to connect the misery she witnessed in her mother with her own being. As a child, I made such a powerful commitment to be just the opposite of my mother that it has influenced my character in major, dysfunctional ways. I addressed this in my visit back in time. I was one adult in her young life who rewarded her with more than words reinforcing her stoicism. And I showed her how to pick and choose her responses. Most of all, I loved her and accepted her for who she was.

"My Death Shield symbol is a hospital bed with lots of equipment on it. 'I am a hospital bed. I've held a lot of pain and terror. I'm a place to suffer and die. I can keep your lungs working with my oxygen pumps. I can fill you with saline and glucose solutions and keep your electrolytes in balance. I have catheters to empty your bladder into a flabby yellow bag, and I have oversized diapers for you to wear. I have a button you can push, and, sooner or later, someone will come to roll you over or wipe the slobber off your chin. I can support your every function from breathing to digesting to moving, but I'm a place to die, not live. I am very, very threatening.' "

Robert's Journey Back in Time and His Death Fear Symbol. "I went back to a nightmare I had when I was very young. I'm not sure if it was a memory or just my imagination, but it felt real enough. I was gripped by an immobilizing terror. I wanted to scream, but I couldn't. I could barely open my mouth. It wasn't that I was inhibited the way my mother seemed to be in the other exercise—I was frozen.

"The picture that emerged from the cold sensations in my chest was, at first, a big cube of ice. Then it became a heart. It was my heart. Frozen. Cold. Scared. I remembered the word 'chilling' from my experience with John Parnelli.

"When the adult me went back to find the child, the child's chest and heart were frozen. Out of fear, it seemed. I placed my hands over the heart. The heart started to thaw. The child started to scream and cry. I just held him and provided understanding and comfort. Being able to scream, cry, and be understood made the whole predicament a little less terrifying. Nothing needed to be said. Perhaps that thawing of the child's heart also helps to thaw this adult's heart of a coldness that goes all the way back to once having closed down against horrendous, unnamed terrors?"

Personal Ritual 6: Creation of a Death Fable, "Death in the Shadow of Fear"

In your journal, or speaking into a tape recorder, write a death fable. Death fables have universal themes. They depict a poignant scene of a person who is dying; they speak to the particular and to the universal, to the conscious and the unconscious; they are not bound by ordinary rules of logic; and they are often typified by extremes (the main character may be very, very rich or very, very poor, very young or very old, very simple or very wise). You may set your story in any particular period of history, in a tribal culture, within a family of animals or elves, or in any other context you wish. In your Death Fable, the main character is dying and knows it. Moreover, this character happens to have the exact same fears about death that you have identified. All other details are up to you. Your character may be male or female, young or old, and about to die from any cause.

Once you have read Peg's and Robert's Death Fables, center yourself, relax in a comfortable spot with your journal nearby, and contemplate the Death Fable you are about to create. Allow your story to emerge from deep within you. Set the scene, and fully describe how the person first learns that death is fast approaching, the way he or she reacts, how the process of dying progresses, and what the final moments are like. You may also recount the funeral or memorial service and describe the eulogy. Develop a story that—in following this person through the process of dying—emphasizes how the person's fears (fears similar to your own) influence that process. Creating this story, in which the main character's fears of death are shaping the way he or she is to die, will provide you with a parable about the importance of coming to terms with such fears, and perhaps some clues about how to come to terms with them yourself.

Peg's Fable.   "The old hag cowers in the darkest corner of her hut, glaring with red-rimmed eyes at the creeping shadows. Within each pulsating, flickering shadow is the essence of some evil deed she herself has perpetrated. Prowling the wall, approaching her corner, is the ghost of her spite, lusting for blood. Groans of anguish fall from the ceiling— voices echoing her malicious gossip, her slandering of neighbors, her vilifying others' honest efforts. Greed sits in the hag's chair, lapping up a beggar's meager meal to feed its soft bulging belly.

"Her breath comes with the rasp of curses cast at thriving children, blighting them. The stench of pride, acrid as burning hair, fills the room. The hag feels bowel-emptying terror; the greasy skin of her back raises stiff quills of gray hair in dread. Death is at the door, and these memories are but Death's lackeys, come to torment the dying hag with the dregs of her life.

"The hag falls to her knees as Death enters the hut. Death comes as an open black mouth, filled with shark's teeth and a bitter purple tongue. Its pallid lips reach out for her as if she were a morsel on a fork. The hag screams and buries her head, too frightened to bargain or confess repentance. One flick of the fearfully livid tongue and she is devoured. The shadows of greed and slander and hate caper in her empty room, unexorcised."

Robert's Fable.   Robert wrote his Death Fable the week after the terrible earthquake in Armenia. Survivors were still being rescued after being buried alive for ten days. One vivid news account told of a woman, trapped under the rubble with her young daughter for over a week, who made incisions in her skin with a piece of broken glass so her dehydrated daughter could suck her blood. Robert could not stop dwelling on such accounts, and they provided the setting of his Death Fable:

"Robchinko Ryzhkov was on the phone in his third-story office in Leninakan when the tremor began to build. Within two seconds he was under his desk. First a moment of respite—then the heavy desk was sliding across the room, rudely pushing him along with it. All at once he heard a deafening sound as the walls shook apart. Suddenly the floor was giving way. When he awoke, all was dark. He did not know where he was, only that his head hurt, he could not move his right leg, and he was pinned under something large, cold, and hard, perhaps four inches above him. Imprisoned on his back, he was unable to move.

"At first he thought he was in a dream. Then he caught an image of having dived under his desk, and in a moment of stark horror, he realized that this was very real. He screamed for help. All was silence. He screamed and screamed and screamed and screamed. He pushed with all his strength at the fallen beam that was pinning him. There was no give. He tried to wriggle out from under it. His right leg was hopelessly tangled in something he could neither see nor reach with his hands. Again he screamed and screamed and screamed until his screams had worn down to a soft moan.

"Then came the realization that he might slowly die in this terrible manner. More alone than he'd ever felt, his mind grew dark with terror. Hearing a shriek well up from deep inside, he could not think. Because he was unable to collect himself, he could not pay his last silent respects to the life he had lived or to those he had loved. And he could not attempt to come to peace with his fate. He was suspended in panic for endless hours. He began going in and out of nightmarish fits of sleep. Before passing out for the final time, he was still wearing an expression of horror and dread as he fought desperately to maintain consciousness and stay in his body."

With these three personal rituals, culminating in the morbid endings of their Death Fables, Peg and Robert have certainly been rattling their systems of death denial. They have each uncovered deep fears about death and looked at them directly. In the following stage of the program, they will be exploring ways they can more effectively deal with and begin to transcend such fears. You too will be guided to shift your focus toward a constructive response to the fears you have identified up to this point in the program.

The Second Stage: Transcending the Fear of Death

"Man is poised midway between the gods and the beasts," observed the ancient Roman philosopher Plotinus. Ken Wilber explains that even if evolution is bringing us up from the beasts and toward the gods, being poised midway makes us inherently tragic figures. The beasts are mortal, but they do not know it. The gods are immortal, and they know it. "But poor man, up from beasts and not yet a god, was that unhappy mixture: he was mortal, and he knew it."[24] With every evolutionary step toward greater consciousness and intelligence, humanity became more aware of its fate, its "mortal and death-stained fate."

A question that divides people is whether we are more like the beasts or like the gods in relation to our mortality. For some, it is intuitively obvious that we all perish as beasts, and that is the end of the story. For others, it is just as intuitively obvious that an aspect of who we are, an essence perhaps referred to as the soul, lives on after physical death. The evidence for each side of the argument is open to interpretation, and each of us is left, finally, to decide around which orientation we shall organize our understanding of life and death. But whether one takes great comfort in one's vision of heaven or other notion of an afterlife, is terrified by images of a demon-infested hell, or is quite certain that there is no afterlife, the quest for "symbolic immortality," to use Robert Jay Lifton's term,[25] seems to be a motivating force for most people.

Lifton describes five modes for attempting to transcend death by achieving symbolic immortality. The first is biological immortality, epitomized by family continuity and imagery of an endless biological chain linked to one's sons and daughters, their offspring, and on and on into eternity. A second mode for attaining symbolic immortality is through one's creative contributions, which may live on "through great works of art, literature, or science, or through more humble influences on people around us."[26] Here we take comfort in the knowledge that our best efforts may become part of human continuity. A third mode of symbolic immortality involves an identity with nature, a knowledge that the natural world will survive our physical demise, and that we, from dust to dust, will be returned to that natural world.

A fourth mode of transcending death involves a belief in "a specific concept of life after death, not only as a form of 'survival' but even as a release from the profane burdens of life into a higher plane of existence." Lifton believes that the "common thread in all great religions is the spiritual quest and realization of the hero-founder that enables him to confront and transcend death and to provide a model for generations of believers to do the same. . . . One is offered the opportunity to be reborn into a timeless realm of ultimate, death-transcending truths."[27]

Lifton's fifth mode, "experiential transcendence," is based on an inner experience that is "so intense and all-encompassing that time and space disappear [and there is] a sense of extraordinary psychic unity, and perceptual intensity, and of ineffable illumination and insight."[28] William James examined the impact of such experiences and reported that "mystical states of a well-pronounced and emphatic sort *are* usually authoritative over those who have them. . . . Mystical experiences are as direct perceptions of fact for those who have them as any sensations ever were for us."[29] We will return to the topic of experiential transcendence, and its provocative implications for our understanding of death, in the third stage of this program.

Stop here, and reflect in your journal on your relationship with "symbolic immortality." Does it make intuitive sense to you that these means of attaining symbolic immortality can lead to a viable sense of peace and meaning about biological mortality? Bring to mind the forms of symbolic immortality that are at work in your life. Do you have sons or daughters who will carry your biological inheritance from your parents into the future? What will live on in the world in terms of your accomplishments or influence on others? In what ways are you able to take comfort in your connection with the natural world and your knowledge that the natural world will continue after your physical being has reunited with it? What beliefs or concepts, religious or otherwise, do you hold that give comfort or meaning regarding death and what follows death? Have you had experiences that suddenly elevated your understanding and acceptance regarding your limited time here on earth? Do you believe that the more meaningful and fulfilling you make your life, the more peace you will find about the certainty of death?

In this second stage, you are invited to participate in three more personal rituals. The first ritual is designed to help you analyze your fears regarding death for the purpose of taking steps to face them more effectively. With the second ritual, you will be exploring the concept of transcendence and focusing on means you have used or might use in your own symbolic immortality projects. The third ritual involves the creation of another Death Fable, this one portraying your vision of successful efforts at symbolic immortality and death transcendence.

Personal Ritual 7: Looking Fear in the Teeth

Yalom emphasizes that anxiety can be a "guide as well as enemy and can point the way to authentic existence."[30] He notes the importance of being able to reduce anxiety to manageable levels while also using it to increase your awareness when facing one of the mature adult's major tasks: coming to terms with "the reality of decline and diminishment."[31] A strategy he advocates for reducing anxiety is to name it and explore it, as you have been doing in the previous rituals, and to break it down into component fears, as you will be doing in this one. He explains that a fear that "can neither be understood nor located cannot be confronted and becomes more terrible still: it begets a feeling of helplessness which invariably generates further anxiety."[32] But he offers the assurance that it

> is a matter of no small importance that one be able to explain and order the events in our lives into some coherent and predictable pattern. To name something, to locate its place in a causal sequence, is to begin

to experience it as under our control. . . . The sense of potency that flows from understanding occurs even in the matter of our basic existential situation: each of us feels less futile, less helpless, and less alone, even when, ironically, what we come to understand is the fact that each of us is basically helpless and alone.[33]

Thus Yalom encourages a "rational analysis" of death anxiety to sort out the various component fears, the major strategy being "to separate ancillary *feelings* of helplessness from the true helplessness that issues from facing one's unalterable existential situation."[34] Among the components of fear he enumerates are the pain of dying, the fear of an afterlife and the unknown, concern for one's family, fear for one's body, loneliness and regression, and the fact that "in achievement-oriented Western countries death is curiously equated with failure." He stresses that "each of these component fears, examined separately and rationally, is less frightening than the entire gestalt."[35] After discussing ways that people can exert tangible control over circumstances that affect their health and quality of life, such as when they involve themselves in social action or "discover with exhilaration that they can elect not to do the things they do not wish to do," he notes that "when all else seems beyond one's control, one, even then, has the power to control one's attitude toward one's fate."[36]

In this ritual, you will be selecting one, two, or three of the most troubling fears or areas of anxiety you identified in the earlier rituals. Recognizing them as components of your fear of death, you will discuss, in your journal, the steps you can take to approach them with understanding and a sense of mastery. Review your experiences to this point in the program, and identify your most significant fears. Use each of them as a heading in your journal, and under each heading, explore the following three questions about each fear:

To what assumptions is it linked?

What are the probabilities that the fearful circumstances will occur?

What can I do to decrease their likelihood or intensity?

Complete the ritual by discussing what you have written in your journal with at least one person who cares about you.

Peg's Analysis.   Reflecting on the assumptions she linked to her fears of aging and illness, Peg wrote: "Sickness and old age are times of diminished power. Without power, there is no dignity. Thus dignity can be eroded by physical circumstances." As to the probabilities of the fearful circumstances occurring: "They are pretty high, judging by the general population, and if I want to put my faith in statisticians. Mitigation would be to stay in good health, die sooner, or somehow find internal resources greater than the provocations of my worst-case scenario. Maybe the dementia of old age is merciful. When Hilda broke her hip in the nursing home, she believed she'd stumbled over a bale of hay in her goat barn. In a real way *she* wasn't in the nursing home at all."

Reflecting on what she could do to decrease the likelihood or intensity of her fears coming to fruition, Peg offered herself the following advice: "Live well. Stay active. Be attentive to my body's needs. Take care of my spirit. Let my friends and family know what I want. Trust. Plan a decent way out if I don't like the hand I'm dealt. Practice visualizations so that I have somewhere to go if I'm ever trapped in that hospital bed. Be cunning. Be wise. Be trusting of the ultimate good that comes from all adversity. Breathe."

Robert's Analysis.   Robert reflected on how the fear of being maimed was such a strong element in his death anxiety. "That sure breaks down one important component of my fear of death. Giving more attention to the fear of being maimed separates it out, gives me a chance to see where I can exert some control over that potential fate. First, it is helpful to know that it is a potential fate, not a certain fate. And it is also important to know that it is a fate that does happen to people—and to look it in the teeth by accepting that it could happen to me. 'There but for fortune.'

"I'm starting to see how, when others are struck by tragedy, my response gets all entangled in my fears. I try to shield myself from what happened, to emotionally distance myself from people who have been badly injured. I'm embarrassed that I haven't 'found the time' to pay a call on Neil Johnson since his accident. Part of it is I was just afraid of the awkwardness—I didn't know what to say. Maybe I'd better figure out what to say. Maybe I'd better deal a little more realistically with my own terror of losing an arm or the ability to walk.

"I'm reminded of that meditation retreat at which the Vietnamese holy man [Thich Nhat Hanh] talked about how the suffering we see around us provides an opportunity to develop the compassion that the Buddhists think of as the noblest emotion. Instead of responding to others' misfortune with fear or pity or guilt—all of which create distance—he teaches that we can turn such events into opportunities to practice opening our hearts, to know our oneness with all other beings. It seemed kind of abstract at the retreat, but it is making more sense to me now. I liked the blessing he did before meals; after appreciating the aesthetic beauty of the food, you take a moment to feel compassion—*not* guilt— toward all those who could not enjoy such a meal this day. Maybe to recognize the 'there but for fortune' aspect of my compassion for others who are struck by tragedy would make me a bigger person regarding such matters and better prepare me for whatever is to be. Perhaps it would be very good for me—not just an obligation or a courtesy—to hear through my own ears what the struggle has been like for Neil. It might even be a good 'emotional inoculation' to hear the gory details of his accident, of what it was like for him to learn of his losses, and to hear with an open heart his struggle to come to terms with them.

"I can do other things about my fear of mutilation as well. I can't prevent an airplane crash or act of senseless violence, but I can take appropriate precautions and operate with greater awareness that much of what I value and take such pleasure in is fragile. If I can raise this to the level of acting with appreciation for the blessings I have, I think it will make for a much better attitude. Also, by maintaining an awareness of the fragility of what I value, I will live so that if I am seriously injured, I at least don't have to blame it on my own stupidity. I guess there are some situations in which I would take major risks, but even there, a tragedy would be different if I were making a free and conscious choice.

"And, of course, there's the 'count your blessings' part of the issue. The awareness that a sudden and terrible downward shift in the quality of my life could be around any corner reminds me, again, of the preciousness of the moment. It particularly makes me want to spend more quality time with Dawn, more time in nature, and more time with good music and good books. I don't know why I don't sink into those cherished spaces more often. 'Too busy' seems lame in the face of Neil's plight."

You can see Robert struggling with his recognition that he would be well served to "sink into those cherished spaces more often" and his awareness that he simply doesn't. Later he will be challenged to take effective steps to change this pattern.

Personal Ritual 8: A View of "Symbolic Immortality" Through Sacred Time

Many spiritual traditions make a distinction between *ordinary time* and *sacred time*. Sacred time is not of the clock but of the heart. To be lost in wonderment watching a sunrise is to enter sacred time. Sometimes we will awake from a particularly moving and inspiring dream and sense that this dream belonged to sacred time. One of the most enchanting qualities of love is its ability to transport us from our ordinary world of work and relationships into sacred time. This also is a goal of spiritual disciplines such as meditation and prayer. Other inward-focused techniques, such as self-hypnosis and guided imagery, can also be routes into sacred time. We encourage you to use the following guided imagery instructions as a gateway to sacred time.

Prepare by setting an atmosphere that is evocative of your highest emotions. Find a space that brings you comfort, peace, and inspiration.

Consider having spiritually uplifting music playing in the background as you read the instructions into your tape, as you have them read to you, or as you create an experience that accomplishes the intent of the ritual. Use candles, soft lighting, inspiring art, and any other objects that might enhance the experience for you. Have your journal, Death Shield, and colored markers nearby. Also, wait to perform this ritual until your mood is receptive to entering sacred time. Sometimes yoga postures or aerobic exercise such as running, swimming, or free-form dancing help open such a space. When you are ready to begin, find a comfortable position, take a deep breath, and close your eyes.

The path you will be following into sacred time is marked by physical relaxation and uplifting memories. Settle in comfortably—finding an inner quiet, peace, and warmth. [Pause.] Thank your body for its hard work and good service. [Pause.] Find the parts of your body that need special attention, healing, or rest. Picture a warm, wise hand filled with fragrant ointment gently touching and appreciating those parts. [Pause.] Focus your attention and sense the melting, calming relaxation that comes into those sore and tired places. [30-second pause.]

As you focus on my voice, other sounds fade away. All is well with you for this journey into sacred time. You are always free to return to ordinary consciousness by simply opening your eyes and exhaling fully, and you are just as free to explore the riches of your inner world. You will recall all you need of this experience, and you will emerge from it with insight and power. You can move and adjust yourself at any time, yawning and stretching, rearranging until your body is peaceful and satisfied.

Begin to reflect on the holiest, most sacred times of your past. [Pause.] Remember a moment of shared love. [Pause.] Recall seeing a newborn child. [Pause.] You have felt yourself awed by a sunset, a waterfall, or the seashore. [Pause.] You have heard inspiring music [pause]; seen great art [pause]; savored a creative breakthrough [pause]; sat in an awe-inspiring cathedral or other place of reverence. [Pause.] Focus on a time that was particularly inspiring. [Pause.] Recall it vividly. [Pause.] Relive it in each of your senses. Breathe into the vision [pause]; the sounds [pause]; the feelings [pause]. Let go into the memory. [20-second pause.] Soon you will hear counting, from one to seven. When you hear the number seven, you will be fully relaxed and deep in sacred time.

One. As you bask in the inspiring feelings of the scene you have remembered, the healing hand sensitively massages your back, shoulders, and neck. You sigh, content.

Two. The healing hand moves to your face, massaging your forehead, eyes, cheeks, scalp, mouth, and jaw. Each breath fills your awareness. Unhurried, your sense of sacred time deepens.

Three. The muscles and joints of your arms and legs are rejuvenated by the healing hand. You exhale fully, feeling vitally alive and relaxed.

Four. The healing hand finds wounded or weary parts in the trunk of your body—pelvis, hips, buttocks, genitals, stomach, spine, ribs, heart—nourishing them with tender touch.

Five. The healing hand continues to touch away your pains as you exhale your tiredness, hurt, and disillusion. Your breathing is deep and pleasurable.

Six. Fully relaxed, you notice a pleasant tingling on your skin. As you smile, you feel a deep sense of peacefulness.

Seven. Your heart is open. You are absorbed in the comfortable, warm sensations. Your breathing fills the moment. You have entered sacred time. [20-second pause.]

Continuing to breathe deeply, watch your breath rising and falling. [Pause.] Your mind is clear as you savor the heightened awareness of this open moment. [60-second pause.]

From this heightened awareness, you find a sense of peace about life and about death. It is possible to find much to appreciate about your life and to take pleasure in who you are. [Pause.] Recall your earlier reflections on your relationship with "symbolic immortality." What attitudes or activities give your life the greatest meaning? [30-second pause.]

You are also, from this space, able to glimpse other attitudes or activities that would offer greater fulfillment and a more viable sense of "symbolic immortality." Let yourself become aware of attitudes and actions that could make your life richer. [20-second pause.] Now imagine yourself living from these attitudes or carrying out these activities. [Pause.] See, feel, and sense yourself living in a way that will give you greater peace about your existence and greater meaning to your mortality. [Pause]. Breathe fully into this experience. Enjoy it. [60-second pause.]

Focus on a sensation in your body that relates to living a life that is satisfying and fulfilling. Identify the part of your body where this sensation is most intense. Find the shape of the sensation—notice its borders. [Pause.] See its color. [Pause.] Explore its texture. [Pause.] In a moment, you will recognize a symbol emerging out of these shapes and colors that represents living with a profound sense of peace.

Watch as the symbol appears. [Pause.] You may actually see the symbol take form, or you may simply sense what it is. It will further evolve over the next few moments. Relax as it becomes increasingly clear. [20-second pause.]

As a fitting symbol of this richer way of living emerges, prepare to draw it on your shield. [Pause.] Take several deep breaths and begin *to stretch your body. [20-second pause.] Open your eyes, and draw the symbol on the portion of your shield that is labeled "Transcending Death Anxiety." As you draw this symbol, you may find that it is changing even as you are creating it or that you have more than one image to draw. Draw whatever comes. When you have completed your drawing, you will find that you have returned to full waking consciousness, feeling refreshed, confident, and able to effectively and creatively meet the requirements of your day.*

In your journal, under a heading called "My View Through Sacred Time," describe your experiences with this exercise. Reflect particularly on the means of symbolic immortality you reviewed during the experience and the new attitudes and actions you explored. How did these look from sacred time, and how do they seem to you now? Also, consider the meaning of the new symbol(s) you drew on your Death Shield. Additionally, consider using the "creative projection" technique for further examining their personal significance. You would "become" the symbol as you did earlier and describe yourself as that symbol, using first person, present tense.

Peg's View Through Sacred Time. In thinking about ways she was maintaining a sense of death transcendence, Peg wrote: "My life is filled with meaning. It matters that I work as I do with people. My writing has meaning. My family relationships are meaningful. I have precious friends. My connection to The Land [a large forest tract in the Coast Range of Oregon, with the Yaquina River running through it, for which she and her husband are steward-owners] is sacred. I use my mind and experience well. I have not lost my sense of wonder and surprise. I find it easy to appreciate. I love to learn and to craft beautiful objects and artful phrases.

"I have adult offspring. They are neither 'mine' nor 'children.' They survive well and show promise of continuing growth. I was a factor in their being. I have been a good teacher, often by my blunders, impetuousness, and intransigence, but sometimes by intent as well. Ah, the natural world—that is my home, my sanctuary—it is where I belong. I know that. I'll be planted there, dissolved, reabsorbed, reborn. Or at least my chemicals will. I believe this is not a wasteful or a random universe. I believe in Meaning and Intent. I do not know the pattern of which my life is a part, but I believe that the synchronicities of being are too frequent to be chance. Something is in charge. Something Knows. I've had numinous moments and dreams; there *is* sacred time and sacred space. The only difficulty is slowing down enough to enter it."

Her symbol for "Transcending Death Anxiety" was a fallen fir giant in the forest. She reflected: "It is a 'nurse log.' In its death it becomes shelter and food for other life forms. Fungi grow on it, reducing its coarse cellulose to a finer form, the better to rot back into the earth. The creek it partially dams flows over it, aerating the water for the fish and craw-dads. Baby cedars take root in the moss of its bark, sinking their root tendrils deep into its body. The hollow core that caused it to fall becomes the home for a raccoon family. Beetles thrive under its bark. Wind-blown soil collects in the crevices, and bird-sown seed sprouts huckleberry bushes. Slugs and ferns find habitat. A heron perches on its submerged branches, alert for scuttling crawdads lurking in the shallows. Bacteria, beetles, mushrooms, and fungi digest it and live their lives in vital harmony with death. In the great pan of its upturned rootball, stones caged in roots see the light of day, and the soil erodes enriching the river. There is no waste here."

Robert's View Through Sacred Time.   "The memory I went to when I scanned my experiences with sacred time was powerful. It was Dawn's twenty-fifth birthday. We weren't certain yet that we would be life partners—there were so many other things we each needed to work out before we could make that commitment. I had invited her to my home for dinner. She arrived to candlelight and twenty-five presents—from trinkets to treasures—hidden Easter-egg style throughout the apartment. After a very special dinner, we spent the evening with her searching for a gift, opening it, and then being told there was still one more. After the fourth or fifth gift, and all the way up to her birthday number, she would look at me incredulously each time, or squeal with childlike delight as she eagerly set out to find the next surprise. The whole evening was a prolonged high. I savored her enthusiasm as she opened each gift. Her expressions of pleasure and appreciation seemed so real and heartfelt that every gift deepened our bond. I took pleasure in having found gifts that really pleased her, and I could tell that she felt appreciated and deeply recognized in the selections I had made.

"In the exercise, I realized that although I've never looked at that birthday, memorable though it was, as a milestone, it really was. I think we made a commitment to each other in the ethers that night. Although it was only after separations and years that we came to merge our lives together, I had the sense that something very spiritual had occurred between us that evening. In the midst of this thought, I felt suddenly uplifted into what I think of as a spiritual feeling. It's hard to describe, but it gives me a glimpse of what words like 'awe' and 'rapture' can mean.

"Answering the question about what I do that best prepares me to come to terms with my mortality was simple. I was doing it right at that moment. By bringing back memories of the intensely loving moments Dawn and I shared on her twenty-fifth birthday, I was transported into a wonderful sense of joy and peace. In response to the question of what I could do more of, nothing made greater sense than to protect the time and create the atmosphere so I could go into this sacred space more frequently. It's clear to me from my memory of Dawn's birthday that love is a major point of entry into that spirit world."

From this account, we get an intimate view of Robert gaining greater sensitivity to deep but subtle longings as he reawakens to realms of his being that he considers "spiritual." On his Death Shield he drew a picture of the candlelit room. He found that by meditating on it, he could re-capture the ethereal feelings to which his memory of the experience had brought him in the exercise.

Personal Ritual 9: A Second Death Fable, *"Death in the Light of Transcendence"*

You are about to write a second Death Fable. It will begin in the same setting and will portray the same main character and the same impending death as your first fable. But in this story, the person has found some effective ways of transcending the fear of death. These happen, in fact, to be the same ways of living that you imagined in the previous personal ritual, when you viewed life and death through sacred time. In this story you will be exploring the difference in the dying process between one who is leading with the fear of death and one who is leading with peace and acceptance. The pioneer of family therapy, Virginia Satir, in her parting message to friends, colleagues, and family, said "I send my love. Please support me in my passage to a new life." She thanked them for playing a significant part in the development of her ability to love: "As a result, my life has been rich and full, so I leave feeling very grateful." The main character of your Death Fable is to have found as much peace about dying as is reflected in her statement.

Like the first Death Fable, this story will describe the way the main character first learns that death is fast approaching, his or her reactions, how the process of dying progresses, and what the final moments are like. You may also include a funeral or a eulogy. But the two stories will be a study in contrasts regarding the dying process, dramatizing the effects of changing a single variable. In the second story, the emphasis is on living so as to transcend death rather than living based on a fear of it. After reading Peg's and Robert's stories, again begin by relaxing in a comfortable spot and contemplating the Death Fable you are about to create. Allow your story to emerge from deep within you.

Peg's Second Death Fable. "The old midwife-herbalist sits by the fire, her weary body leaning doggedly to her task. Before her is a vellum book, thick and substantial. Holding her goose quill pen, she copies down the years of her learnings. She writes of healings and losses, of children born and mothers dead. She draws pictures of herbs in bloom and signs to watch for in harvesting them. In the margin of her book she writes a jest at herself, to bring a smile to the reader who will inherit her wisdom.

"The room darkens. The candle flickers and the air cools. The midwife looks up. Death, a long-familiar ally, is coming through the door carrying a lamb's wool blanket to warm and cradle her. She smiles in recognition and draws a last flourish under the final entry in her Life Book. In the shadows, mercy and curiosity and service circle close to calm her heart and quiet her breath. A smile comes as she folds inward, her work complete.

"The funeral is attended by those she's healed and taught, all telling stories of her goodness and humor and telling how they themselves are the better for her having lived. They mark her grave with four redwood trees at the cardinal points and a thousand daffodil bulbs; then they set in place a forest of wind chimes and prisms that sing in the night and flash rainbow light in the daytime."

Robert's Second Death Fable.   "Once Robchinko Ryzhkov realized that his fate was sealed, he ceased his frantic digging, and a sense of peace fell over him. He knew he had done all he could to free himself from the rubble. He knew he could not. And he knew his time was very limited. 'This is when a review of my life is supposed to flash in front of me,' he thought. But it did not, so he began the review in his mind. He saw how his life had directed him toward certain lessons. He took satisfaction in how much he had learned, and he noted his failures, accepting that the time to right them had passed. He remembered particularly the most loving moments along the way. Those seemed to be the important landmarks from this vantage point. As he began to say good-bye to those whom he had loved the most, the tears seemed to pour out endlessly from deep in his being. Finally, he directed his attention toward his faith that his life and death were part of a larger plan. He realized that this was perhaps his hardest moment ever for maintaining faith in a good and greater Power. He willed himself to imagine a light beyond, like he'd read about, and he fell asleep with that image in his mind. In his dream, a beautiful, ornate, horse-driven carriage was taking him above the clouds and toward that light. He never returned."

In the first stage of the program, Peg's and Robert's fears of death were emphasized and explored. In this stage, they each examined ways of contending with their fears and formulating viable ideas and images of death transcendence. Their second death fables both ended on the opposite note of their fables about "Death in the Shadow of Fear." In the following stage of the program, you will watch as they each consciously and willfully mediate between the fear of death and the wish to transcend it, and you will also be invited to find a path toward reconciliation.

The Third Stage: A Confrontation Between the Fear of Death and Images of Transcending Death

Death, according to Yalom, is the ultimate "boundary situation."[37] Like a nation's borders, boundaries give definition. Psychological boundaries define our identity and our sense of limits. One of the infant's first definitive cognitive achievements is to distinguish between self and other, to create an inner image that maps the physical boundaries separating infant from mother and from the rest of the world. This inner image becomes the prototype for a variety of psychological boundaries that will be important as the infant matures.

Your concept of death, your internal image of where your existence will end, is a pivotal psychological boundary because of how much it tells you about the nature of life. Your concept of death and your concept of life share a common border. As your comprehension of the boundary that marks death evolves, so does your understanding of life. This psychological boundary, separating existence from nonexistence, will be our focus in this stage of the program.

One force that determined where you, as a child who was unconsciously constructing inner images about death, drew the boundaries on life is the instinctive, biologically rooted sense that death is the end of existence. Images of death whose boundaries are confined to this rather narrow interpretation of the possibilities are often laced with fear or a sense of emptiness. They require that life's meaning be found exclusively within the observable facts of existence. A counterforce that provides a more expansive contour for personal images about death is the innate desire to somehow transcend the certainty of death, coupled with some vision of immortality—whether derived from intuition, wishful thinking, sophisticated theological conviction, or successful "symbolic immortality" projects.

To this point in the program, you have explored some experiences and premonitions that influenced you to draw the line closer to the "death is the end" position and others that favored the "death is a transition to another state of being" side. Here we ask you to temporarily suspend whatever beliefs you have held to this point in your life regarding how this boundary is best drawn and to examine the issue afresh. Because the question eludes a rational solution, the challenge in this stage of the program is to open-mindedly arbitrate between both sides of the issue. We believe that the greater the reconciliation of these opposing internal forces, the more balanced and resilient will be the mythology that ultimately provides you with guidance on matters of life and death.

The issue is at the core of the differences between secular-existential and spiritual-religious attitudes. If there is "no exit" into some notion of death transcendence, as the existentialists claim, we are required to find whatever meaning we can along the way, with no hope for a better existence somewhere else.[38] The motto of this philosophy might be "The existence you see is the only existence you get—make the most of it." If, on the other hand, you believe that you will persist in some form even after death, and that you will eventually reap the consequences of the life you are now living, as the religious position invariably contends, you may be equally motivated to make the most out of your life. Although each side can ultimately lead to a life-affirming stance, both positions also have their hazards. The existential position does not foster the sense of an inherently meaningful connection with the cosmos or much hope for a dramatically better future, and it can lead to a paralyzing sense of isolation and hopelessness. The religious position is vulnerable to promises of a future paradise that divert one's energy from getting on with the business of creating a better life here on earth.

We believe that a version of this existential-spiritual debate goes on in each individual, although often beneath the level of conscious awareness, and many people resolve the ambiguities by strongly identifying themselves with one position or the other. You may consciously accept or reject the notion that some form of existence extends beyond physical death. Such beliefs serve to overshadow conflict in the psyche between unnamed primal fears of death and archetypal images of death transcendence. You have already been uncovering and examining your thoughts and feelings about the question. Here you will further explore each side and initiate a dialogue between them so that your personal cosmology may become better informed by considerations on both sides of the issue. Through these efforts, you will gain conscious access to a more integrated outlook as you proceed with this program for recreating your mythology about death.

Before asking you to begin your dialogue, we will review the existential-spiritual debate in some of its contemporary manifestations. The debate exists not only between scientific and traditional religious voices, to whose divergent views of creation and afterlife you may have been exposed since grade school science classes and Sunday school. It is also being vehemently waged between those who hold to an orthodox view of empirical science and those who, while also claiming scientific rigor, depict a vision of consciousness that transcends the life of the body and sometimes resembles mysticism more than it does the Newtonian worldview.[39] Traditional science has supported a secular outlook, and the modern thinker, inevitably impressed with its accomplishments, is swayed toward accepting the basic empirical premise that for the rational mind whatever cannot be observed does not exist. /

The debate is alive today within the scientific community as the nature of scientific thought has been changing radically in recent years. Many of our models of reality are still based on a Newtonian view of the universe. But concepts that are on the cutting edge of modern science—such as an "implicate order," "morphogenetic fields," and "superstrings"—begin to seem more consistent with the mystical notion that there is another order of existence than they are with the traditional "universe as a machine" perspective. But contemporary science does not *prove* the existence of other realms or of life after death. Coming to terms with the question remains an individual matter.

Ernest Becker was an articulate spokesperson for the existential view that existence ends with physical death. He identified an integral relationship between the hoarding of wealth and power that blights much of civilization and the attempt to psychologically deny the reality of death: "All this seemingly useless surplus, dangerously and painstakingly wrought . . . goes to the very heart of human motivation, the urge to . . . transcend the limitations of the human condition and achieve victory over impotence and finitude."[40] This part of his thesis offers a profound, often quoted, and rarely disputed insight into the nature of human motivation and social organization. But Becker extends his argument, asserting that all conceptions of immortality can be understood as simply the psychological denial of death as our ultimate fate. On this point there has been heated debate.

Ken Wilber, for instance, has challenged the existential position represented by Becker, arguing that an essential aspect of the self persists after physical death. Wilber summarizes Becker's viewpoint: "Because man fears death, he responds with death denials, and thus creates the pure illusion/lie of Eternity."[41] Wilber parts with Becker by claiming that all attempts to transcend death through some vision of eternal life cannot simply be reduced to death denial or illusion. He reverses Becker's argument: "Because man is presently ignorant of Eternity, he fears death, and thus constructs death denials." According to Wilber, visions of life after death are not only psychological defenses to counteract our fears; we intuit some of these images because they reflect our "true and prior Nature."[42]

From this perspective, before coming into the physical body, the self exists in some form—either unified with or in harmony with the cosmos, like a drop of water in the ocean—and it will eventually return to that state. But in order that we may establish a separate identity after birth and move out into the world, we relinquish our awareness of this unity with the cosmos. In order to find our way as individuals, we experience ourselves in isolation. At some level, however, we yearn to transcend

this temporal self and to be transported back to a spiritual reunion—
"comin' for to carry me home." But it is the nature of the conscious
ego to stand in trepidation of knowledge that the hard-earned boundaries
it has forged in the world might someday be obliterated. Wilber explains
our ambivalence about recognizing what he believes to be our infinite
nature and our essential unity with the cosmos: "Above all else, each
person wants true transcendence . . . ; but, above all else, each person
fears the loss of the separate self, the 'death' of the isolated ego. All
a person wants is Wholeness, but all he does is fear and resist it (since
that would entail the 'death' of his separate self). And there is the dilemma, the double-bind in the face of eternity."[43]

The resolution to this dilemma, from the spiritual perspective, has
traditionally required a religious faith about one's part in a larger plan.
The German philosopher Wilhelm Leibniz thought of this faith as belonging to a venerated tradition that he termed "The Perennial Philosophy." The expression refers to an essentially mystical worldview that
has been shared by many of humanity's most luminous moral and spiritual leaders throughout history, though widely separated by time and
place. Aldous Huxley, in his anthology of writings by saints and other
seers who expressed the Perennial Philosophy, presents a big picture of
widespread accord regarding an "ethic that places man's final end in
the knowledge of the immanent and transcendent Ground of all being."[44]
He claims this view is not more widely maintained because, according
to his reading of history, this "ultimate Reality is not clearly and immediately apprehended, except by those who have made themselves loving, pure in heart [and] spirit."[45]

Though the idea that humanity's most evolved souls have independently come to a similar view about the ultimate nature of reality is
based largely on religious and philosophical literature, psychological in-
vestigations also lend support to the notion of a Perennial Philosophy.
In studies of "self-actualizing" people, Abraham Maslow observed that
many of the most psychologically vibrant individuals he could identify
reported intense, mysticlike episodes, which he termed "peak experiences."[46] He found certain common features in how these persons
perceived the world during these episodes, which are similar to Lifton's
description of "experiential transcendence." Maslow thought of these
common features as the "facts of Being"—observations that penetrate
into the nature of existence. These perceptions generally correspond with
the tenets of the Perennial Philosophy.

During peak experiences or moments of experiential transcendence,
there is a direct apprehension of the essence of qualities such as love,
goodness, beauty, truth, and justice. Though these intense perceptions
may be short-lived, they tend to shape the long view. The transcendent
apprehension of a quality such as love or goodness may forever after

fuel one's impulse to pursue the essence of that quality as it was revealed. Mother Teresa recounts an occasion when, as a young nun and school-teacher riding on a train in India, she "heard God" tell her that her life's work was to bring love to the poorest of the poor. Although the basis of such experiences has been hotly debated among theologians and scientists, she felt touched by a Divine voice that dramatically set her life on an unpaved course that has inspired millions.

Reports of transcendent experiences that involve a sense of death and rebirth frequently appear in the world's mythologies and are the dominant motif of the classic hero's journey. According to Stanislav and Christina Grof, "Heroes descend into the underworld and after enduring extreme ordeals and overcoming obstacles, return to earth endowed with supernatural powers."[47] The Grofs explain that it is possible to induce such confrontations with death in a ritual context:

> Many traditions include the belief that one can do more to prepare for death than just acquire intellectual knowledge of the process of dying. Mind-altering technologies have been developed using psyche-delic substances or powerful non-drug methods that make possible real experiential training for dying. In this context, compelling psychological encounters with death, so profound and shattering as to be indistin-guishable from actual biological annihilation, are followed by the sense of spiritual rebirth. This is the core-experience of shamanic initiation, rites of passage and mystery religions. Symbolic death of this kind not only gives a deep realization of the impermanence of biological existence, but facilitates spiritual opening, and provides insight into the transcen-dent nature of human consciousness. . . . Rites of passage are powerful transformative rituals, usually enacted at the time of biological tran-sitions such as birth, circumcision, puberty, marriage, second maturity and death. Van Gennep, who first defined and described these rites, noticed that they have three characteristic phases. In the first phase, which he called *separation*, the initiates are removed from their social matrix and kept in isolation for weeks or even months. During this time, they are learning through songs, dances, tales and myths about the strange experiential territory they are about to enter. In the second phase, *transition*, powerful mind-altering techniques are used to provide a transforming experience. These methods include combinations of sleep-deprivation, fasting, pain, mutilation, group pressure, social iso-lation, emotional and physical stress, and in some instances the use of psychedelic substances. The initiates experience extremes of anguish, chaos, confusion and liminality, and emerge from the process of an-nihilation with a sense of rejuvenation and rebirth. The third stage, *incorporation*, involves the reintegration of the transformed individual into the community in a new role. The depth and intensity of the death-rebirth experience provides a dramatic framework for the termination of the old social role and the assumption of the new one. However, repeated encounters with annihilation followed by a sense of redefinition

have another important function: They prepare the individual for eventual biological death by establishing a deep, almost cellular awareness
that periods of destruction are those of transition rather than
termination.[48]

Though it is beyond the scope of this work to provide a guide for
inducing an intensive "death-rebirth" experience, such guidance is
available.[49] In addition to planned encounters with one's mortality, the
"life-after-life" reports of people who return from a close brush with
death are particularly germane to our concerns here.[50] Following such
dramatic experiences, people often recall having had so unmistakable
an encounter with a "Being of Light" and with an afterlife that the
existence of each is beyond question for them. These conclusions appear
to emerge independent of any prior religious or spiritual beliefs. People
who have had a life-after-life experience also frequently enjoy a greater
appreciation of other people and of their own lives, become less ma-
terialistic, less concerned with pleasing others, and more concerned with
ultimate questions such as the meaning of life. These changes are often
lasting. Perhaps most remarkably, they "enjoy an overwhelming increase
in self-confidence, security, and self-esteem."[51] Other evidence supporting
the life-after-life position includes the accumulation of increasingly well
documented reports of "past-life memories" and of clinical break-
throughs after such "memories" emerge.[52] Particularly impressive are
the "memories" of children, as young as two or three, who in describing
a past life are able to provide verifiable details about people and places
to whom they could have had no exposure.[53]

Each of the basic phenomena of the life-after-life argument can be
explained in alternative ways. For instance, "the brilliant light that
doesn't hurt one's eyes may arise directly from the visual cortex," and
"experiences of intense joy, profound insight, and love may be caused
by a flood of endorphins designed by evolution to blot out pain when
pain's message is too frightening to be functional."[54] Hallucinations,
carbon dioxide overload, and other biochemical explanations have been
posited. The implications of near-death phenomena are still being fervently debated. The above discussion is presented not to persuade you
that the case for an afterlife has been established, but to offer some current
views in humanity's enduring attempt to overcome the instinctual terror
of death and to fulfill its yearning for an everlasting identity with the
cosmos. Where these arguments support or differ from your own beliefs,
you may find it valuable to explore how you came to accept or dismiss
them. The issues involved are central to your understanding of life and
death. You are, at some level, continually dealing with them, and we
believe the act of bringing the process into consciousness will ultimately lead you toward a more viable and empowering mythology regarding death.

Personal Ritual 10: A Dialogue Between Your Fear of Death and the Prospect of Transcending Death

In this ritual, you will personify, in a role-play both your fear of death and the greatest peace about death that you can image. The character who will portray your fear of death is in vivid contact with the biological terror of annihilation. The character who will personify an acceptance of death is aware that some of the wisest and most illuminated individuals in humanity's history have found emotionally and intellectually viable ways of transcending that terror and takes heart in their example. The two characters will engage in debate and dialogue about their differences. You will, for this dramatization, physically enact each character. You will, alternately, speak for one of them and then the other. Do not be surprised if their dialogue in some ways resembles the existential-spiritual debate discussed above.

Prime yourself for representing the first character by reviewing your exploration of "the fear of death at its foundation," the "death fear" symbol on your shield, and your fable about "death in the shadow of fear." Contemplate the fears that are the most troubling to you. Prepare yourself to represent the other character by reviewing the perspective you gained as you viewed mortality through "sacred time," the symbolism on the portion of your shield called "Transcending Death Anxiety," and your fable about "death in the light of transcendence." Recall the modes for death transcendence or symbolic immortality that seemed the most gratifying or plausible for you. The two sides will be taking part in a debate. On one side will be the primal part of you that is terrified of death and annihilation. On the other side, you will give voice to the intuitions and beliefs you hold or find most palatable regarding peace about death and the prospects for transcendence of death.

Allow yourself to explore the two sides of the issue by alternately identifying fully with each position. For each side, invent a character, or use the character from one of your death fables, and create a role-play. Find physical postures that depict the life stance represented by each side. Wholeheartedly dramatize the dialogue. The impact of this exercise may be increased if someone whom you trust and who cares about your personal development serves as a witness. The presence of another can both affirm and ritualize your experience. The person can later share observations and impressions. New insights about the relationship between your fears of death and your hopes of transcending it may emerge from reviewing the exchange. If you do not arrange to have a partner, you can use a tape recorder to serve as mirror and witness. Familiarize yourself with the following instructions. They end with a summary that can guide you as you proceed.

The first step is to find a physical posture that expresses your fear of death. Move into the posture and experiment with it. Find a fitting facial expression. Should you grimace, scowl, frown, stare, twitch? What kind of gestures would be most appropriate for this character? Will you point? Put your hands in your pocket? Hug yourself? Shake nervously? Dance? Jump? Pray? Crawl?

Once you have found a posture for the first character, become acquainted with the other character in a similar manner. Take two steps forward, turn around, and "face" your first character. Move into a posture that represents peace about death. Experiment until you find the most fitting gestures and facial expression. Establishing this character is a drill in sensing your way beyond primal, fearful images about death. Give yourself all the time you need.

After establishing the postures and facial expressions that best represent each character, move back and forth a few times, becoming more comfortable in each role. Then give each character a chance to begin observing and sizing up the other. Finally, allow a dialogue to begin.

In the initial interchanges, highlight the differences between the two characters. You can begin the dialogue by stepping into the position of one of the characters, finding its posture, and making a statement that reflects this character's basic stance regarding life and death. Speak while looking at and reacting to the other character. Be conscious of using an apt tone of voice. Find the words that express your feelings and thoughts as this character. Then step into the other position and respond. Keep your facial expressions, posture, gestures, and tones appropriate to the character you are portraying.

As the two characters encounter each other, allow the words to flow unrehearsed. Keep the dialogue going without long pauses or planning. Trust your spontaneous comments. Continue to move physically between the two characters as you let the dialogue develop.

In the early part of the dialogue, you will be exploring where the two sides hold incompatible beliefs, values, or feelings. Eventually, you will be attempting to establish improved communication between the characters. If the dialogue gets bogged down, have one side ask the other, "What do you want of me?" Provide a thoughtful response. Have each character listen with increasing care and compassion to the other's position.

In summary: (1) Find the posture and gestures of each side, and experiment in moving from one to the other; (2) give words to one side so the character can make a clear opening statement, then move to the position of the other side and begin with a clear opening statement; and (3) let the dialogue develop. Read the following accounts of Peg's and Robert's dialogues, and then begin your own.

Excerpts from Peg's Dialogue.   Peg's dialogue was between the Hag and the Healer from her death fables.

HAG: Goody-goody!

HEALER: Goody-goody? Me?

HAG: You! Thinking that if you're just good enough, then dying will be okay. Fool! You need to gather more things and make yourself plump, the better to withstand the lean times.

HEALER: You really think that'll make you safe? I don't! I believe that being helpful is the answer, not riches, when Death comes.

HAG: Don't talk to me of Death! Death can't get me if I'm clever enough—I can hold him off indefinitely.

HEALER: Foolish old woman! Death is a soothing ointment on the scalded flesh; it is rest at the end of toil; it is a friend leading us into a bright place. And Death comes when it will, not at our bidding.

HAG: You'll sing a different tune when pain tears your guts and ideas elude your grasp. Better to wrap yourself in silk clothes, eat rich food, and drink wine before your throat closes forever.

HEALER: What of love?

HAG: Fairy tales! Fantasy!

HEALER: What if I rub your poor tired back and bring you a bowl of fresh vegetable soup? Let us tell stories of being young and juicy—will you laugh with me?

HAG: Rub my back? Where it aches? What will you charge?

HEALER: How about a smile and one sentence about the goodness of life?

HAG: A hard bargain.

HEALER: Oh I'll rub you without it, but it's what I'd like most in barter. After all, fair's fair.

HAG: For a goody-goody, you're a tough cookie. All right. How's this for a smile?

HEALER: Not bad, but you could use some practice—happy eyes are part of a smile, you know, not just baring your teeth. Try again; it'll feel good. And don't forget the sentence ...

HAG: You're right, it does feel good—how curious! Here's my sentence: Life is good when you're in touch—like now, with my back being rubbed.

HEALER: Wait until you rub mine! The big secret is that it feels better to give than receive, odd as that may seem to you right now. You'll get your chance.

Excerpts from Robert's Dialogue. "The fear side was huddled up in a fetal position, trembling, screaming, 'I don't want to die; I'm not ready to die.' On the other side was a big man — standing tall, breathing fully, and expanding into this space. He was very serene about the whole thing. He even exuded a strange kind of peace as he cryptically said to the trembling character, 'It is not death that you should fear.' The two began to speak with each other:

FEAR: What do you mean, implying that there are worse things to fear! I'm so fully consumed by my fear of death that I can't even get a handle on how to begin to contain it. And you want me to find something else to be afraid of!

PEACE: I'm not meaning to make light of your terror. I just want you to know that you would find comfort if you could grasp the full picture. You are part of a bigger plan. Death is but a doorway to the next stage. A glorious realm awaits you on the other side. Take peace in this knowledge.

FEAR: I don't experience death as anything but terrifying! I have no reason to believe in fantasies of another world, much less a "glorious" one. You're not going to create false hopes in me! I think the foundation of all your supposed inner peace is built on wishful thinking.

PEACE: You know, that's the basis of the whole debate. Someone full of fear, like you, sees everything teeming with danger and decline. Those who have been touched by the world of spirit have a different take. They still see the suffering, but they also see the opportunity to quell that suffering with a sense of deep connection to a larger plan. The question comes down to deciding which position to believe.

FEAR: That's no problem for me. I don't trust the wishful fantasies of the self-proclaimed spiritually evolved.

PEACE: Of course not. If you've not been touched by that realm, it's not very convincing. But you see, there is more than what you experience. I've had moments when I have been touched by a sense of spirit that is infinitely greater than what is encased in my body. It's not wishful thinking — it's direct experience. But when you hear such reports, however vivid and sincere, they are quickly discounted and forgotten.

FEAR: Why should I believe you?

PEACE: Which one of us is happier? You have to admit that between the two of us, I'm the one who's found serenity and
joy. By my criteria, that merits a certain amount of authority. The kind of happiness that grows out of deep
peace even in the midst of great distress is found in the
saints, like Gandhi and Schweitzer. They all believed in,
had direct knowledge of, the spiritual, death-transcending
foundations of their lives.

FEAR: Hey, hearsay doesn't convince me. I'd like to be able to
believe what you believe, but I can't find a shred of convincing evidence.

PEACE: Come here, Fear. Let me just hold you for a minute. Let
my energy calm you. I'll hang out with you in your world
until enough of me has rubbed off on you that you feel
secure enough to venture into mine.

FEAR: What makes you think it is not I who will rub off on
you? Just watch as your rose-colored glasses darken in my
presence until you finally have to whip them off and gaze
directly at the stark, terrifying truths of existence.

PEACE: There is no question for me that it is I who is tuned into
the eternal truths of existence. They are beyond your
wavelength. But with those truths backing me, it is I who
will rub off on you. You will be pleased.

FEAR (feeling mocked and mobilized for a fight): We'll just see
who's going to rub off on whom . . .

After completing your own dialogue, summarize it in your journal,
and reflect on the way these characters representing your relationship
to death were able to communicate with each other. Were they able
to inform each other or come to any resolution of their differences? We
suggest that over the next several days you extend the dialogue with
two or three more rounds of at least ten minutes each. Commit yourself
to attaining greater integration between these two sides of your primal
response to the fact of being mortal.

Personal Ritual 11: Opening the Space for a New Integration

In the previous ritual you consciously engaged in a dramatization
of your conflict. In this one you will invite your unconscious mind to
open itself to the conflict and help facilitate a resolution. You will be
performing a ritual dance to open within yourself the space for a new
and deeper integration between your primal fear of death and your in-
tuited or acquired ways of transcending it. One way to open a space

for new and creative insight is to temporarily put aside the concepts you currently hold, to more or less peek beneath them so you can freshly perceive the issue. In this ritual you will invite yourself to go deeper than the ideas about death you have been examining, to travel below your conscious mind and into the realm of your intuition and creative imagination.

You have heard of the trance dance used in many tribal cultures to attain altered states of consciousness. In this ritual, you will also be using patterned movement to bring yourself into a preverbal state of openness and receptivity. Begin by selecting a piece of music with a fast beat. Rock music or percussion music with a tribal beat, such as "Totem," by Gabrielle Roth, or "Drums of Passion," by Olatunji, can serve the purpose.

With the music playing, stand in the position and posture of the character who symbolizes your fear of death. Explore the way this character dances to this music. Then move about ten feet across the room and into the posture of the other character. Explore this individual's dance. Once you have established the two separate dances, begin to move in a circle with the positions of the two characters being points on opposite sides of the circle. As you approach the position of one of the characters, allow your movements to become that character's movements. As you leave that position, release those movements, and then find the movement patterns representing the other character. Go around the circle at least three times, alternating your movements as you reach each character. Finally, continuing to go around the circle, pick up speed and allow the movements to blend into a new movement belonging to neither the first character nor the second. As this occurs, begin to chant, out loud, "Let the change begin!" Allow the circle to become smaller, until you have spiraled into its center. No longer spinning around, allow your movements to be free in their form.

For several more minutes, continue your movements while chanting, "Let the change begin!" Know that you are opening a space for new insight and a new relationship with the basic questions regarding your mortality. If different words want to come, allow them. Move so as to embody the words you are chanting. Feel them deeply. Move rapidly and emphatically to the beat. Continue until your body is tired and your mind is clear (if you have any physical limitations, pace yourself accordingly). Finally, lie down and immediately embark on Personal Ritual 12, following.

Here is a summary of the steps for initiating your Trance Dance: (1) Establish the dance of each of your characters, placing them about ten feet apart; (2) move at least three times around a ten-foot circle, taking on the movement of each character as you approach its position; (3) picking up speed, allow the movements to blend into a new, unrehearsed pattern; (4) begin to chant, "Let the change begin!" as you begin to spiral in toward the center of the circle; (5) from the center, continue dancing freely, allowing your chant to evolve as it will; and (6) lie down, relax, and begin listening to the guided imagery instructions of the following personal ritual.

Personal Ritual 12: A Body Metaphor of Resolution

You will need to have familiarized yourself with this ritual or prepared a tape or made arrangements so someone can read it to you immediately after finishing your Trance Dance. With your journal, Death Shield, and markers nearby, feel your body calming as you focus your mind on these instructions:

Bring your attention to your breathing. [Pause.] Listen for and feel each in-breath and each out-breath. [Pause.] Notice how your stomach and chest fill . . . and empty. [Pause.] As you continue to breathe and relax, you are better able to concentrate on my voice and on the suggestions I will offer. If outside sounds or passing thoughts cross your mind, they fade quietly into the background just as they occur. Your breathing is slow and deep as you relax more completely with each of your next five breaths. One [pause]; two [pause]; three [pause]; four [pause]; five [pause].

Let one side of your body represent your primal fear of death. Sense if it is your left side or your right side. Do not pull back; there is vital information here for you to have. [Pause.] This side of your body is immersed in the energy of fear. It is reacting to your primal fear of death. As you tune into this frightened side of your body, an image that represents your fear of death may emerge. Give it some time, and if an image does appear, examine it. [20-second pause.] Focus again now on the feelings in this side of your body, and explore your body's response to the energies and images of fear. [30-second pause.]

Imagine now that the other side of your body represents confidence, hope, and harmony about death. [Pause.] Focus on this side of your body. You may experience feelings of acceptance or tranquillity. As you tune into this more peaceful side of your body, an image that represents serenity about dying may emerge. Give it some time, and if an image does appear, examine it. [20-second pause.] Focus again now on the feelings in this side of your body, and explore your body's response to the energies and images of peace and serenity. [30-second pause.]

Compare the sensations between these two sides of your body. [Pause.] Notice where the two sides meet. The energies of the two sides may repel each other along this line, or one side may be reaching or pushing over into the other side. Or they may already be starting to blend and merge.

In a moment, the energies on the two sides of your body will be merging into a single energy. As your intuition guides the process, be open to your innermost truths. A creative resolution will occur between the two sides. First the energies around the fearful side of your body and those around the peaceful side start to mingle and merge. [Pause.] As they blend more completely, a new, unifying energy swirls around your entire being.

Securely surrounded by this unifying energy, the sensations within your body begin to blend into a single energy. A merging of the energies on each side of your body is occurring. Know that this blend is coming about for your highest good. That which is wholesome and valid of the transcendent, peaceful side mixes with the harsher realities from the other side, raising them to a higher level. The two forces synthesize and become a single integrated energy that retains the most important qualities of both. The new mixture will offer peace, wisdom, and strength. The integration between the sides becomes stronger with every breath. You sense newfound hope and understanding. [30-second pause.]

As the new harmonies permeate your body, you may notice that a feeling of resolution and a new direction has become strong in you. As the integration deepens, you may sense a new tranquillity about being mortal. Identify the part of your body where the feelings and sensations of serenity and integration are most intense. Find the shape of this part of your body—notice its borders. [Pause.] See its color. [Pause.] Explore its texture. [Pause.] In a moment, you will recognize a symbol that represents a new relationship with death emerging out of these shapes and colors.

Watch as the symbol appears. [Pause.] You may actually see the symbol take form, or you may simply sense what it is. It will further evolve over the next few moments. Relax as it becomes increasingly clear. [20-second pause.]

As a symbol that represents your new relationship with death emerges, prepare to draw it on your shield. [Pause.] Take several deep breaths, and begin to stretch your body. [20-second pause.] Open your eyes, and draw the symbol on the portion of your shield that is labeled "A Renewed Mythology About Death." As you draw this symbol, you may find that it is changing even as you are creating it or that you have more than one image to draw. Draw whatever comes. When you have completed your drawing, you will find that you have returned to full waking consciousness, feeling refreshed, confident, and able to effectively and creatively meet the requirements of your day.

In your journal, describe your experience with the Trance Dance and with your body metaphor of resolution. Reflect on the meaning of the new symbol(s) you drew on your shield. Additionally, consider using the "creative projection" technique for further examining its personal significance. You would "become" the symbol, as you did earlier, and describe yourself as that symbol using first person, present tense.

With this ritual, you will have completed the symbolism for each section of your Death Shield. Add any borders or decorations that will make it more complete for you—people have affixed items ranging from feathers, pine cones, and crystals to heirlooms and photographs. Keep your Death Shield where you will see it regularly. It will help sustain your awareness of the transformative inner work you have been doing regarding your relationship with death. It also provides a touchstone that can offer emotional protection when you are troubled by existential questions regarding your mortality and your place in the universe. Find confidence and solace in knowing you have taken the journey it records. Meditate on its symbols. They were generated from deep in your psyche, and they can connect you with inner wisdom. Add new symbols as your relationship with your mortality continues to evolve.

Peg's Symbol. A pair of spawning salmon was Peg's symbol of her renewed mythology about death. "Having lived out their lives, in their last acts they deposit roe and milt on the gravel bar where they were spawned a lifetime before. Their last movements ensure the future of their kind. A cycle is completed, and life ongoing is assured. There is power and renewal in death: dignity and completion. Their uninhabited bodies feed crawdads, snails, bear, 'coons, birds, and bacteria. Nothing is wasted."

Using the creative projection technique, she wrote: "I am a female salmon, symbol of Great Wisdom in Celtic tradition. I have survived profound hazards, been hunted for my flesh, have known the depths of the sea. I was born in sweet water, matured in salty, and return to my origins at death. My return has been arduous, as I was drawn upstream over sharp rocks, surmounted cascading waterfalls, eluded cunning fishermen, swooping eagles, and clawing bears. I know the terrors of low water and the power-sucking force of sudden run-offs from winter rains. I've suffocated in the silt of eroding banks, and I've seen the full moon shine on the river at flood. I persisted, drawn by destiny and delight, for despite its hardships, life has been good. I've known my freedom and my power. I leave a legacy of full living to my offspring."

Robert's Symbol. "My left side represented my fear of death. I saw my strong and healthy left arm begin to wither. It became old, pallid, atrophied. On the other side was pure light—some of the light was from Dawn's twenty-five birthday candles, shining through nearly two decades.

When the two energies merged, I had in an instant an astoundingly complex and informative vision. I saw the progression of evolution from the past into the future. I was as though all God's creatures were in an endless line and on a long journey. The line began with reptiles emerging from the ocean. Every species of the animal kingdom was represented. Each creature was a bit further along on the path of evolution than the one before it. I realized that each step forward represented a greater capacity for intelligence and, after a certain point in the line, for compassion as well. The mammals led up to the place where humans began. First were cavemen with clubs. Very close behind me were the early Greeks and Romans.

"The procession also extended ahead of me—as far as I could see into the future. From my place in line—in the present—I could see that off in the future would be people who have evolved much further than we have. I sensed the difference. They emanated a strong, spiritual light in their compassion, serenity, and understanding of the interconnection of all beings. They inspired peace and cooperation. Believing we are evolving toward becoming more like them did not erase the horror of the atrophied arm and oncoming death, but seeing what was up ahead showed a way to become and offered comfort in the rightness of things.

"Being part of this chain gives meaning to life that the fact of personal death cannot erase. The suffering I see along the chain is still beyond my comprehension, but the entire vision at least allows me to place that suffering into a context that gives it some meaning. Also, surprisingly, I found relief in seeing myself as a mere building block—no more than a link in the chain of evolution. I sensed at a deeper level that it is not necessary to be the finished product. My 'perfectionism demons' lose some of their grip with that realization, and I can appreciate who I am rather than dwell on all I am not."

The Fourth Stage: Toward a Renewed Mythology About Death

Your personal mythology is shaped by your experiences in the world. It is a bodiless monument to the way you have engaged with life. In turn, it gives structure to the way you will perceive subsequent situations and how you will behave in them. It thus behooves you to attend to this ephemeral keepsake, this evolving mythology. Myths are continually being created and updated by the psyche, and we participate more or less consciously in this natural process. But even if we live with little awareness of the mythology that is developing within us, we still think and act according to its invisible guidance. We come to depend on it for the direction it offers and the structure it lends to what we experience.

You will find that in many respects your mythology is wisely formulated and well suited for you. The explanations it offers are usually sound, and you have good reason to take comfort in much of its ongoing guidance. In a few areas, however, your mythology may not be serving you well, and you have good reason to initiate changes so it can offer better guidance.

There is also a fundamental paradox about personal myths. Though we need the myths that guide us, we are also required, if we are to stay vital, to perceive the world afresh, to set aside preconceived models and engage fully with what is. Such engagement produces moments of clarity in which we may receive new insight about how to meet a particular situation or how we may need to revise a particular guiding myth. On the one hand, it is necessary to create guiding myths so that we are able to give order to our experiences, develop strategies for meeting life, and avoid repeating past errors. Your personal mythology spares you from having to keep rediscovering the kinds of lessons that can never be gained from books or study—the fundamental knowledge about life that cannot be adequately expressed in terms of someone else's experience. On the other hand, there is hazard in holding on too tightly to your hard-earned insights, rules of behavior, and ways of perceiving. However pertinent your myths may be, clinging to them can prevent you from making changes dictated by your more recent experiences or, in special moments, moving beyond the boundary of what you already know and seeing with fresh eyes.

In discussing the healing process, Stephen Levine suggests that if a person is able to experience directly his or her "original nature, healing becomes a lens that focuses the potentialities of the moment."[55] He stresses the importance of being able to set aside our inner models and directly contact the truth of the moment. He explains that it is our desires and our fears—our models of what we want and what we do not want—that create the greatest emotional suffering. He extends these suggestions to the acid test of encountering physical pain. He teaches people the value of meeting even their physical pain with direct awareness—breath full, tightness released, heart and mind open.

It is this attitude of directly meeting your inner experience—not unlike the meditation practices that are our legacy from antiquity—that we hope you will adopt as you complete this program for renewing your mythology about death. Accept with an open heart even your fears, confusion, and unfulfilled longings. It will always serve you to be mindful of revising your mythology as you have been doing—exploring its roots, unearthing the conflicts contained within it, and generally evaluating how it has been serving you. But do not grasp too tightly even the best of that mythology. It is a tool for navigation, and it can serve you well, but it can also interfere with your immediate experience of the voyage.

There is a time in every journey for putting the maps aside and calling upon serendipity to lead the way. So even as you are reworking your mythology, maintain an openness to the process as well as a focus on the task. We suggest that as you go through the remainder of the program, you frequently repeat the mantra that Stephen Levine teaches for moving beyond the fears, desires, and expectations created by the inner models we all hold: "Notice breath. Soften belly. Open heart."

In this stage of the program, you will be introduced to three more personal rituals. They are designed to help you synthesize your experiences to this point into a truly empowering mythology about death. In the first you will receive a Death Chant that can give you instant access to your renewed mythology and the comfort and good guidance it has to offer. In the second, you will formulate a vision of your own death. There is power in creating a thought form, and holding a positive vision about death will favorably impact your life. In the third ritual, you will review the philosophy of death you formulated at the beginning of the program and elaborate upon ways it has developed and deepened.

Personal Ritual 13: Receiving Your Death Chant

In most religious traditions, death is seen as the critical moment of transformation from life in this world to another existence. The thoughts one holds when taking the final breath are accorded great importance. Lifelong training and preparation may be dedicated to ensure that one will die with the name of God on one's lips, thus returning to the source already filled with God's presence. When Mahatma Gandhi was struck by an assassin's bullet, he uttered the name Ram, one of the appellations for God, as he fell.[56] Millennia of Jewish people have died with the words "Sh'ma Yisrael, Adonai Elohaynu, Adonai ehkhad" ("Hear, O Israel, the Eternal is our God, the Eternal—'that which always was and always will be'—is One") on their lips.

Levine describes "an extraordinary technique" some Native American tribes devised to prepare for death. Young warriors received—from a grandfather, a dream, a meditation, or a vision quest—a death chant to use throughout their lives to maintain contact with the Great Spirit in times of threat or fear or when in need for healing. The death chant was "an instant centering technique to keep the heart open and the mind clear even in great adversity."[57] Upon falling from a horse, on being attacked by a wild animal, or when burning with fever, the death chant was a constant companion. "Imagine," Levine suggests, "after having sung your death chant perhaps a hundred times in various close calls, when one day you find yourself immobile in the shade of a great boulder, your body burning with snake venom and no one there to help you as the poison begins to paralyze your limbs. But you are not helpless.

You've got a powerful channel, a path you can follow, each moment unto death."[58] The death chant created a familiarity with the unknown and prepared a serene entry into the world of spirit. Having made this practice for integrating living and dying a part of life, many Native Americans faced death with great peace and clarity.

Both your Death Shield and the Death Chant you are about to receive can be companions that give comfort in relationship to your mortality. With practice, your Death Chant can become a vehicle to transport you to the inspiration of the best of the mythology you have been developing about your eventual death and into the open space that is beyond it, where your perceptions are clear and your contact with reality is more direct. It provides a form for enlarging your life with greater peace and awareness. Use it whenever you face threat, loss, or a need for healing.

You will be returning to the "maximum sense of integration" you experienced in the previous ritual. Your objective will be to associate that experience with your Death Chant. One way of achieving this is to allow the Death Chant to grow out of this "maximum sense of integration" and the feelings of peace and understanding that are part of it. You may need to repeat the previous ritual a number of times before you are satisfied with the degree of peace and integration it offers. The following instructions will take you through a modified form of that ritual and lead you to your Death Chant.

Recall the Trance Dance you used to open the space for a new level of integration in your mythology regarding death. You will begin here with a similar dance, designed to open—in body, heart, and mind—space to receive your Death Chant. Select the same or similar music to that which you used for your Trance Dance. Move to the music with an awareness that you are inviting your deeper self to devise a Death Chant, a sound you can invoke to draw solace and healing. Move rapidly and emphatically to the beat. Continue until your body is tired and your mind is clear (again, if you have any physical limitations, pacing yourself accordingly). Finally, stop the music and find a spot where you can lie down as you prepare to receive your Death Chant.

Your body is already becoming calm as you focus your mind on these instructions. Bring your attention to your breathing. [Pause.] Listen for and feel each in-breath and each out-breath. [Pause.] Notice how your stomach and chest fill . . . and empty. [Pause.] As you continue to breathe and relax, you are better able to concentrate on my voice and on the suggestions I will offer. If outside sounds or passing thoughts cross your mind, they fade quietly into the background just as they occur. Your breathing is slow and deep as you relax more completely with each of your next five breaths. One [pause]; two [pause]; three [pause]; four [pause]; five [pause].

Recall how in the earlier ritual one side of your body represented your primal fear of death. Again, the sensations symbolizing your primal fear of death become vivid. [Pause.] They may include coldness, tightness, heaviness, or darkness. [Pause.] These sensations become particularly vivid in the hand that is on the fearful side of your body.

Recall the sensations you felt in the other, peaceful side of your body. [Pause.] These sensations, symbolizing tranquillity about death, also become vivid. [Pause.] They may include warmth, light, or tingling. [Pause.] These sensations become particularly vivid in the hand that is on this peaceful side of your body.

Recall how the sensations in the two sides of your body blended into a single unified energy. [Pause.] This time, the blending can begin in your hands. Raise your hands, palms facing, about two feet apart. Explore the sensations in the hand that represents your fear of death. [Pause.] Shift your attention to the sensations in the hand that represents a sense of peace about death. Just as opposites attract, there is a force that is drawing your hands together.

Slowly, your hands will come together. The instant they touch, you will feel a merging of the energies between the two sides of your body. A single, unified creative integration of these two energies will encompass your hands, permeate your body, and leave you with a deepened inner harmony. [Pause.] Hands coming together now. [Pause.] When your hands meet, your fingers may intertwine. [Pause.] The two energies are now synthesizing, integrating, becoming a single energy, retaining the best qualities of both. Feel them merging with every breath. [30-second pause.]

As the newly integrated energies permeate your hands and body, you have stronger and stronger feelings of resolution and of new direction. Lowering your hands, the energy flows between the two sides of your body, and the sensations merge into a single unified feeling. [Pause.] Identify the part of your body where this feeling of integration is most intense. [Pause.] Begin to breathe into this feeling. Your breathing is slow and deep.

Allow your breath to pass over your vocal cords with each exhalation so a sound results. [Pause.] Allow the sound to develop in such a manner that it expresses a harmony between the two sides of your body, a constructive integration of primal fears and serenity. [20-second pause.] Experiment aloud with this sound. Play with it until the sound becomes a chant or a song. The chant will express this feeling of integration, along with whatever peace and understanding you have come to about the nature of life and death. The chant may be made of words that you recognize or sounds you do not recognize. It will involve you physically,

*emotionally, and spiritually. Receive your Death Chant now, and allow
it to develop. Repeat it until you come into a deep sense of peace and
inner harmony.*

You may recreate this space any time you wish by taking three deep
breaths, bringing your hands together as you recall the feeling of integration, and squeezing them as you repeat your Death Chant. Do this
now. Take three deep breaths. As you recite your Death Chant, bring
your hands together and squeeze them. Continue chanting as a feeling
of integration and wholeness moves through your body. Repeat this
practice frequently over the next few weeks, until your Death Chant
is able to take you reliably into the space of your renewed mythology
about death and its attendant tranquillity, openness, and understanding.
Like the Native American warrior, you will invoke your Death Chant
in times of threat, fear, sorrow, need for healing, or need for connection
with the Great Spirit.

Peg's Death Chant.   "Though characteristically I wanted to be thor-
oughly 'original,' the theme of my death chant is very familiar:

> This is a good day to die
> The Sun will rise tomorrow
> This is a good day to die
> The River flows endlessly
> This is a good day to die
> I follow my bliss into the Earth.

Death Chants are highly personal, and Peg's chant has different meaning for her than the same words might have for another person. Asking
her to elaborate on the personal significance of her Death Chant, she
equated "This is a good day to die" with "I have no regrets, no unfinished
business; I am not afraid." In affirming to herself daily, and in proclaiming
to the universe, that she *is* prepared to die, she is also reminding herself
that because life is part of a larger cycle, she can proceed with a looser
grip on her attachments to the earthly world. With the middle lines,
Peg affirms her belief that "there is no ending." The "waters of life flow
endlessly and inexhaustibly." The final line, "I follow my bliss into the
Earth," offers Peg a pleasing and comforting image: "I complete my
cycle, release my spirit, recycle my chemicals."

Robert's Death Chant.   "I started with a deep, solid resonant sound
that came up from my toes and seemed to vibrate every cell of my body.
It brought about a warmth that enveloped me in a unified, pulsating
feeling. It was very pleasurable. Then I sensed that some part of me

wanted to speak. I sensed that I should keep making the sound, more quietly now, and allow it to form into words. I had an image that I was handing over the controls to this part deep inside. The first words that sort of tumbled out, and in a rather pleasing melody were these:

> Come listen to my song for you.
> Come listen to my song for you.
> Come hear your death chant.
> Come hear your death chant.

"The words certainly got my attention. I listened inwardly. There was a silence for a long time. Then I began to glimpse or hear—I'm not sure which—another verse. Soon it was coming through, in a similar melody.

> You who do not feel ready to die.
> You who do not feel ready to die.
> Come hear your death chant.
> Come hear your death chant.

"I kept listening, and new verses kept coming:

> Death like life is real.
> Death like life is real.
> Death like time is false.
> Death like time is false.
>
> You must stop to see
> What's been always there
> You must stop to see
> What's been always there
>
> So you know the timeless
> As you live your life.
> So you know the timeless
> As you live your life.
>
> You must stop to see
> What's been always there
> So you know the timeless
> As you live your life.
>
> From your depths
> You find
> The timeless space
> That transcends death [repeated perhaps a dozen times].

"This last verse seems to say it all, and it is the part I take with me as my Death Chant. It is a reminder for me that death is there to be reckoned with, however much I keep it out of my mind. It is a fact of life. And it is also a reminder that the 'timeless space' that reveals the nature of death and shows me that death is not the end is always within me. The primary effect as I'm deepening my understanding of death is that I am getting internal agitation and support, perhaps I could call it inspiration, to more frequently find the 'timeless space' that exists in my depths, and to live from it as fully as I am able."

Personal Ritual 14: Personal Death Fable, "A Vision of a Good Death"

Recall the death fables you wrote earlier: "Death in the Shadow of Fear" and "Death in the Light of Transcendence." For this ritual, you will write a third story. It will reflect an integration between your primal death anxiety and whatever sense of serenity you have achieved regarding your awareness of death. This story, however, rather than featuring the character from the first two fables, will be about you and an event that is in your future. In this personal death fable, you will generate for yourself a vision of a good death. In that vision, you will have come to terms with your fears, and you will have been successful in finding an inner sense of peace about your eventual departure from this world.

William Irwin Thompson describes the relationship between our inner images and the life we live: "Like a lure-casting fisherman, man seems to cast a fantasy far in front of him and then slowly reel himself into it."[59] Our inner images and thought forms hold a magnetic charge—they draw us toward performing the very actions that will bring them into being. Your life imitates your personal mythology as much as the other way around, and intensely positive consequences may ensue from transforming your mythology so that it is more constructive, more supportive of your highest potential, and more attuned to your deepest wisdom. If your life's journey is organized around a vision of declining health, diminishing pleasure, fading opportunities, and a dreadful ending, your path into the future will seem different and *be* different than if your guiding vision about aging can offer hope and highlight opportunities. Some people hold a vision of themselves in old age as enjoying a time of increased wisdom, as being able to slow down and bask in the simpler pleasures of life, as taking satisfaction in past achievements, and as savoring the relief of no longer being responsible for making the social wheel spin around. Though such visions do not ensure one's fate, they inspire choices that maximize the chances that the vision will become reality.

By using your imagination to fashion a plausible death scenario, you will have an opportunity to create a positive and constructive vision about your own death. You will also, in your imagination, be able to experience how your Death Chant might provide you with comfort and strength in your final hour. First read about Peg's and Robert's death scenes. Then find surroundings that evoke inspiration and peace, perhaps a place with great natural beauty. Place the heading "My Personal Death Fable" on a fresh page of your journal. Take time to relax. Tune inwardly to a deeper voice. Imagine the setting of your final hour; note your age; recognize how you look and feel; and be aware of who else is with you. You are seeking a vision that you will *want* to "cast far in front" of yourself, a vision you can "reel" yourself into with the daily choices that shape your life.

Peg's Personal Death Fable.   "I am very old. I am used up, not broken or diseased. My body is used up like a fallen fir log, nurse to ferns and a thousand life forms, dissolving formlessly into Earth.

"I have used up my ambition, ego, foolishness. What is left is love without boundaries and experience. The belly and breast scars of my childbearing, my forehead lined by countless frowns of anger and puzzlement, my mouth's brackets shaped by ten thousand laughs, my bony feet, veterans of many the long mile walked, are fading snapshots of my living.

"Today is my death day. Long years of wonderment watching the forest's seasons have removed my fear. There is only longing. It is midspring, perhaps my birthday, and the daffodils are nodding enthusiastically under the alder trees. I sit among them, my palms touching the earth, my back pressed against the moss-clothed bark of a great maple's trunk.

"Before me is the shining creek, turning sinuous curves through reeds. I feel the salmon's call to give life even as I die. My body will melt, but be no more wasted than the fir log. Beside me is my husband, old now too. We are the only two human forms here on the banks of the Yaquina, but we are not alone—the Spirits of the land attend us. I raise my eyes to his a last time; our life has been long and good. He will miss me, but he will find his way. We know each other's thoughts.

"I think of my parents and forgive them their humanity as I forgive my own. It is a good day to die. I rest my head a last time on my husband's chest, feel his long arm snug me close. One tear falls for words of love left unspoken in my life. The sun catches the falling tear, lights a star within, and I am part of it all—again."

Robert's Personal Death Fable.   "I'm at home. For the last time I inspect each of the sacred objects that adorn my room. Each holds fond memories, pleases the eye, and offers inspiration. I tell my children and my grandchildren what every item means to me. And I tell them what each of them means to me, each as unique and special as the sacred objects that surround us. They each have some parting words for me. They tell me some of their memories of times we've spent together, and they tell of qualities in myself that they value and will remember. I say good-bye to each of them. Also, two of my closest friends are there to say good-bye. One of them tells me that 'good-bye' means 'God be with ye.' We are in deep peace with one another.

"I know my time is very near, and I ask to be alone with Dawn. We have been preparing for this moment over the past few weeks. We conduct a ceremony with candles and pictures and talk about the best parts of the life we've shared together. I begin to sing my Death Chant, feeling its solid, resonant tone welling up from deep within me:

> From your depths
> You find
> The timeless space
> That transcends death.

"Although I am weak, the effect is profound. Like so many times before, my Death Chant brings me into my "timeless space." Dawn begins to sing her Death Chant in harmony with mine. Our eyes meet. The sounds merge into one, and our spirits seem to join as well. Time stops as we come into communion with each other and with the forces of life and death. From this holy union, we say a final good-bye. I close my eyes as I softly continue my Death Chant. A tranquillity comes upon me. I am complete and content. I drift peacefully out of my body and into the light."

Personal Ritual 15: Your Philosophy of Death Revisited

"Let death be thy teacher," advised Saint Augustine. Your philosophy of death codifies what you have learned from death's counsel. At the beginning of the program, you described your philosophy of death. Here you will describe new developments in that philosophy. First enact another round of the dialogue between the characters representing your fear of death and your resources for transcending that fear. Unrehearsed, continue for at least ten more minutes. Explore whether the work to this point has made it possible for the two characters to achieve a better mutual understanding and an ability to support each other's concerns. Summarize such progress in your journal. Then review the symbols on your Death Shield and reread what you wrote earlier in your journal under the heading "My Philosophy of Death." Place the heading "My Philosophy of Death Revisited" at the top of a new page. Write freely for at least ten minutes, focusing on areas where your philosophy of death may be starting to evolve from what you wrote earlier.

From Peg's "Philosophy of Death" Revisited. "I can bring back my fear by conjuring ugly images. I can make cases for uncertainty. But if life has taught me one thing, it's the awareness that it is better to feel good than to feel rotten. I believe all creation is energy—things, space, and forces—all are energy. Physics teaches us that energy is neither created nor destroyed but that it frequently changes form. Nothing is wasted.

"I believe that there is more to me than the body I gratefully occupy. This *something* includes and transcends my consciousness and personality. How energy came into being and what (if anything) is its destination are questions too difficult for me: I cannot know the face of God. I can only recognize that the orchestration of the cosmos and the cells of my body are purposeful. Because I have the capacity to feel union with the creations that make up the earth, and because feeling good is better than feeling terrorized, I choose to invest my energy in the ways that feel holy (whole) to me.

"My life task lies in knowing and directing the energy that is *me*. I do not believe I exist or can function without relation to the energies around me—environmental, human, and spiritual. Therefore, it follows that I will direct myself toward the goal of harmony. No simple task for a rebel, a pragmatist, and a coward. I must become a healer, a mystic, and a courageous woman if I am to have a good death."

From Robert's "Philosophy of Death" Revisited.   Robert discussed some of the changes in his beliefs and attitude that occurred while he was going through the program. For one, he had begun to read extensively the teachings of the various great religions regarding afterlife. He reflected: "I'm less sure now than ever that the life hereafter is a heavenly shift into uninterrupted peace and joy, as I'd previously imagined. But I feel more sure that there *is* a life hereafter and that there is some Plan, some Intelligence larger than anything I can imagine running the show."

Robert also reflected on the difference between people who have good deaths and those who do not. "Those who do their part to have a good death have learned some important things about living. They have learned how to be in the moment and to face whatever is there with, as the program advises, an open heart and an open mind. They are able to work through and let go of past disappointments, to not live in their expectations for the future, to just be in the eternal present. I don't know why it is so hard to just slow down and 'be here now.' But somehow it seems to have a lot to do with whether I will ever make peace with my mortality."

Another topic Robert addressed concerned the contribution his life would make to the world. "I once believed that all the world's problems would be solved by technological advances, and I had a religious fervor for my work helping design [architecturally] the world in which we would live. Now that technology emerges as much the villain as the savior, my work doesn't provide meaning for me the way it once did. I keep coming to the realization that if I am to help the world, there is truth to the old cliché about starting with oneself. Developing more compassion, love, and serenity within myself is my best bet."

The Fifth Stage: Bringing Your Renewed Mythology About Death into Life

You have now completed the major portion of this program for cultivating a more empowering mythology for confronting death. The program was designed to show you how to actively participate, within the light of conscious awareness, in the stages through which we believe your mythology naturally evolves. In observing mythic-level changes in several thousand people, my colleagues and I have learned that by walking people through this process once or twice with mindfulness, we can help them come to understand the deeper mythic forces acting upon them. They also grow to be more capable of influencing these forces and of living in a positive relationship with them. By developing such facility with their guiding mythologies, people become more effective in handling a broad range of life problems.

Each of the five stages in this program has a specific purpose and corresponds with one of the phases by which personal myths seem to naturally develop. Though the personal rituals used here were designed to keep your focus on your mythology regarding death, they are organized within the same five-stage model that was devised for working with personal myths pertaining to other topics as well. In the preliminary work, you gained an overview of your mythology regarding your mortality by writing your philosophy of death, journeying back in time to some of your earliest memories about death, and creating a Death Shield to symbolize and keep track of the discoveries the program offered about your relationship with death.

Having established this background, you were brought into the first stage of the program. In this stage of our model for self-guided transformation of a person's mythology, the task is to discover the areas in which the individual's mythology is out of date, is steeped in internal discord, is causing conflict in one's outer life, or is otherwise creating difficulties. The first stage of the program was organized around the theme "Rattling Your System of Death Denial" because some of the difficulties people have regarding death are closely related to repressed or unconscious fears. Therefore, we had you excavate this anxiety, using personal rituals designed to "open your heart to your deeper fears," to take your awareness to the historical "foundation" of some of these fears, and to create a death fable called "Death in the Shadow of Fear."

In the second stage of our program for helping people work with their personal mythologies, the mythic conflict identified in the first stage is explored in depth. In the very areas in which the person's mythology is not working well, the psyche is typically generating alternative mythic structures, often below the level of consciousness. We teach people how to investigate those fledgling mythic structures by examining their potential contribution and by consciously participating in promoting their wholesome development. In the second stage of this program, "Transcending Your Fear of Death," you searched for counterforces to your fear of death, and you focused particularly on your psyche's quest to find ways of transcending death, such as in attempts to achieve symbolic immortality. You closed your work in this stage with a second death fable that was the polar opposite of the first: "Death in the Light of Transcendence."

The third stage of our model attempts to bring resolution to the natural conflict between the prevailing myth identified in the first stage and the emerging countermyth identified in the second stage. In the program presented here, the conflict was described as "a confrontation between the fear and images of transcending death." The task in this stage, once the differences between both sides have been highlighted, is to promote a process of deep reconciliation in which the best of each side is integrated and elevated into a new and more effective mythic image. You did this by conducting an inner dialogue between your fear of death and prospects for transcending death, by opening an internal space for a new and deeper resolution of this conflict, and by establishing a body metaphor of this resolution.

In the fourth stage, a renewed mythology that reflects the deep resolution of inner conflicts, which was the focus of the previous stage, is further articulated, expanded, and anchored in one's being. Receiving your Death Chant, creating a personal Death Fable, and expanding your philosophy of death all served these ends.

In this, the fifth stage, the task is to weave your renewed mythology into your life. It involves stepping out into the practical world and making changes at that level. It comprises three personal rituals that involve "Attending to That Which Will Survive You," "Creating Ceremony for the Final Hour and Beyond," and "Establishing a 'Right Relationship' with What You Do Between Now and the Final Hour."

Personal Ritual 16: Attending to That Which Will Survive You

The wisdom of the ages suggests that to live in peace about death requires that one be ready in an instant to let go of life in the physical world. Ritual preparation for death to come at any moment can be found in many traditions. The ancient warrior went into battle fully prepared to meet death. Among some Orthodox Jewish groups, sleep is spoken of as one sixtieth of death and dream as one sixtieth of prophecy. Thus, going to sleep can become a training ground for dying. Some of the prayers designed to be recited before death are also said each night before going to sleep. There is, for instance, a nightly liturgy for forgiving anyone to whom your heart is closed, though they have committed a transgression against you, and another to confess your own transgressions and ask forgiveness. Thus, each evening, one performs a ritual of purification and is ready for death if it comes in the night.[60] You can take these liturgies a step further by holding in your heart those people and things you love the most and, before you go to sleep, appreciatively bidding each farewell. Through such practices, not only does one have an opportunity to cherish what one loves and to make peace with what is difficult, but also, each night before entering the "little death" of sleep, one becomes a bit more prepared for the final passing.

Putting your worldly affairs in order is another way of preparing for death. As you move through the following ritual, you will be considering a number of steps that can be taken in order to live with greater preparedness for the inevitable last hour. If you have not taken these steps, we suggest that you do. Simply having attended to these matters, and having made the decisions they require, serves to bring more peace and acceptance about the eventuality of death. If you have already attended to these items, we suggest that you rethink the decisions regarding them from the perspective of your new mythology about death.

In either case, address the following topics in your journal. Cover only one topic at a sitting, or at least give yourself some space before going from one topic to the next. Begin your work with each topic by meditating on your Death Shield and then repeating your Death Chant, along with any ceremony (such as your Trance Dance) that might open you to your deepest wisdom as you address each issue. Only then, begin to write.

1. With whom do I have unfinished business that I want laid to rest while I am still alive? Regarding each person you identify, create a plan that specifies what you will do and how and when you will do it.

2. Are there letters or poems or other forms of communication I want specific people to receive after I die? What arrangements must I make for this?

3. What would I like done with my best works (art, writing, creations related to my profession, etc.)? How will I make these intentions known?

4. What are my desires regarding burial or cremation? Would I like to have any of my body parts donated for transplant or medical research? How will I make these intentions known?

5. What would I like to leave others? If I do not have a will, how can I go about writing one that is in proper legal form?

Other issues may also come to mind—from checking that your life insurance is in order, to making arrangements so that extraordinary measures will not be taken to prolong your life if you are in a coma with no reasonable expectation for survival, to making peace with yourself about a transgression you committed three decades ago. Add other topics as you are moved to do so.[61] Begin your work on each topic by bringing yourself into a clear and peaceful internal space, using the kinds of activities suggested above. Appreciate the process of entering this space. Though it may have consisted primarily of internal activities, think of entering the space as itself a creative ritual. This will put such sacred efforts into proper perspective. And by conceiving of the process as a ritual, you will be more likely to remember it and to repeat it so it may again transport you to a state of inner clarity and peace.

Peg's Intentions for That Which Will Survive Her:

1. I have unfinished business with very few who are still alive. I want to release my anger (and righteousness) at several people, even though I take some sort of perverse satisfaction in rejecting them. My plan is to rechannel my energy. When I think, "Greg is a brutal, selfish man," I will repeat until I believe it, "Greg's essence is good." Hard.

2. I want my children, particularly, to listen to me read *Blind Raftery: Seven Nights of a Wake*. I've made tapes before and sent them, but as far as I know they haven't taken time to hear me. I will make new, better recordings. Wrap them nicely, put them with my things to be found after my death. I'll enclose a personal, private note to each. I want a few others to have copies. I'll see to it.

3. My best works are walking around laughing and living; they are beyond and free of my "intentions."

4. Regarding burial, wrap me in unbleached cotton cloth and put me in moist ground on The Land. Put me deep, where the taproot of a redwood can be nourished with the minerals of my body, so that when a great grandchild looks up at a massive trunk, he can think "This place feels familiar, and it feels safe."

5. I will make a list of what to do with my "things" and entrust the list to my husband.

Robert's Intentions for That Which Will Survive Him:

1. My own death feels so far off in the future that it was hard to get into this assignment. Then I thought about my parents, whom I expect

to outlive. My parents are well along in years. Although they still enjoy good health, they decline noticeably between our annual visits. I have sat in judgment of what I consider to be their inflexible and outdated values during these obligatory visits, occasionally allowing a contemptuous remark to slip out. I've never quite accepted them for not taking what I consider the higher road in the second half of their lives. I've been unwilling to forgive them for not letting go of attitudes and securities that have been their companions for a lifetime. Right now that looks really dumb on my part. They gave me the best they had. They are about to leave forever, and I sit around allowing my judgments to put a wedge between us! They may irritate me, but I do love them, I will miss them deeply, and I want them to feel my deepest love and appreciation for all they've given me while they are still here. The visit next month will be very different.

2. I've always thought I'd like to write something toward the end of my life, a kind of "Important Things About Life from the Vantage Point of One of Your Ancestors," to be passed down through the generations. I'm forty-two. This is probably at least the halfway mark. I wanted that essay for future generations to contain my wisest, so it has always been something I'd do sometime off in the distant future. But maybe I'm ready to begin the first draft. I could put it on the word processor and revise it annually. That would help track any advances in wisdom from one year to the next, and it would keep me attuned to promoting such advances. It also gives me something constructive to do with my awareness of my mortality.

3. Oh God, here we go again with an assignment that calls for preparation as if death is just around the corner. Okay, it could be! I'll pull together a little scrapbook of the highlights of my life. I'll include photographs, mementos, news clippings, and little narratives. I'll find three or four of the best letters I've ever received. I'll include copies of a few of the best letters I've ever written. I will give it to Bobby [his first child] for his next birthday to keep as a legacy for future generations. Maybe each year I'll use the week of his birthday to add anything new to it and also to update my "Important Things About Life" statement.

4. I remember discussions with my father about the way cremation helps free the soul of earthly attachments. Seems sort of farfetched right now, but nonetheless, I've thought of cremation as the proper way to dispose of a body ever since. But now that I'm always looking for the "natural way" to do things, the idea of being laid to rest in the ground, with no coffin separating me from the earth, seems more natural. I'm not sure. Cremation still offers an image of being released that is more appealing than rotting in the ground. I guess it's time to make a decision about burial or cremation. I'll discuss it with Dawn. Whether it's cre-

mation or burial, I think I'd like them to wait about three days so there is plenty of time for the life energies to peaceably leave my body—as in the Kirlian photographs where you see how the energy of a leaf fades each hour after it's been picked. I've also been very ambivalent about donating my body parts. It's a little silly, because I'll be somewhere else, but I feel unsettled when I think of various parts haphazardly dispersed. What came to me as I was reflecting on it this morning is that I'd feel good knowing that one of my organs, whatever is needed most, would be available for transplant.

5. No question here. Dawn and then the kids get everything. And I pray that the way we're steering this planet will take a sharp turn for the better so that Bobby and Jill can make good use of my hard-earned assets for a long, long time.

Personal Ritual 17: Creation of a Ceremony for the Final Hour and Beyond

For this ritual, you will go on a guided imagery journey in which you create a fantasy about your final hour, your funeral or memorial service, and your eulogy. First reread your personal death fable. The vision of your final hour will be similar to the one in your death fable, but this time, in addition to experiencing it in deep fantasy, you are to focus on the kind of ceremony or ritual you would like to have occur. These visions of your final hour, service, and eulogy will be created while you are in "sacred time."

The following guided imagery instructions begin in the same manner as the earlier ritual "A View of 'Symbolic Immortality' Through Sacred Time." Again, wait to perform this ritual until your mood is receptive for entering sacred time. Your Trance Dance, Death Chant, or an approach you devised in a previous ritual may help bring you to such a space. When you are ready to start, find a comfortable position, take a deep breath, and close your eyes.

The path you will be following into sacred time is marked by physical relaxation and uplifting memories. Settle in comfortably—finding an inner quiet, peace, and warmth. [Pause.] Thank your body for its hard work and good service. [Pause.] Find the parts of your body that need special attention, healing, or rest. Picture a warm, wise hand filled with a fragrant ointment gently touching and appreciating those parts. Focus your attention, and sense the melting, calming relaxation that comes into those sore and tired places. [30-second pause.]

As you focus on my voice, other sounds fade away. All is well with you for this journey into sacred time. You are always free to return to ordinary consciousness by simply opening your eyes and exhaling fully, and you are just as free to explore the riches of your inner world. You will recall all you need of this experience, and you will emerge from it with insight and power. You can move and adjust yourself at any time, yawning and stretching, rearranging until your body is peaceful and satisfied.

Begin to reflect on the holiest, most sacred times of your past. [Pause.] Remember a moment of shared love. [Pause.] Recall seeing a newborn child. [Pause.] You have felt yourself awed by a sunset, a waterfall, or the seashore. [Pause.] You have heard inspiring music [pause]; seen great art [pause]; savored a creative breakthrough [pause]; sat in an awe-inspiring cathedral or other place of reverence. [Pause.] Focus on a time that was particularly inspiring. [Pause.] Recall it vividly. [Pause.] Relive it in each of your senses. Breathe into the vision [pause]; the sounds [pause]; the feelings [pause]. Let go into the memory. [20-second pause.] Soon you will hear counting, from one to seven. When you hear the number seven, you will be fully relaxed and deep in sacred time.

One. As you bask in the inspiring feelings of the scene you have remembered, the healing hand sensitively massages your back, shoulders, and neck. You sigh, content.

Two. The healing hand moves to your face, massaging your forehead, eyes, cheeks, scalp, mouth, and jaw. Each breath fills your awareness. Unhurried, your sense of sacred time deepens.

Three. The muscles and joints of your arms and legs are rejuvenated by the healing hand. You exhale fully, feeling vitally alive and relaxed.

Four. The healing hand finds wounded or weary parts in the trunk of your body, nourishing them with tender touch. Your breathing is deep and pleasurable.

Five. The healing hand continues to touch away your pains as you exhale your tiredness, hurt, and disillusion.

Six. Fully relaxed, you can notice a pleasant tingling on your skin. As you smile, you feel a deep sense of peacefulness.

Seven. Your heart is open. You are absorbed in the comfortable sensations of warmth and heaviness. Your breathing fills the moment. You have entered sacred time. [20-second pause.]

Continuing to breathe deeply, watch your breath rising and falling. [Pause.] Your mind is clear as you savor the heightened awareness of this open moment. [60-second pause.]

From this heightened awareness, your appreciation of life is amplified, along with a sense of peace about death. You can feel yourself, now, moving forward in time. You are moving forward to the occasion of your own death. In this death scenario, precisely the atmosphere you would desire for your last moments on earth already exists. [Pause.] Visualize yourself now in this final hour. [Pause.] As you survey the situation, you can vividly see or sense yourself in the scene, along with any others who are there. People are relating to you and to one another just as you might wish. [Pause.] You are about to imagine a ceremony or ritual to maintain or heighten the mood. It may be performed by you alone or with others. [Pause.] In the following silence, you will experience the entire ceremony. [45-second pause.]

As the moment of death approaches, you begin to recite your Death Chant. Start to use it now, and continue it as you imagine your consciousness moving out of your body. In your imagination, allow your Death Chant to be the bridge as you leave your body and come into a space from which you will be able to view your funeral or memorial service. Slowly move into that space now. [Pause.] From here in your imagination, you can see your funeral or memorial service. Again, the atmosphere is exactly as you would like it to be.

Survey the scene, noting who is there. [Pause.] Your eulogy is about to be given. Look at the person who is beginning to deliver it. In the following silence, you hear it. [30-second pause.]

From this privileged vantage point, you realize that you will be returning to your body, and continuing with your life. [Pause.] Consider how you wish to live differently. [Pause.] What insights from this unique perspective do you intend to bring back with you? [20-second pause.] Now it is time to reenter your body. [Pause.] You return fully to your normal body awareness, noticing your breathing, sensing your weight against that which is supporting you, feeling your hands and feet and neck. [Pause.] You have fully returned to your present age.

Peaceful in your body now, you will soon bring your awareness back into the room. Counting from seven back to one, you will be able to recall all you need of this experience. When you hear the number one, you will be fully awake and aware of the present moment, as if returning from a wonderful nap. Seven, taking a deep breath. [Pause.] Six, moving your toes and feeling the circulation. [Pause.] Five, moving your fingers. [Pause.] Four, stretching your shoulders, neck, and face muscles. [Pause.] Three, breathing deeply, smiling as you return. [Pause.] Two, bringing your attention back to the room. [Pause.] One, opening your eyes, feeling refreshed, confident, and able to effectively and creatively meet the requirements of your day.

In your journal, describe the ceremony or ritual you would like to have as part of your final hour, the nature of the funeral or memorial service you envisioned, the eulogy you heard, and any insights or resolutions you brought back with you. As you complete this section of your journal, be tuned in for the wording of an epitaph. Write an epitaph at the end of your journal entry. If any instructions should be given to your loved ones about plans for your final hour, funeral, memorial service, or epitaph, make plans to convey them.

Peg's Death Ceremony. "First, it's a wake. A wake is a time to remember, to feast, to clear the air, and to summarize the lessons of the life lived. I've said my intentions in my book *Blind Raftery:*

> For my wake, you're to gather the neighbors seven nights runnin.' Each night seven songs will be sung in memorium, seven kinds of cakes eaten, seven glasses of the good stuff drunk in toast to my blessed memory and seven stories told each night that show my character off in a pleasin' light. Seven auld women will keen as though all their sons were going into exile. Seven pipers will flail and abuse the atmosphere with mournful tunes until all present have taken aboard enough of the good stuff to tire of the lamenting and demand a hornpipe or jig. Through it all the fiddlers of the countryside will stand at one side and play the songs that fit the stories, so that all may wonder at the wake of Blind Raftery and remember my doings at least until they're planted themselves. At the end of the seventh night each one present will lay a hand on my fiddle, listenin' the whole time with heads cocked to one side. I'll play a tune from heaven—or wherever I find myself—that will bring a blessing of a peculiar nature to them as hears.

"It is fine with me for details to be changed to fit the circumstances, but decorum will *not* be maintained, pleasure will be had, and harmony promoted. I want my children—now grown and separated—to love and see the good in one another.

"Plant me deep in the earth on The Land. Put redwoods at the cardinal points, not more than thirty feet from where I'm dissolving. I'd like ferns, spring bulbs in plenty, lilacs, and my loved ones' favorite plants 'round about. I'd like a stone lintel made like the dolmens of Ireland erected and hung with bells, wind chimes, prisms, bright ribbons, swinging pots for burning sage and lavender, and other objects of beauty and ceremony. I'd like a little shelter, a gazebo or such, set close by. It should be suitable for sleeping, lovemaking, or quiet times of contemplation in all weather. A winding path, with comfortable seats in pleasant bowers, suits me well. There should be no fence, but a hedge of fruiting plants to feed the birds and deer is desirable."

This was Peg's epitaph:

Hear me in the wind
Feel me in the river
Touch me in the ferns
Taste me in the blackberries
See me in the season's change
Be glad in the moment
And remember me with smiles

Robert's Death Ceremony. "First I saw the ceremony with Dawn that I described in my personal Death Fable, except we were outdoors on a sunny day. She was wearing a flowing purple velvet gown. I was in loose white clothing, lying on a mat surrounded by grass and trees. The most powerful part of the vision was when we were singing our death chants in harmony, eyes and hearts locked together. I knew our hearts would remain connected long after our eyes had separated.

"Again, it was hard to envision my memorial service because I think so much is supposed to happen between now and then. But I forced myself to imagine a memorial. It is a warm day on the Oregon coast. The spot I envision is within two hours from our home. I have been dead three days, watching from up here with compassion and love as various people react to the news of my death, and now I am ready for today's ceremony because I know it is time to move on. Dawn carries my ashes in a porcelain vase made for us years earlier by a dear friend. She will keep the vase. The ashes are to be buried under a sturdy spruce tree where we've watched bald eagles light on the cliffs overlooking the rugged coastline. A goblet filled from my precious 1974 bottle of Mt. Eden cabernet sauvignon is passed among the twenty-some relatives and close friends who are present. Taking the goblet, each one reminisces about me.

"I find it gratifying that they have such good stories to tell. I am pleased that my friends remember me in terms of my humor, compassion, and intelligence. I experience my love for each of them with a purity that I realize I wish I could have expressed down there on earth. Maybe I still can. I also appreciate the role each has played in my journey. I send blessings from beyond as each drinks of the goblet. It is clear that I will be missed, but it is also clear that I have lived fully and enjoyed my life. Being carved on the spruce tree is a sort of epitaph, adapted from my Death Chant: 'Behold the timeless space that transcends death!' "

Personal Ritual 18: A "Right Relationship" with What You Do Between Now and Your Final Hour

You are coming to the close of this program for opening your heart to the fact of death, and thus to a richer understanding of the foundations of your life. We believe that such openness and understanding is vital to maintaining a "right relationship" with death. A right relationship with death leads, in turn, to a right relationship with life. This program has been one pathway for cultivating such a relationship. The process is lifelong. From time to time, a life event or inner change will bring these questions back to the forefront of your attention. The techniques you have used can be repeated, and the principles you have learned can be adapted to new areas of concern.

This step-by-step guide, however, has escorted you as far as it can on your journey toward a right relationship with death and life. It is time for you to initiate the next steps. In this final ritual, you will commit yourself to take action toward further establishing a right relationship with death and life. Some possibilities may have occurred to you while you were going through the program. There may be a ritual you would like to repeat or a difficult issue that requires further attention. You may decide upon additional steps for making your environment more receptive or your daily routine more supportive of the guidance your new mythology offers. You may need to affirm your intent to protect space for your inner exploration. Sabbaths and other holy days have, in the past, ensured that time was consecrated for nurturing one's spiritual life. Our culture, for the most part, no longer supports such traditions, and you may have to firmly commit yourself to guarding such time and space. Because you are this far in the program, you already have had some success in keeping a focus on inner work.

For this ritual, once again begin with your Trance Dance and/or your Death Chant to enter a space from which your deeper spirit will illuminate your understanding. From that space, ask about actions you might take to establish a more fulfilling relationship with life and with death. Quietly listen for the answers that are within you.

When you have returned to your normal waking consciousness, describe in your journal the actions that came to you. Consider the purpose or positive intent of each. Decide if you believe this action is the best way of accomplishing its positive intent. If it is not, envision an action that would be. Come to one, two, or three actions that you believe would benefit you. Specify when, where, how, and with whom you will carry out these actions. Commit yourself to doing them. Rationally decide on the first steps that are needed for each, and describe them in your journal. With someone who cares about you, make a contract regarding the first steps you will take. Verbally commit yourself to specific actions you will complete this week. At the end of the week, meet with the person, discuss what occurred, and if you wish, make a contract for the following week based on what you learned and what you know you still need to learn. Make a ritual of meeting each week, attending to the atmosphere, perhaps involving food, candles, or nature. Continue to update and renew your contract for as long as you find having a contract to be of value.

Peg's Contract. "My cries that 'I need more time' and that 'I've been a laggard scholar in terms of too many lessons of appreciation, patience, generosity, honor, mercy, humility left to learn' defines my contract.

"My time is precious; I must be thoughtful, intuitive, protective, and generous in allocating it. I must keep my body healthy, having squandered much of my genetic advantage in casual disregard of its well-being. I know how to improve my ways of self-nurture, and I will allocate my time so I can make those improvements.

"I dare not hurry as a result of failing patience or out of fear of missing something. Stinginess with things or with my energy serves no purpose, but I must not be grandiose about my resources. I deserve a generous portion of my own hours. To learn my lessons, I cannot indulge in hateful cleverness or self-serving shady practices. I would be dishonorable, most of all, to myself. Compassion must not be stifled. I must give myself exposure to others' pain in order to be filled with loving-kindness, a most joyful experience. And humility. It is too easy to bask in the glow of the need of others to have me be wise—to have the illusion that I, having lived this long, know the answers. I know some of my answers—for right now. But the hunger to be loved has sometimes led me to the mistake of inflating myself so I feel big and in some ways 'better' than others. I must be modest from the heart, where I know that we are all part of the One, and none is greater or lesser than the other parts.

"This week I will drink fresh orange juice instead of wine, I'll hike on The Land instead of vegetating in a chair, I'll hug a neighbor rather than hiding away with my books. I'll say 'thank you' instead of 'I want.' And I'll swim each day. I will affirm these words daily:

> This is a good day to die
> The Sun will rise tomorrow
> This is a good day to die
> The River flows endlessly
> This is a good day to die
> I follow my bliss into the Earth."

Robert's Contract. "First of all, I am going to give myself some time before jumping into another two-year project. Having just completed the Larson contract, I have plenty to do without attaching heart and soul to another all-consuming commitment. I do feel I make a real contribution to the world with such projects, and there is certainly a great aesthetic satisfaction—but it costs me so much in relationship to being in the present moment. As a loin-clothed bull, sitting cross-legged and gurulike in a 'Far Side' cartoon puts it, 'Don't forget to slow down and eat the roses.'

"Putting all my striving into the context of my limited time on the planet changes my outlook about it. If I'm not totally overcommitted to performing good works, I start to feel empty and worry. I intend to *not* overcommit myself and to face the emptiness and worry straight on. Dawn has been begging me for years to shift my priorities. I will announce today that from this point onward I will consult her before taking on any new large projects, and we will talk each one through until we come to a consensus about what is best for me and for us, not just for my career.

"I will use the freed-up time and energy wisely. I have training in meditation, but I rarely meditate. I love nature, but I don't spend much time in it. I am always welcome to just lie back and play with the kids and with Dawn, but I'm always too busy. I will no longer steal from such activities to support my career goals, nor will I fill up the free time with other devices I've used in the past to avoid facing myself, such as spending endless hours writing clever computer programs. One other thing I will commit myself to doing, although it really scares me, is to find some kind of vision quest or outward bound experience that pushes me to my limits. I'm afraid of a true 'death-rebirth' encounter, but I don't know any better way to forge into the deeper truths about who I am."

*   *   *

We hope that by completing this program you have found new sources of meaning and vitality in your life, attained a greater sense of peace regarding your mortality, and become more resourceful for creating personal and shared rituals for you and your loved ones when death's shadow falls into your lives. Where this section of the book has focused on coming to terms with your own mortality, coming to terms with the death or loss of a loved one is another of the terrible challenges life reliably seems to dispatch. Overwhelming grief follows naturally in the wake of a loved one's death. Sir Edwin Arnold's wonderful epic poem chronicling the life of The Buddha describes death as "that curse which makes sweet love our anguish."[62] In the following section, Peg Elliott Mayo offers a poignant guide to "expressive grief work" that includes a set of powerful and practical personal rituals for elevating the agony of loss into the transformative alchemy of wholesome bereavement.

Part Three
The Alchemy
of Transmuting Grief
to Creativity

Peg Elliott Mayo

There is no birth of consciousness without pain.

—C. G. JUNG

The terrible fire of grief is an energetic furnace, refining character, personality, intellect, and soul. It is a catalyst for creation. What is created may be dreadful—a distorted, unapproachable monument to despair—or a distillation of experience that is wholesome, useful, bright, and even wise.

The alchemist of antiquity was absorbed in the elusive task of transmuting lead to gold or pig offal to pearls. While alchemy may conjure up images of sorcerers, boiling caldrons, and dark medieval laboratories, it was a sophisticated spiritual discipline. Painstaking experimentation was conducted with a meditative attunement to the chemical changes being produced. Transformations in physical matter corresponded with changes in consciousness and were meticulously devised to foster healing and spiritual development. To give a measure of the status of alchemy, Leonardo da Vinci was a practicing alchemist, and Sir Isaac Newton had a laboratory designated for alchemical research. In this section of the book, I use the ancient tradition of alchemy as a metaphor for transmuting anguish and sorrow to wisdom and creativity.

Life presents us with repeated opportunities to take "base" or common events—disillusion, outrage, grief—and shape them to our benefit or detriment. The profound emotions associated with deep loss may affect the mourner's character in ways that are devastating and destructive, or they may open the heart to deeper truths.

The principle of transformation is a central concern of philosophy, mythology, and psychotherapy. All religions portray some image of salvation or positive change at the core of their message to the world. The politician, preacher, or counselor who extinguishes optimism fails. To be effective, teachers and leaders must offer hope for a different, more desirable future.

Whether we turn frogs into princes, watch acorns become oaks, or weave vines into baskets, each of us lives daily with examples of energy changing into new forms. Of course, it is also possible to imagine princes becoming tyrants, ancient oaks falling to a woodsman's ax, and baskets crushed under heavy loads. What is not possible is for life to advance unaltered. The only thing that seems certain is eternal change.

My intent in this final section of the book is to show some ways that others have learned to transmute the anguish of loss to wholesome, creative living and to provide a set of techniques and personal rituals by which you may find such a path within yourself. I refer to this process as expressive grief work.

A Personal Philosopher's Stone

The alchemists of medieval times attempted to create or discover a "philosopher's stone"—a chemical preparation with the power of transmuting base metals to gold. All human beings need a personal philosopher's stone: its name is hope. Hope is the alchemical ingredient required by the psyche if life's base experiences are to be transmuted into creativity. Without hope, problems go unsolved; systems of law, religion, and philosophy lose their meaning; and the burden of life becomes intolerable. Without hope, the instinct for survival, which keeps us stubbornly resisting death, weakens.

The medieval alchemist was himself a vital part of his "noble experiment." His enlightened attitude and full-hearted devotion to the task were considered essential to the process. The alchemist had to responsibly direct personal energy and choices in order to be master of himself and to be capable of orchestrating the miracle of metamorphosis. Today, all men and women are their own alchemists. We are presented daily with opportunities for transmuting the tests and tribulations of life into meaning, wisdom, joy, and compassion. We each need to create from our experiences in life a personal philosopher's stone—hope—to spark the alchemical transformation of loss into emotional growth and creative action.

To develop, sustain, or rebuild hope, we must nurture a core of optimism and see ourselves as capable of learning, even amid daunting challenges. We must cultivate a personal mythology that affirms our ability to work through our despair and find fresh meaning. Hope grows out of the experience and practice of making life-supporting choices. We can train ourselves to incubate trust in the positive powers of existence. In the following pages you will be developing mental habits that support hope, and you will learn how to deal more effectively with elements of your inner life that defeat it. Hope—the philosopher's stone—is the irreplaceable catalyst in the alchemy of transmuting grief and agony to wisdom and creativity.

Loss as Alchemical Fire

In addition to base material, the philosopher's stone, and a worthy practitioner, alchemy has another essential element: fire. Fire cleanses, purifies, alters, and prepares the base material.

Sorrow and anguish are the elements of grief. In the alchemy of transmuting grief to creativity, sorrow is the base material to be transformed; anguish is the flame. Their combustion causes unspeakable pain, tests endurance, challenges assumptions, and refines us. When we add hope to the mixture, our response to disaster becomes immeasurably more creative.

I know something about this process from several vantage points. I am a psychotherapist, a widow who has remarried, and the parent of both living and dead children. As a therapist working with emotionally wounded people during much of my career, I have an intimate involvement with human despair. Several clients chose to die; many more threatened to do so. Much of the human pain I have seen has been that of people learning to live with and transcend loss. Many have learned to disarm their discouragement and invoke hope. I have profound respect for their strength and courage to undergo this transformation to vital living.

My credentials for writing this piece were also hard earned in my personal life, through the excruciating lessons that grew out of my husband's suicide and, four years later, that of my son Patrick.

I have had to learn a great deal about how to face grief, and I also have trepidation about holding out my experiences as a model. What was useful for me may or may not be useful for you. Each of us must come to terms with grief in our unique way, so I invite you to take what may be of value from my experiences and to discard what is not. I also feel reluctant to expose my own warts and vulgarity, but dealing with death and grief is a great equalizer. To pretend that I have some kind of "professional immunity" to base responses and to present only my finer insights and moments of emotional reconciliation would neither ring true nor fairly portray the process.

Grief is a universal experience, shared by all of humankind—present and past, civilized and savage. We are born weak, unskilled, and dependent. As we mature, we gain physical, emotional, spiritual, and intellectual strength. We learn to provide for ourselves, and we seek mates. We reproduce ourselves and nurture our young. We become elders, teaching by example. We lose powers, and finally we die. Carl Jung once commented, "To the psychotherapist an old man who cannot bid farewell to life appears as feeble and sickly as a young man who is unable to embrace it."

At any point in our cycle, however, we are vulnerable to personal extinction. An apparently random accident, war, sickness, a genetic flaw, savage aggression, or a personal choice may interrupt our progression toward a merciful death in old age, potential fulfilled. At birth, we suffer the loss of the security and protection of the womb; later we suffer the loss of our mother's breast and her constant attention as we are displaced by younger siblings or by our own need to explore. We have all suffered loss as we involved ourselves with the world. Some of our losses were tangible; others not. If our second-grade teacher made false accusations of cheating against us, we may have lost our faith in justice. Our best efforts sometimes don't measure up to another's standards. The loss of innocence is the price of experience.

In maturity, we suffer the loss of our earlier dreams. We may find that we must abandon our aspirations to save the world. We may darkly suspect that we will not have a perfect marriage, achieve a dazzling level of success, or achieve enlightenment by forty. The disillusion of failed dreams, the loss of perceived truths, and the recognition of personal limitations are catastrophes that may devastate our optimism and self-esteem.

We are required to transform such losses into a refined awareness that enhances our inner strength and enlarges the meaning of our accomplishments. Would Ray Charles's piano music be as elegant if he were not blind? Would Mother Teresa's luminous face shine the same way in a "safe" convent far from the festering slums of Calcutta? Helen Keller, blind and deaf, set an example of the transmutation of tragedy to an exemplary productive and joyful life. We are bound to follow their example or to regret not only our losses but our inability to use them as alchemical fire.

Grief and fear of grief are constants in human experience. Tribal people the world over and across time have invoked powers beyond the commonplace and have practiced rituals to postpone and soothe the pain of grief. We modern sophisticates are no different in our needs. We fear loss, and we experience anguish when it inevitably occurs. We, too, may be fortified by rituals for transmuting and transcending our losses and finding meaning in them.

Loss takes many forms and is most poignantly felt for that which we hold most dear. We may mourn the loss of "being in love" or of comforting ideas such as "the world is fair." I have wept over the loss of an object—Grandmother's watch—and of a place—the house my father and grandfather built and in which I was born—and, of course, people—a son, husband, mother, grandparents, father, friends, brother-in-law, clients, and victims of disasters. The more intimate and valued the idea or person, the greater the fear of loss and the greater the anguish when it occurs. The death of a child wrenches a parent's soul harder than any other personal catastrophe.

In 1732 Thomas Fuller wrote, "No man should be afraid to die, who hath understood what it is to live." When we believe death to be inappropriate—unfair—the pain of bereavement is particularly harsh. The death of a dewy bride wracks us far more than the death of an exhausted old woman. When my brilliant and creative son Patrick died, a particularly bitter pill for me was the loss of the books that would be forever unwritten, the artistic statements that died with him, and the unconceived children he might have fathered. It was the loss of his potential—that fragment of my hope—that I was most reluctant to yield to the awful reality of his death. I felt that he had not understood what it was to live, and I could not reconcile his voluntary embracing of death.

Failed relationships, faded youth, destroyed homelands, loss of independence, disillusion with God, lost promises, abandoned talents, spent passions, and deaths of intimates—all carry their baggage of sorrow.

When we are bereaved—left alive when someone dear has died—we are sorrowful. Anger, confusion, denial, terror, and despair may invade our hearts. Our feelings will be powerful, perhaps foreign, and will dominate our existence.

If we think of our grief as a *condition,* we live as if being sorrowful, abandoned, or wounded is our identity. We can have a condition for a long time, even a lifetime. Thinking of grief as a condition creates stagnant energy. If we think of our grief as a *process,* we emphasize movement and change—including a beginning, intermediate steps, and a hope of resolution to our anguish. Thinking of grief as a process creates dynamic energy. Love, creativity, grief, and maturation are processes.

The Path Toward Creative Transmutation

Energy can neither be created nor destroyed. It may, however, be stagnant, misdirected, unrecognized, or unruly. Negative energy tarnishes hope and can overwhelm us. Negative energy is often directed toward revenge or other ultimately self-destructive activities.

At some level, each of us is aware of hidden and destructive forces, the unclaimed and disowned parts of ourselves that Jung referred to as "the shadow." The shadow sabotages our best efforts and whispers messages of destruction that are at odds with our finest aspirations. The shadow is pure energy, often flowing in directions inimical to the well-being of ourselves and others. The grieving person does well to focus energy on the parts of life that nurture and heal while being wary of the alluring seductions of the shadow.

We have all known people whom we found draining. As a psychotherapist, I have worked with people who wanted so much from me that I felt my veins were open and my vitality was draining out of me. The next client, however, might present a parallel problem yet be so determined and actively engaged in the healing task that I come away uplifted and excited.

The first is passive and looks to me for change. I must guard against the grandiose and foolish temptation to believe that I can be the magician he or she is seeking.

When I work with the vital client, we enter the fire together, each shielded by our life experience, each cooperating with the other, each trusting of the other's goodwill. A mutually enriching process is under way. The changes are clearly for the client to make, though I will be enriched and altered by entering another's fire, even as a guide.

The Irish have a saying, "The same fire that melts the wax hardens the steel." We must each choose whether to be flabby, quickly consumed wax or resilient, tempered steel. Moreover, the alchemical grief furnace may produce the gold of empathy, spirituality, maturity, and creative expression. This gold is refined from common sorrow.

To speak of common sorrow is not to suggest that it is easier to bear—or less profound—because it is a universal human experience, any more than to say that war is banal because of its commonness, or that the havoc worked on Earth's living body is trivial because of its pervasiveness. The abscess in your jaw hurts no whit less because your brother has one too. Just as I cannot adequately describe the flavor of licorice, the color amber, or the sound of a waterfall, there is no way to make sense of a comparison between your pleasure and mine. Neither is there a yardstick to measure which of us is the more sorrowful. Nor does it matter. We have each stumbled into the searing fire and must endure and transcend, comforting each other as best we can. Sorrow is our common ground.

Casualities of grief are those sad people overwhelmed by despair who have not made choices leading them to refinement and cleansing. The common feature among them is unremitting anguish; they build, consciously or not, a bitter memorial to their dead loved ones. The memorial is made of pain, anger, desolation, abandonment, resistance, and stagnant energy. They worship at this shrine, giving up their own lives to twist memories into the emotional equivalent of paper flowers in "everlasting" funeral wreaths. They see no path, no hope, no reason to stir themselves. I feel compassion for their grief and am restless that they be up and about, growing into the next phase of their lives.

How is it that some people—"survivors"—come through hideous challenges with their lives enriched and spirits renewed? Some common themes appear when we look at those who not only survive but flourish after the testing fire. We will draw our lessons from their experiences. One quality they seem to share is a perspective that nourishes hope and optimism.

Trust in a Larger Plan

Spiritual awakening, as used in the subtitle of this book, is a coming into awareness of empowerment and direction *beyond that of ordinary consciousness*. The rational mind is supremely useful in ordering our daily lives, in problem solving, and in speculative musings. Without its ability to plan, analyze, and process factual information, the advances that distinguish us from other species could not have occurred. But our rational abilities do not account for our capacity for rapture, nor can they sustain us in the throes of profound loss.

When we grieve, we find ourselves asking, "Why?" "Why him?" "Why not me?" We are compelled to find answers to give meaning to our loss. Coming to view our own life and the life of the person lost to us as part of a larger plan is humankind's venerable solution for bringing order to the emotional chaos of bereavement.

An axiom often heard during World War II was that there are no atheists in foxholes. The primal awareness of impending death elicits pleas for assistance from beyond and confronts us with the need to make meaning of our lives. For uncounted generations, humankind has derived that meaning in terms of a divine or overarching Intelligence that directs our destiny. We resist notions of randomness about our lives and deaths. In our vulnerability, we seek ways to give meaning and purpose to these inevitabilities we cannot control.

Modern people are no different from their ancestors in needing guiding myths to provide frameworks for leading purposeful lives. Myths are not simply comforting (or terrifying) stories; they are the *result* and expression of deep, often wordless experience. A *numinous* moment is one that connects us with parts of ourselves ordinarily hidden. We may experience blinding insight, firm inner instruction, or a "knowingness" that surpasses any previous convictions. When we have had such an opening of consciousness, we are forever changed. This sort of awakening brings us to an unassailable understanding that there is reason and purpose in our existence. How this purpose is revealed, how we describe its origins and power, and how sturdily we live our intentions is an individual matter.

Such numinous experiences can offer a sense that Something is in charge and can give meaning to the most profound losses. So may religious consolation. Whether we call to "God," "the Father," "the Tao," "the natural order," or to a Power larger than our minds can grasp, we are comforted in our isolation, even as we grieve. The sense that "everything happens for a purpose" or is "part of a plan"—even though the pattern or purpose is hidden from us—offers solace and helps to bring order to disorienting confusion.

The crises of life strip us of our conventions, platitudes, and avoidance, either facing us cruelly with our spiritual poverty or leading us into a deeper sense of our connection with all creation. Bereavement is both a ripping away of denial and an endowment of opportunity to connect with a deep wisdom. We need to trust in a larger plan. Whether that trust grows out of religious beliefs tempered by Job-like faith, or whether it is earned in a creative engagement with the trials of life, it is of immeasurable benefit in facing and transforming the agony of grief.

Expressive Grief Work

In the alchemy of transmuting grief and anguish to wisdom and creativity, *emotional expression* is a central activity. *Psychological discharge, ventilation,* or *catharsis* are terms for describing the core emotional process in conscious, ritualized grieving. In Orthodox Jewish tradition, "sitting shiva" allows seven days for the family and other bereaved during which they are supported, expected, and encouraged to experience and *express* their anguish. All other duties are suspended. Details of living are attended to by others. Mirrors are covered to symbolize the need to turn inward; black is worn in mourning; burial is prompt. Weeping, keening, talking, remembering, regretting, appreciating, *emptying out* feelings are in order. These are basic ingredients in the grief process.

Whether we "sit shiva," sob into our pillows, confide in our spiritual advisers, or seek professional psychotherapy, emptying out is part of the growth necessary to transmute grief to creativity. To contain, deny, or repress our pain may lead to personality-distorting depression.

There are two main sorts of depression: reactive and chronic. Reactive depression is a natural, transitory response to physical or emotional loss. The body husbands its resources, and the mind works desperately to blunt the anguish. Energy is unavailable, feelings are muffled, and helplessness overwhelms the sufferer. Time will, to a degree, naturally heal this sort of depression.

Chronic depression is an insidious stagnation that does not yield easily to time, fresh stimuli, or inspirational talks. It may be genetic and unremitting, or it may begin as a reactive depression and become entrenched. The body "turns off" and distorts natural needs for sleep and food into excesses or denials. Hopelessness is the pervasive experience of the chronically depressed. A meaningless, featureless apathy distorts life. The juice is gone. Death is attractive, but we are afraid and double-condemn ourselves as cowards.

A semblance of normality is maintained by keeping to ordinary routines—get up, go to work, be polite, shop for food, fix supper, go to bed. But repressed misery will leak into our thoughts, actions, and emotions. Tears may start unexpectedly—as they did once for me, when I saw a tall, red-blond man sitting pensively on a park bench. The quick impression resurrected my son Patrick's image before me. With the vision came the realization that I would never, ever again sit with him under a eucalyptus tree and watch the sunset, commenting on the charming accent of Russian countesses.

Strange fears may grow in us when we are heavy with grief. Danger seems all around. Nowhere are we safe. Dread anticipation poisons the mind and body. Sleep may be elusive, and bad dreams may haunt the hours that should be bringing rest and renewal.

"After all," I reasoned, "if it could happen to Patrick, it could happen to Katie, Stan, or Peter." The pleasure and comfort I might have taken from them was burned away, leaving ashes. Terror at the thought—even the expectation—of their deaths distorted my love. Fear became my companion. I was comfortless. Un-comfort-able. I was acutely aware of my own mortality, the tick of the clock, the turning of calendar pages. These are some of the painful qualities of sorrow.

New commitments may feel too dangerous. Bottled up, we see death as a treachery, a violation of an unwritten contract with God or with the dead person. The contract, unspoken and unacknowledged until it was broken, stated that either *we* were to be permitted to die first *or* that death would come in old age as a welcome release. How can we commit to anything after such a betrayal?

Unexpressed, this anger is a coal scorching our capacity to express love. Resentful suspicions about the meaning of life and the motives of God turn us bitter. We isolate ourselves. Sometimes we even think that "no one understands."

It is clear that body and mind interact intimately. Many a peptic ulcer has been traced to an agitated mind. Containing grief carries a fearful danger of physical and emotional sickness. We do literally have wounds from our sufferings—the broken heart we feel in our chest is the real, beating organ that pumps our blood. Unrelieved sorrow has led many to seek solace in alcohol and drugs or to retreat into the living death of mental withdrawal.

We may feel guilty for being alive, or we may become obsessed with the ways—fancied and real—we failed our dead companion. Guilt is an acid etching our self-respect, hope, and good memories away into oblivion. It works its brutality on our souls and may demoralize us so fully that we forget our virtues, our sacrifices, our successes, our love. Unexorcised, guilt is a foul, debilitating presence in our lives, turning us away from all that is wholesome and healing.

It is not necessary to live with guilt. Guilt can be exorcised, restitution made, absolution self-granted. For some of us it takes a strong expressive effort to do so. We may need outside help.

I have experienced the alchemical fire of grief many times in my life. I am not unusual in this. After having listened to literally hundreds of people dealing with their lives—their confusion, grief, outrage, inadequacy, love, and spirituality—I know that we are all given repeated opportunities to refine ourselves. I believe that the failure to learn and grow from these tests is the supreme tragedy of life. Not to do so is to risk—even invite—physical and emotional disability.

In one four-year period, my stamina and courage were tested severely. My beloved father had an accident with his radial-arm saw, leaving four fingers on the bench. Three months later, he died of emphysema and a stroke. My husband killed himself with a 30–06 rifle in our bedroom. My four children were in the throes of adolescence, and I lost my job. It looked as if I was going to lose the home my father and grandfather had built and in which I was born. Then my brilliant, charming, depressive son committed suicide. Through it all I appeared to function reasonably well —with time out for private despair—but my body couldn't be deceived.

My physical movements reflected my bitter grief and eroding courage. I totally broke down and had to stay in bed for three months, my back nearly destroyed. I'd gamely "referred" my tension to my spine.

I believe that the primary reason I've become a survivor is my incredible good fortune in having a circle of wise friends, skilled in the healing arts, who challenged me to live. The existence of my other children was, of course, a powerful motivation. Later, I'll discuss various personal rituals for healing that I have either used myself or have seen used with great effectiveness.

In the pained confusion of our bereavement, we may fear that we will be disloyal if we express our grief, transcend the moment, and go on with our lives. Somewhat absurdly, we fear that we will forget. I remember well the first time after Patrick's death that I had a liberating belly laugh at some silly movie; the world stopped in a frozen frame of time. I heard my voice laughing, felt the release in my chest, and knew that I had forgotten for a few minutes.

Questions flooded in. Was I disloyal? A negligent mother? Had I forgotten? Was I wrong to be amused by the pratfalls on the screen? For me, the answer was "no"—not when I remembered the laughs Patrick and I shared, his wicked sense of humor, and his pleasure in goofiness. Enjoyment was part of him and part of me. Fun was a bond that held us close. Far from "forgetting" him, I was able, at long last, to smile when I thought of my son.

As we express our guilt, anger, loneliness, and fear appropriately, we become less obsessed, less compulsive, less haunted by miserable images and unhappy conjecture. The refining fire of grief can clear much room for laughter, creativity, affection, and curiosity. I find that my stamina and compassion have grown, and most important I believe there is purpose in my life and in all life. And there is a community of survivors who have come to the same conclusion.

The word *appropriately* in the last paragraph has special importance. First, appropriate grief work furthers the grieving process. It *accomplishes* something—ventilation, insight, planning. Something. It is not a fruitless, endlessly chanted mantra of misery.

Second, appropriate grief work doesn't exploit others. Comforters may feel empathic pain, but the mourners are not parasitically feeding off the comforters' energy. Rather, the mourner is eliciting understanding and sharing. The transactions are clean, and the caring is received with recognition that it is not a substitute for remaining actively involved in furthering one's inner work.

When our energy becomes stagnant, we may try to revive it by reaching out to others. It is one thing to lament and keen while sitting shiva or grieving in the arms of a friend, when pain is tearing at our hearts and guts. To allow a friend to provide genuine comfort is to confer a great privilege. But it is quite another thing to wring pity and concessions from our companions by drearily displaying our wounds. We become beggars, casting aside dignity and exploiting those who care for us when we repetitively describe and display our pitiful "condition."

I had a client, a woman whose third child, a longed-for son, had died at sixteen months of SIDS (sudden infant death syndrome). Her suffering was undeniably genuine, but her treatment was, by my standards, unsuccessful. I never doubted her pain. Marie was unwilling to move forward in the grief process by any path I was able to provide. She literally "took to her bed" and became a voluntary invalid.

At the time I saw her, both her daughters and her husband, as well as her mother and several neighbors, were involved in "protecting" her. She had become a petty tyrant, complaining of her great loss and demanding the others' complete devotion. She was frighteningly depressed. Her husband was emotionally exhausted by two years of this behavior. Her daughters had both run away several times, feeling devalued and unloved in comparison to their mother's bottomless, self-serving grief over her dead son.

Note that I did not say Marie was *unable* to make progress in her grief work. If I, as therapist, had believed she was incompetent or entirely immobilized, there would have been no basis for attempting expressive grief work. As therapist, I had to have hope for a positive outcome or I would have been defrauding her of time and money in our sessions. And I did see reason for hope. But my attempts to get her to assume enough responsibility for her emotional condition so that she would take effective action were defeated. By placing the responsibility to change on Marie, I was not being hard-hearted. I was being respectful of her dignity as a person with considerable potential and resources, including a loving family and good physical health. But in the end, Marie's energies continued to be bound up in the unwholesome mileage she derived from her loss, and her refusal to move through her grief seemed obstinate. She did not visibly benefit from the therapy. I believe she could have benefited had she been willing to engage grief as a *process* rather than entrenching herself in the secondary gains she derived from having others organize their lives around her woeful *condition*.

The third characteristic of appropriate grief work is that it cannot be rushed. Simply coming to genuinely *believe* death has occurred is difficult. And acceptance cannot come before belief.

Neither can we skip the steps of self-disclosure and self-examination, which will bring changes—adaptations—to our new, bereaved reality. We will not be able to avoid our confrontation with our faith and view of God. When I say understanding cannot be hurried, I don't mean to promote a wait-and-see approach. In grief work I am an activist.

As feelings emerge, there is no more constructive response than to acknowledge and appropriately express them. The energy of painful feelings needs to be discharged. I have known people who condemned themselves for wishing for the death of a sick partner and, particularly, for longing to be relieved of the burden of care. If peace is to be found, such feelings must be recognized and worked through. I knew a woman whose son, like mine, had committed suicide. She had been *sensing* his unacknowledged intention and had felt frantically impotent, wanting to intervene and having no means. When she recognized that among her complex feelings about her son's death was relief at no longer being in this helpless position, she condemned herself terribly. She had to face these emotions when they emerged. Her recognition of the feelings could not have been hurried. Nor could the feelings have been pressed back down without great cost to her psychic equilibrium.

Finally, appropriate expressive grief work must be suited to the individual. We each have our own pace, our own characteristic way of going about the business of life. That one is quick does not mean that another is wrong to be deliberate. It only means that we are unique and will do our grief work differently.

Rituals for Transmuting Grief to Creativity

How can all the roiling emotions and terrible lassitude of bereavement be channeled creatively and wholesomely? The first essential is *commitment to heal*. A commitment to heal can, in the terminology of the previous section of the book, become an empowering personal myth. All inner experiences and new developments in one's world come to be viewed through a lens that highlights the implications for healing, and new choices are made with this purpose in mind. The commitment to heal requires hope. If we lack the commitment to heal, all else is wishful thinking.

I will describe a series of personal rituals through which you may refine, from common sorrow, the pure gold of creative living. In the previous section of the book, you were presented with eighteen interlocking personal rituals, designed to move you into a new relationship with your mortality. The rituals presented here are also designed to be highly personal, creative, and transformative. You need not do them in any particular order. They are to be tried as you are drawn to use them.

Also, I do not suggest that these are the only ways or even the best ways to accomplish the alchemy of transmuting grief into creativity; they are means that have worked for me and for others I have known. Each shows you a particular way to focus your attention and direct your energy so that the alchemical fires are more likely to engender a positive transformation.

All these paths through the flames can be traveled alone or with friends. Since we first sat around a campfire together, groups of people have pooled strength and wisdom, providing comfort and companionship. Therapy and self-help groups can be of tremendous value. I made grateful use of skilled professionals in my grief process, and I believe that counseling is important for many mourners.

Ritual is a way of formalizing and setting apart significant events. It may be used for memorializing (as in the Jewish Kaddish), celebrating (as in Christmas), sanctifying (as in marriage or christening), initiating (as in the bar mitzvah acknowledging that a boy has come to manhood), welcoming (putting down the red carpet), or worshiping (the Roman Catholic Mass). In rituals, time is set apart, and ceremonies that have deep personal or collective significance are performed. There is a solemn sense of purpose and recognition that the ritual is important. Memories are refreshed, time passed is marked, changes noted, dignity enhanced. Successful ritual is deeply moving and involves a feeling of mystery. At its best, ritual has a "numinous" quality, which means it evokes feelings of sacredness.

The alchemist's rituals were designed to transmute the base material from its common form to something precious. Each of us must learn, as part of our maturation, to become more adept in directing our life energies. Failure to do so permits the shadow's dark, fearsome, passive forces of entropy and decay to dominate our being. Success means directing energy toward growth. *Taking charge of the direction our energy flows is the refining task of our lives.* It is our challenge to direct our own energies in order to be survivors of the alchemical fire. A grieving person is weary. Sleep comes hard and may be troubled with terrible or restless dreams. Grief saps energy while creating none. An exhausted mind and body distort reality and alter perspective. By directing one's energies wisely, rest will finally, blessedly, come. The remainder of the book is devoted to creating personal rituals for developing and directly the energy of grief into growth and creativity.

Creative Visualization

Shakti Gawain has written a disarmingly simple book titled *Creative Visualization*, which I frequently recommend.[1] Her language is direct, and the pleasant exercises are entirely "do-able." The book makes accessible those basic psychological and spiritual principles for developing the capacity to rechannel energy in creative directions.

Each of us can be thought of as a unique energy field. Sophisticated medical technology can measure our brain waves and the electrolytes in our body fluids. Our bodies give off heat and, according to sensitive scientific instruments, generate invisible electromagnetic fields. Chinese medicine, through the use of acupuncture and the study of subtle pulses, claims to have demonstrated discrete energy zones and pathways within the body. An individual's particular pattern of energy is as unique as his or her fingerprints, dental work, or blood chemistry. Death is the absence of perceivable *moving* energy.

All creation—from objects to the primary laws of nature—can ultimately be understood in terms of energy. As iron is drawn to the surface of a magnet, so do we either repel or attract different "energy fields." The principle behind the "self-fulfilling prophecy" is that we draw to ourselves those conditions toward which we have, in our imaginations, directed our energies. In studies where a teacher was told that a particular student of average intelligence had an exceptionally high IQ, that student excelled. This illustrates the uncanny power of the underlying myths that structure our perceptions and our behavior. The teacher, believing the student was intelligent, was able to perceive the student's existing intellectual strengths and to foster them.

Our self-image and habitual patterns of thought are products of the way we have directed our life energies. If we believe and act in life-enhancing ways, we will greet the twists of fate with greater confidence and proficiency. We "create ourselves" by interpreting and managing our own energies and the energies we meet in the world. Consequently, it is invaluable in times of trial to have already cultivated positive psychological habits such as expressiveness, honesty, and empathy.

Habit is both a terrible taskmaster and a wonderful conservator of energy. If we had to relearn or rethink each of our routine daily tasks, life would be laborious and uninspired. I can think about writing this paragraph while brushing my teeth. If I didn't have the habit of brushing, I'd have to focus my consciousness there, sacrificing both energy and time. Noxious habits, as we all know only too well, are difficult to break. Good habits, like the competent staff of a successful executive, allow us to focus our energies in creative directions and improve the quality of our lives immeasurably. Psychological habits such as disciplined self-examination, honest expression of emotion, and the taking of measured risks for self-development are valuable beyond price.

We create our self and our future by our thinking and feeling and behavior. Our actions tend to bring about whatever we anticipate, so we are best served when we *consciously take charge of our expectations*. We are the sum of our choices.

But, you protest, I certainly didn't choose to have my loved child or life partner die. Of course not. Fate deals each of us a different hand — we're born into comfort or poverty; we are good-looking or plain; we sing gloriously or are tone-deaf. We may be bright or foolish. We are male or female. These are givens.

However, within the structure of our particular set of givens, we perceive in our own unique way, and we *choose* our responses. If five people eat the same meal at a restaurant, and all become ill upon reaching home, they will have five different reactions. One may be furious and sue. Another may blame herself for breaking her diet and consider the sickness divine retribution. The third may decide never to eat away from home again. The fourth may decide the poisoned food is part of a communist plot, and the fifth may philosophically decide that once in every ten thousand meals something like this is bound to happen — it's the odds. Each diner has *chosen* an explanation and a response. *It is what we do with our own energy that defines our experience.*

If, as bereaved people, we believe it is our fate to suffer the rest of our lives, the future will certainly be darker. We may even think we *should* hurt endlessly. By fervently visualizing perpetual anguish, we create a mind-set that will make long-term affliction inevitable. When taking up fresh challenges, contemplating the future, or facing death, our attitudes and expectations color our perceptions and shape our behavior.

Expectations are formed from experience and fantasy — a blend of memory of past events and imaginings of what emerging circumstance will bring. Attitude is the posture we assume in relation to what happens to us. We may be spiteful or generous, self-protective or vulnerable, demonstrative or subdued. Though we may be swept along by events we would never have chosen, the way we respond to them is our *self-defining* responsibility. I want to emphasize that mind-set is a choice; an individual's internal images have consequences; and choices and images direct energy. It's vital to choose wisely.

A first step in making a genuine commitment to heal our grief is to imagine and visualize a fulfilling life for ourselves without our loved one. This is an enormous challenge to our fortitude and creativity. By holding a picture in our mind's eye of good things happening to us — trips to be taken, holidays enjoyed, friendships deepened — we are redirecting our energies. We are taking a critical step forward through the alchemical fire.

Creative visualization is one of our most powerful tools for directing our energies to positive ends. It is not, however, "magic" that brings its results without effort or balance. Like all tools, it is latent until activated.

Without action, creative visualization can degenerate into the pleasant but fruitless exercise of wishful thinking. If I visualize myself as slender while gorging daily, I will not lose weight. If I visualize myself slender *and* eat wisely, get appropriate exercise, and deal with any inner resistance to becoming slender, I will succeed and be hopeful while doing so. We must provide the conditions for the success of our visualization.

Meditation

Electroencephalograms reveal a changing array of brain-wave patterns. Shifting from one to another is natural and spontaneous, depending on our activity at the moment. We are in one state when we are engaged in problem solving. When we listen to music, we switch to another. Creative writing or watching a sunset will produce other patterns. Meditation is associated with a brain-wave pattern that is believed to be helpful to both emotional and physical healing.

Meditation is a vast subject. It comes with an exotic reputation. You may be put off by nontraditional spiritual practices, the idea of "losing yourself" in a strange, unknown mental state, or by Zen masters speaking in riddles. A woman in one of my groups thought meditation was a trap set by Satan, and if she ever experienced it, her soul would be lost. She didn't mind prayer, but that, she said, was different.

My reluctance was not as strong as hers, but I certainly was apprehensive when friends first encouraged me to meditate. I had an automatic resistance to the idea. Nor did I believe I could "do" it. I was too rational. These arguments proved to be self-fulfilling until I learned that a meditative state is really quite natural. Meditative practices need not be at all esoteric. Meditation, according to Joan Borysenko, "is any activity that keeps the attention pleasantly anchored in the present moment."[2]

By this sensible definition, our lives are rich in opportunity for meditation. It is not necessary to have a forest, an altar, or a vast amount of disciplined time. A bubble bath is a meditation *when* we attend consciously to the delightful sensory details of rainbows in the foam, subtle fragrances, our comfort in the warmth, and other pleasures. Shifting our attention to the present moment elicits the "relaxation response," a bodily reflex that is both enjoyable and healing.[3] We release from our minds the clutter and endless chatter of analytic observation that characterize ordinary waking consciousness. Attending to what we see, hear, touch, taste, and smell is a present moment activity. When we are in the hereand now, we are not troubling ourselves with "what ifs," vain regrets, or catastrophic visions. We renew our power.

Another dimension of meditation can be discovered by ritualizing the experience. When we select a special place, perhaps a corner of the bedroom used for nothing else, set up an altar, and return to it regularly to focus on our immediate experience, the setting itself activates our search for deeper wisdom. Objects on the altar should have beauty and meaning. My altar is backed by a mirror that reflects four candles (one for each of my children), a bird's nest found on a forest walk, seashells, a brass chime, several river stones, and precious objects I've been given. A friend has placed pictures of spiritual masters (Jesus, Buddha, Gandhi, Sai Baba) on his altar. Another simply carries a small rock she found on a sacred mountainside in Asia. She touches it with her fingers and recalls that powerful place. By keeping a flower, a shell, or a special picture on your desk at work, you give yourself the opportunity for minimeditations—islands of peace—several times a day.

What is there "to do" in meditating? Meditation requires the release of ordinary intellectual processes. According to one of my favorite T-shirt slogans, "Meditation is not what you think." Nonthinking is a tough concept and a strange practice to us who have been rewarded and required to be constantly processing information. We worry that we may not "come back" if we "bliss out," that we will be helplessly vulnerable and perhaps unable to defend ourselves—or maybe go crazy. Nothing like this will happen in a positive meditative state. What we will do is rest the ever-active and ever-interfering rational left side of our brain, just as we might rest our aching back after digging ditches all day.

Periodically, we need to let go of the Möbius strip of thinking– reacting–judging–considering that is common to waking consciousness. We need to allow the internal critic-commentator an hour off. We are able to come back into ordinary reality instantly when there is a need or desire to do so. After fifteen or twenty minutes of meditation, I am calm and mildly elated. My senses are refreshed. Air tastes like mint, and colors are brilliant. I am energized and eager to move, usually to dance or walk. Daily concerns are in reasonable perspective, and I think better. Meditation heals.

There are many methods for achieving a meditative quiet—a state that is associated with positive psychological changes. I'll share one of my favorites. I sit on the bank of a creek. I hear the sounds in stereo— letting the music of the water run through my head, in one ear and out the other. I breathe consciously, enjoying the effort it takes to empty myself, giving thanks for the moist forest air that enters me. I lean on a tree and experience the mosses under my hands. My eyes wander, tracing the progress of a limb from trunk to twig, following the move- ments of a hawk, studying a piece of white alder bark embroidered with red and yellow lichen.

Leaning forward, I see three tiers in the creek. Reflections, whorls, bubbles, eddies, leaves, and water bugs occupy the top level, a fluid canopy. The middle level holds a trout nosing sleekly into the current, leaping for a gnat, returning to conserve energy through proper po- sitioning in the flow. I sense a metaphor and let it slide as intellectual.

The lower level is an intricacy of flat stones in a thousand shades of green, gray, brown, and black against which I see red crawdads scuttling on their purposeful way. At last I am quiet enough to want to begin my meditation. I smile in anticipation, and when I share such a moment with a friend, we experience a profound wordless, touchless intimacy.

I sit comfortably erect and lay my hands open, palms up, on my knees. I may pick one spot on the rippled water and keep my gaze there, or I may close my eyes, directing all my attention to a certain sound, often my own breathing. Thoughts come circling in like crows at a picnic, but I've learned that they'll fly off on their own if I leave them alone, paying them no mind. And if they don't, I return to listening to my breathing or watching the red crawdad walking on a gray rock. Time has no relevance; I am no more aware of time when I am meditating than I am aware of baseball scores in my ordinary life. My body relaxes without being troubled by my intervening mind's judgments and demands. When I come back to ordinary consciousness, I am intensely aware that I have done something nourishing, something designed into my essence and too long denied.

There are many paths to meditation—chanting, watching a candle flame or the miracle of rainbow light in a prism, focusing attention on one's breath. T'ai chi, yoga, and Sufi dancing are common paths "into" that calm and healing space. Meditation may be a private matter or a group experience. I believe any committed person can do it.

Generally a teacher is helpful. This may be a friend, a professional meditation instructor, a spiritual guide, or a book. Larry LeShan's *How to Meditate* offers an excellent introduction to meditation and an overview of meditative practices.[4] *Seeking the Heart of Wisdom: The Path of Insight Meditation*, by Joseph Goldstein and Jack Kornfield, is a sophisticated, engaging, and eminently helpful commentary on the topic.[5] *The Miracle of Mindfulness: A Manual on Meditation*, by Thich Nhat Hanh, provides a simple and highly personal guide to a form of Buddhist meditation that many Westerners have found to be particularly useful.[6]

Mantras

An important tool in expressive grief work is the development of a personal verbal amulet—a mantra. A mantra is a sound, word, phrase, or sentence that directs and attracts a particular energy. Some meditations use particular sounds or Sanskrit words.

Another term for the sort of mantra used in expressive grief work is *affirmation*. The mantra that will most effectively direct your energy will affirm both who you are and who you *will be*. It focuses power and energy toward self-acceptance as well as toward a desired result.

As affirmations, mantras are always expressed in positive terms. Wrong: I will never be late again. Right: I will be on time. Wrong: I won't eat junk food. Right: I will eat healthful food. Affirmation mantras should be short, easy to remember, and rhythmic. With a little practice it becomes natural to compose your own mantra. Use it until you see reason to make another. It is wise to use only one at a time, so you will keep your focus and avoid diffusing your energy. Here are some examples:

I am a decent woman, worthy of serenity, satisfaction, and love.

I am a peaceful person, able to understand, accept, and grow.

I am a caring man, growing in spirituality, emotional power, and prosperity.

People often protest that such statements aren't true, or that to say such things feels false or conceited. This mind-set denies hope and misses an opportunity to constructively direct energy. If we do not have a vision and a belief in positive outcomes, then we live formlessly, reacting to life's contingencies but failing to actively set a positive direction for our development.

Just as we can "program" ourselves for failure by continual self-criticism, so we can "program" ourselves for success by taking charge of our own energies. If we feel it is conceited or egotistical to say, "I am a good person," we are missing the point that we must invite the changes we want in our lives by opening our hearts and minds to them. If our behavior and habits have been unproductive, it does not mean that we are doomed to perpetuate what was. But first we must *choose* to change.

When we direct our power toward our own growth, we may feel awkward from lack of practice. But like all habits, it will become easier with repeated application. Anything worth doing at all, advised the great psychologist Abraham Maslow, is worth doing awkwardly at first.

An affirmation mantra *affirms* and shapes expectations. It is wise to test the power of your personal mantra with an open heart, anticipating success.

Your mantra should travel with you and provide a refuge when stress or exhaustion cause trouble. It should be with you when things go right. It should be repeated at least twenty times a day, with full attention to the words, the meaning, and the rhythm.

I like to say mine as I walk, putting emphasis on each word in turn. "*I* am a loving woman . . . ," "I *am* a loving woman . . . ," "I am a *loving* woman . . . ," and so on. The mantra should be the first thing summoned into consciousness in the morning and the last released in dropping off to sleep. It should be said aloud. Though saying your mantra in your mind is valuable, there is extra confirmation and potency in actually hearing the words.

Commit yourself to your mantra. When doodling, scribble your affirmation. Sing it in the shower. Write it out and paste it on the mirror in your bathroom and on the dashboard of your car. Chant it. Carve it in wood, inscribe it in clay, paint it with water colors. Chew your food to its wisdom, and brush your teeth repeating it. Swim to its rhythm, and say it, say it, say it — out loud and in your heart. Make your mantra an integral part of your life until it is accepted into your essence and you *know* it is true. Then assess where you have come and how you wish to direct your development from there, and consider developing another mantra.

Movement

We know the world through the many senses housed in our bodies — among them hearing, seeing, smelling, tasting, and touching. We also have a time sense and a sense of rhythm. We sense the energy of other persons, knowing instinctively whether we are attracted, repelled, or indifferent to them. We sense danger.

Beyond this, we are designed to move. In fact, we need to move. Mobility is necessary for health. It can also be a powerful tool in expressing grief and developing hope. We experience movement through our kinesthetic sense. It tells us our position in space and provides balance. If we do not use the wonderfully complex instrument we occupy, our joints calcify, our muscles atrophy, and our spirits wither.

Any movement can be useful — stretching, walking, athletics, yoga, or aerobics. Dance is a spontaneous, natural human expression. As used in expressive grief work, dance is a highly individual, unpatterned series of movements, with or without music, that reflects the emotional life of the dancer. We are not likely to call on the discipline and formality of ballet or other highly technical steps unless they are part of our past. The dance of expressive grief work may involve either the entire body, with large, open movements, or only the hands, trunk, arms, or another part of the body. There is no need to please an audience. Each dance reflects ever-changing feelings of the moment emerging from deep within.

If you are inexperienced or self-conscious about your dancing, begin with hand dancing, done privately. Put on a favorite tape or record, preferably an instrumental piece. Lyrics tend to impose their own structure; the dancing is meant to express an intensely personal statement. Soft light, perhaps a candle in a dim room, causes moving hands to cast long, interesting shadows on the walls and ceiling. These become partners in the experience.

Begin without a preconceived notion of what you will do; simply follow the music and your own impulse, persisting long enough to rest the rational part of your mind and to permit your emotional life to take form in your movements.

Exercise *alone* has been shown to improve the condition of depressed people. In one program, patients who had been confined to the back wards of mental hospitals, some so deteriorated that they were incontinent and couldn't feed themselves, were required to participate in twice-daily exercise. Their passivity and resistance was massive—the staff had to work hard to keep them involved in the program. But the patients were kept active until they were sweating and their respiration and heart rates increased.

After two weeks there was marked improvement. They looked and felt better physically, and almost miraculously, some began to respond to the world they had previously blanked out. They became accessible to other treatment. When the exercise program was dropped for lack of funds, the patients returned to their pathological depression.

We are different from those patients only in degree. It is when we are most apathetic that we have the greatest need for exercise—and the most resistance to it. We require physical activity to relieve our tension, get our juices flowing, and stimulate the brain chemistry that enlivens thought. One of the great inducements of extended physical exertion is what is called the "runner's high"—a euphoria produced naturally in the brain through the release of endorphins. Bestirring ourselves from our sad lethargy takes commitment. The rewards will encourage us to repeat the experience. Physical movement, appropriate to the condition of the individual, is a central element in the rituals of expressive grief work.

Certain movements and postures are natural to particular situations. When we are in love, our step is bouncy, our shoulders back, and our faces lifted upward. When we grieve, we may be literally bent over under the weight of our sorrow. Our shoulders droop, our chest caves in, our steps are slow and dragging.

I was brought up to be stoic, praised for my self-mastery and admired for my ability to carry through even under difficulties. The farce that "everthing is under control" cost me much pain and was a contributing factor in laying me up for three months with degenerative disc disease.

The profound interaction of body, emotions, and mind should not be underestimated. When we inhibit our bodies, we also inhibit our emotional range and our intellectual vigor. When we make a positive change in just one system, we are helping all of our systems. The body is a tangible place to begin. It is accessible. You may not know how to lift your depression or increase your optimism, but you can lovingly encourage yourself to move your body and to care for it well.

Expressive movement is also a way of working through and discharging experiences that are too deep, frightening, chaotic, or intimate to describe in words. When I tried hand-dancing in my room, I came to a freedom to move as I felt—not as I had been taught or thought "right"—to music and to sounds I generated myself. In my hand dance, I have cowered and threatened, shaken my fist at the sky, and dug allegorical graves.

Sometimes, in other movement activities, I've pounded a drum, and I've stamped my feet. I've crouched and jumped and rolled on the floor with my arms wrapped tightly around myself. I have spun around and around until I collapsed on a beach, sailed high on a playground swing, and skipped on a city sidewalk. I have exaggerated the rocking, holding posture of a mother comforting a hurt child—and then experienced myself as the child. I have danced in the moonlight, seeking to describe in my motions the horror of outliving my precious son. Always, *always*, I have felt the stagnant, gouging energy move out and life flow into me.

Stretching movements that loosen the spine, articulate the limbs, and free the neck make us more flexible. They are vitally important. As in many new things, we may do best with a teacher. Beware of one who demands a military rigor—the emotions of grief are powerful but not regimented. "Soft" yoga is excellent; the broad, sweeping movements of free-form dance will meet other needs. Aikido and t'ai chi are wonderful ways of experiencing the energy of "ki," or the "vital life force." Experiment with moving to your mantra, to music, and to the sounds of the forest and sea.

Sound

Snuffle, grunt, yawn, sigh, sob, gulp, cough, sneeze, hiccup, cackle, pant, whistle, smack, growl, scream, whine, wail, keen, hum, chant, groan, chortle, giggle, laugh, howl, snarl, sing, intone, whisper, cry, speak, choke, gag, retch, yell, screech, gargle, trill, praise, lament—these are words of action. In this case, each verb describes an action for the human voice. Of course, we also make personal sounds by clapping our hands, gnashing our teeth, cracking our joints, and expelling flatulence and other excretions.

Of the partial list above, which do you do freely, impulsively? Which do you inhibit? Do you stifle a yawn in company and enjoy it in private? Why? Part of becoming civilized is to learn which behaviors are and which are not "polite." We learned too well what is "correct" in the sounds we may indulge. "Don't belch at the dinner table." "Ladies keep their voices down." "Stop yelling at your sister." "Whistling girls and cackling hens always come to the same bad ends." "Be quiet around your betters."

In learning so well, we have had to deny that we even *feel* the inner stirrings. We were vehemently trained to repress our noisy, expressive sounds. Tragically, we have lost part of ourselves in the process.

In learning these "civilizing" inhibitions, we had to constrict our throats, immobilize our chests, make our breathing shallow, and block our feelings. As adults we are frightened by the emotional sound of our own voices. We stifle our groan of pleasure in lovemaking, block the scream of terror when startled, or censor our wail of profound sorrow. We have forgotten the full and natural use of breath and voice we knew as children.

As we reclaim our breath and voice, we draw air into our chest and consciously release it. Focused awareness on breath and voice vibration is a central technique in many meditative practices and can lead us to greater release in our emotional expression. Such awareness is calming, centering, and satisfying.

Breath supplies us with oxygen to fire our metabolic furnace. Just as important, it carries away the by-products of combustion. When we are in the alchemical fire, if our grief is to be transmuted to creativity, we must rid ourselves of wastes and unfinished business. The cleansing power of breath is tied to sound.

Appropriate expression in grief work discharges negative energy. As a psychotherapist, I put the utmost value on expressive sound. When a woman who is furious though inhibited can *sound* authentically angry, I know she is well advanced in her emotional work. When the sounds are accompanied by convincing expressive movement, then I know she is far along in transforming the terrible burden she has been carrying. A variety of local forms may be called upon in expressive grief work.

Keening. "A lamentation for the dead uttered in a loud wailing voice or sometimes in a wordless cry." In Ireland, China, Crete, and Mexico, and among the Eskimos, old women perform this duty to the dead— calling out the tones of misery in shrill, penetrating voices.

When my friends Bob and Zora came to my house, I knew by their faces that something was terribly wrong. My first question was, "My son or yours?" I don't know where that intuitive flash came from. When Bob said, "Patrick," everything froze for a microsecond. Then my voice filled the room with an animal wail that was utterly foreign to my experience. I had uttered the "wordless cry" and surrendered to loud keening.

Though I didn't recognize it for a long time, that was my first discharge of negative energy. I believe I would have died of horror if I hadn't wailed. Though I keened again and again, never again did I touch the raw reality of that first instinctive cry of a mother whose son had died. It (I) was primitive, uncalculated, rending. I had begun my grief process.

Weeping. "To express deep sorrow by shedding tears." I had as a client a retired Navy captain whose wife of forty-plus years had died suddenly of a heart attack. He sat looking at me tensely while complaining of depression and insomnia. Captain Holbrook had carried out all the "proper" activities. He'd arranged a good funeral, dispersed his wife's belongings to their daughters, sold the house and rented an apartment, and gone out socially. Despite this, he was losing efficiency at his new job. He did not enjoy the women clamoring for dates, had lost his fascination with golf, and "just couldn't sleep" without a tumbler of Old Bushmill's whiskey.

It finally came out that he had never shed a tear. After all, Navy captains don't cry. Not until he finally permitted his feelings of "lost aloneness" to come to consciousness could he cry. Feeling abandoned came when he recognized the little child in himself and the despair he felt at his wife's death. With his tears came anger—at God, at colleagues with living partners, at being "cheated," even at Nellie for leaving him.

The night he wept, he slept unmedicated. With more expressive grief work, he was revitalized. His life took on savor, and he became expressive in other ways. The alchemical fire had altered his perception, and he became more emotionally responsive. He remarried three years later and invited me to the wedding. I cried all through the service.

As a therapist, I'm on the alert when a bereaved client doesn't weep. The swollen eyes, runny nose, and gasping breath of hard crying vividly show the energy involved. After Patrick's death, I feared that if I began to weep I might not stop, an unrealistic concern. For several weeks I was subject to uncontrolled spasms of sadness. I called these "grief attacks." Tears would start flowing down my cheeks at work, in the bank, on the street, in a restaurant, and any time I heard Bach. I would wake up crying, and I cried in the shower.

Working with a therapist, I discovered that I had a deep well of regrets, unbestowed blessings, fears for my living children, guilt over my role in Patrick's death and the death of my husband, Joe—all of which overflowed in wordless tears. I was ready for my next step.

Lament. "Crying out in grief." The Lamentations of Jeremiah is an Old Testament text for howling aloud one's sorrow, anger, and desolation. In chapter 3, Jeremiah laments:

> I am the man that hath seen afflictions. . . .
> He hath led me, and brought me into darkness, but not into light.
> Surely [all] is against me. . . .

He turneth his hand against me all the day.
My flesh and my skin hath he made old: he hath broken my bones.
He hath builded against me, . . . [all is] gall and travail.
He hath set me in the dark places, as they that be dead of old.
He hath hedged me about, that I cannot get out: he hath made my chain heavy.
Also when I cry and shout, he shutteth out my prayer.
He hath enclosed my ways with hewn stone, he hath made my paths crooked.
He was unto me as a bear lying wait, and as a lion in secret places.
He hath turned aside my ways, and pulled me in pieces: he hath made me desolate.
He hath bent his bow, and set me as a mark for the arrow.
He hath caused the arrows of his quiver to enter into my veins.
I was a derision to all my people. . . .
He hath filled me with bitterness, he hath made me drunken with wormwood.
He hath also broken my teeth with gravel stones, he hath covered me with ashes.

There is more. Jeremiah's sense of abandonment and misery are there to read. Thousands of years later, they are the voice of the sufferer in the alchemical furnace. To me, they are familiar complaints. In time, I came to unburden myself of my grievances against my fate, my faith, my family. Expressing my laments was a powerful experience, and I recommend it in protected circumstances: with a counselor, in your journal, or with an absolutely trusted friend who won't try to dampen your expression.

Why do this? Why indulge in an orgy of self-pity, blame, and complaint? What good will it do? And doesn't lamenting work against creative visualization? How could lamenting do any real good since it summons up all that blistering suffering? Wouldn't facing so much pain destroy a person? With these and other fears, we seek to avoid the resentful, confused forces within us.

To contain our wails and complaints, we use great amounts of energy, energy that is then unavailable for creative living. We must discharge what is hurtful. We will make space for other emotions and free the energies that had been devoted to containing the pain. When we are effective in discharge, we unburden our psyche of graceless misery rather than holding it inside like a growing canker.

Sometimes people fear that they are manufacturing or being incited to perform in a way false to their own nature. Often feelings of grief are so terrifying, or their expression is so foreign, that a sense of unreality accompanies the exercises. It is my experience that only the extremely rare narcissistic person enjoys wallowing in his or her misery and wringing concessions out of those around. The majority of us are authentic when we wail out our inner turmoil. It takes courage to break through the bonds of inhibition. It is well worthwhile to begin to move the stagnant energy tied up in frozen emotions.

We *must* express our outrage, confess our sins of commission and omission, and symbolically rend our flesh and tear our hair if we are to empty out the foulness and abandonment we feel.

We must choose our time, place, and companions well, as we "empty out" such emotions. If we deny these feelings, they become like sea worms boring through the wooded hull of a boat. In their silent action, they can destroy us.

We had best begin our lamentations with a clear affirmation that we will complete our old business as a result of expressing these negative emotions. We accomplish several purposes. First, the energy that has been used to fend off expression will be freed to serve us better. The day after my first therapy session following Patrick's death, I was able to walk a half mile without pain. I attribute this to the release of emotional tension stored in my spine.

Second, though the process may be as unpleasant as vomiting up a bad oyster, the resultant relief will repay us many times over. By giving up bitterness—heaving it out—we cleanse ourselves. The evil potions of fear and loathing will be cleared from our system. We must take care not to ingest the poisonous feelings again; we must *visualize them gone!*

For myself, using the tools of creative projection, movement, and sound, I visualized my grievances as stones. They were in an imaginary army green backpack, many times too heavy for me. I was bowed under the weight, my stoic back nearly broken. I threw the first stone, marked "husband," and felt better. I did this work with a therapist, and by the time I had "thrown all my stones," I was exhausted with the clean fatigue of someone who has worked hard. I stood up straight again and looked toward the horizon.

To lament is to actively express difficult emotions, unreasonable ideas, and our most unlovely parts. It is to beg, bargain, and, eventually, accept life as it is presented. It is to cleanse and empty. It is necessary to do this in order to move foward through the alchemical fire.

Sighing. "Taking a deep, audible breath." To draw in a deep breath means we must make room in our lungs by expelling the stale air already there. We attempt to suppress our feelings by holding or limiting our breath. Imagine yourself in the dentist's chair, waiting to feel the pick scrape a crumbling filling. Chances are you held your breath, seeking to minimize the pain. Imagine yourself in an intersection, in a stalled Volkswagen, with a logging truck closing in on you. Chances are you held your breath. Fritz Perls, originator of Gestalt therapy, said, "Anxiety is excitement minus oxygen." It is true.

When we are first stricken by grief, our pain is overwhelming. We literally feel we cannot bear it. We must buffer ourselves and only let our feelings seep through cautiously. Though holding the breath is an unstudied attempt at self-protection, it does not serve our long-term purpose, because it stifles our energy and stops the process of grieving.

Sighing is our body's effort to obtain oxygen and express feelings. An excellent expressive grief exercise is to sigh several times with increasing intensity and with an open-throated sound. Prolong the sound until there is no more air you can push out. The relief is tremendous. Do this four or five times a day. I did (and do) mine in the shower. I feel revitalized and open afterward. Yawning is wonderful, too, if the yawner doesn't stint on the expressive tone.

Singing.   I am one of the people that Roy Blount, on Garrison Keillor's radio program "A Prairie Home Companion," called the "singing impaired." Like many of my kind, I love to sing and am shyly inhibited about doing so in public. Being able/willing to sing marked progress in my grief work. A friend, Marlin Clegg, came to my home while I was in my deepest mourning. He played and sang the Beatles' song "Let It Be"—perhaps fifty times. The song, a favorite of Patrick's, had deep meaning for me. I sang some of its wise words, and my wandering pitch was unimportant. I felt I was getting advice from my son through the moving lyrics and hymnlike melody.

In the intervening years, I have found that for many other grieving people, vocal music is wonderfully apt for expressing feelings. Singing the songs that were shared with the dead person may elicit tears or smiles. It helps heal the survivors. Singing changes moods. I maintain it is not possible to be depressed while singing "Polly Wolly Doodle All the Day" or "Feelin' Groovy." Bright rhythms, familiar words, and a bold approach can mark a definite turning point in grief work. When we choose "Here Comes the Sun" or "Amazing Grace" to serenade the freeway or to echo in the privacy of the shower, we are truly "getting better." When we risk singing with others, we are infused with their enlivened energy, fostering a lovely companionship.

Chant.   "A rhythmic, monotonous utterance or song," chanting has long been used to evoke a sense of God's presence. The splendid Gregorian chants of monastic Catholic orders have the awesome power to bring about a sense of wonder and spirituality. The resonant "Om" of Eastern religions sets up a vibration in the head and body of the chanter that flows seamlessly into a meditative state. "Shabbat Shalom" is chanted in Jewish temples every Friday night with a joyous cadence, reminding people that the day of rest and contemplation has come. Shamans the world over chant to alter and deepen their perception of the hidden world. Chanting may lead to the heightened awareness, serenity, and joy of the mystic's rapture. Chanting a mantra of your affirmation will add meaning; to use breath and sound is deeply confirming.

The blending of one's own voice with others can be a high experience. The relentless continuance of a chant taxes a person's stamina. It takes energy and commitment to chant, but chanting becomes natural once shyness is overcome. Depending on the cadence, chants may be worshipful, mournful, jubilant, or calming. To chant in nature is particularly beautiful, a meditation in itself.

Toning.   A voice that *wordlessly* slides up and down the scale, holding an interval, falling off, growing softer, then louder, is toning. The monotonous, repetitious rhythm of chanting is not present; toning is solely emotional vocal sound. Sustaining and improvising sounds means breath, consciousness, choice, and improvisation. It is, above all, an expression of emotion. A kind of emotional and spiritual clarification comes with toning, as if light is entering the soul.

All children tone, playing with sound. So do jazz musicians. No melody is needed. The voice is an instrument as much as a violin or a saxophone—it does not need a beat, tune, or words to be expressive. Strange and wonderful harmonies develop when people sound their emotional tones together.

Throughout this discussion of sound, I have emphasized the value of breath-consciousness and emotional expressiveness. Words and wordlessness each have their place in the sounds of expressive grief work. Yelling, screaming, and commanding are legitimate ways of expression; so are complaining, confronting, taunting, laughing, shouting, and praising. Do not deny yourself the wholesome healing that may be derived through the use of expressive sound.

Creative Projection and Dialogue

Creative projection is my term for a method of recognizing, understanding, managing, and exorcising repressed feelings. You saw one form of creative projection in earlier sections of the book where the instruction was to "become" a dream image or other symbol, speaking as that symbol and enacting it. Some feelings are beyond words. I may describe the blistering, scouring, scalding pain over my heart when I heard of Patrick's death—but these words are inadequate or even false compared to the intensity of my feeling. By working in clay, a medium that requires no spoken language and that is responsive to every nuance of touch, I was able to work out—and creatively project—my experience.

By discharging the stagnant energy trapped in my hurting body, I felt release, understanding, and the satisfaction of having done something almost impossibly difficult.

It may well be that all creative endeavor is some sort of projection. Certainly a tenderly prepared meal is a creative projection of the cook. Dance, painting, ceramics, music, drawing, building, poetry, gardening, massage, even mending jeans are statements about the doer. We are instructed by our own productions, especially when we can escape bullying self-judgments.

I would like to take the example of my clay work to demonstrate one way to use creative projection. Keep in mind that though I worked in clay, others might substitute a different technique that permits *spontaneous*—unstudied—expression. The mind-set needed is one of openness; there is no requirement to produce "art" or a functional, lasting product.

My moist clay responded to the subtlest of pressures, opening itself before my fingers, taking imprints from the wooden plank I worked on. Tearing off a chunk the size of a grapefruit, I made a ball, pinched out a couple of ears, modeled a nose, and pressed eye sockets in the surface. Under my hands a semblance of a face grew—it was no one I knew. I lost patience and smashed the clay into a pancake, only to have a sense of loss. I re-formed the ball, working human-proportion features on it again. The face that appeared the second time was fearsome—a monster with a witch's hook nose, sunken eyes, and snarl. I was horrified that I had made such a hideous creature.

Holding the witch, I gathered my courage to discover what part of me she represented. I had formed her out of featureless clay; she was clearly a projection of myself. What follows is an example of dialoguing. It is a verbatim sampler from my journal, six weeks after Patrick's death. I ask for tolerance at the gutter language. Katie, Stan, and Peter are my younger, surviving children.

Note, too, that in the primary psychological discipline I practice, Gestalt therapy, the word *it* can generally be changed to *I* or *me* to more closely approximate the truth. I hope this brief and incomplete explanation will make the items in parentheses more comprehensible—they were reminders to myself.

From My Journal—April 11, Evening

I've been staring at this wad of mud sitting on a paper plate on the bench for half an hour. I want to smash the damn thing—it is (I am) hideous.

ME: Christ, but you're an ugly witch—I can't believe I made you.

WITCH: You did more than make me, you *are* me.

ME: To hell with that! You're mean looking—hateful—cruel. You're like something that has possessed the clay.

WITCH: I repeat—I am you—cruel, ugly, and hateful.

ME: That pisses me off . . .

WITCH: And angry.

ME: Angry? Well maybe a little, but I'm nothing like you.

WITCH: Try it on for size, as you so glibly say to your clients.

ME: Try what?

WITCH: And stupid. You're ugly, hateful, cruel, angry, *and* stupid.

ME: (sullen): This isn't getting anywhere. I don't see any good coming of this aimless name-calling. (Turns away.) This is going nowhere—I'm going to quit this asinine dialogue.

WITCH: Good! Leave me in charge, will you? I like that—I can show up in your dreams and in any work you try to do.

ME: Look, you're not in charge. I can smash your ugly face any time I want—I can damn well *dissolve* you. You're mine . . .

WITCH: Exactly. I'm yours. You.

ME: Part of me, maybe. I hate to admit it. But, you're not all of me.

WITCH: I can twist you anytime I want—right now, for instance.

ME: Damn you! Now I'm really angry. I'm a responsible person, and I'm sick of you. (Makes threatening gesture.)

WITCH: Go ahead—what else are you angry about?

ME: I'm mad at politicians—exploiters—users—the rape of the earth—incompetent therapists . . .

WITCH: Now we're getting to it (me). Any particular incompetent therapists?

ME: God damn it! Me. If I were any good, Patrick would still be alive.

WITCH: That's grandiose. Who the hell do you think you are to be holding another person's life—even your own son's—in your control? Don't you believe any of the stuff you've been preaching about personal responsibility?

ME: Get off my back! Of course I believe it (me)—except . . .

WITCH: You don't believe you could have saved him if you were a better therapist, do you?

ME: Or better mother. (Tears.)

WITCH: Bawl if you want, but unless you face up to how righteously angry you are, I'm in charge.

ME: (taking a deep breath): I know it, I've known it all along, but *God* it (I) hurts.

WITCH: (unsympathetic): Tough. Who are you really angry at?

ME: Pat! If I had him here, I'd blister his ear! How dare he make a mockery of the years of love, the support—his own potential.

WITCH: Take his picture from the drawer and tell him.

ME: Do I have to?

WITCH: No. You can leave me in you, eating away at everything, poisoning your work, screwing up your relations with the kids. Be gutless; it (I) feeds me.

ME: I hate you. I really hate you—or me. (Takes picture out—looks at it—weeps.)

Hello, my Beamish Boy. I'm hurting over you. It's your fault I'm hurting. I'm not about to say good-bye. I keep repeating that—selling myself? I can live without you—I already have for six godawful weeks, you son of a bitch. That's funny. Makes me a bitch. I am alive, and you are ashes on the ocean.

Your memorial is in things—leatherbound books, the turquoise hippopotamus from the Met, letters and bunches of dried flowers in my memory book. Not enough, Pat, not nearly enough. Where is your diploma from Yale, the grandchildren, the books you were to write? You left me your journal—and I haven't the courage to read more than a line at a time—I see the pages and know your live hand touched them, your fine mind formed the phrases, your despair colored the sentences.

Your letter said, "Forget me, forget me." Damn you, kid! I didn't try to direct your life, and you can forget that crap in mine! I love you. I remember you. You are my boy and my pride and my shame. I didn't control your body or soul—leave mine alone. I won't be dismissed by the likes of you. Goddamn, Pat, please let this be a dream of unendurable length. Wake me up! Hold me. Laugh at me. Mock me. Enlighten me. Show me your new book.

World! I hurt! I choose to hurt—don't ask me to play myself safe and mild and cool. No. I'm rocking with pain. I'm breathing hard, my neck is straining—I hurt! I want my child. I'm screaming at you, "Give me back my child, you rotten withholders of life." You aren't listening and I'm in pain, and I won't make your life easier by quitting my pain. Don't force the platitudes of Hallmark cards and chicken soup on me. I'm better than that. I will be done with Patrick—with you, son—in my own good time. This is my statement: I will live, and in living I will commit myself to pain. My joys are mine too. Katie and Aaron are playing—she's a superb mother! Peter has outgrown another belt. Stan's earache is better, and the surf is comin' up. I am a hub—a vortex. I do know that deferring experience—whether pain or love—is foolish and not my style at all. I don't know enough—I don't know where to go to learn more. I do too know where to go to learn more—ahead!

I'm angry, Patrick Joseph-Elliott Pleskunas. Angry at you. How could you give up? Because I taught you that you belonged to yourself? What a miserable distortion. Because you despaired and didn't share—didn't ask for help—didn't come home—didn't trust. You had no right—no right at all to distort my universe and to give such a message to Katie, Stan, and Peter. Didn't your father's self-murder show you the havoc death can bring? *Why were you so angry, so hopeless, so foolish?*

It was with this journal entry that I mark the first self-directed progress in my grief work. By reclaiming the ugly, angry, stupid witch in me, I sapped her power, expressed her venom, began her exorcisim from my being.

The process of engaging in dialogue, illustrated here in my journal excerpt, is a useful way to learn the dimensions and strength of emerging parts of personality. Conscious dialogue gives voice to the varied and competing parts of ourselves. Implicit in this process is the idea that what we produce, think, feel, and intuit is *us*. The apple pie I bake or the evil witch I sculpt takes on my particular energy. They come from me. Additionally, we have a range of impulses and needs clamoring to dominate in every situation. Will I be a responsible adult trudging off to work or a happy truant escaping duty to lie in the sun on a warm spring morning? How I settle the conflict directs my day and defines my personality.

We are affected by things, people, and circumstances. It is reasonable to dialogue with them to define our positions, confirm our decisions, and test our options. Throughout the dialogue we must take care to observe which side of our brain is more active—the "logical" left side or the "emotional" right side—and to be sure that each has its say. The more real, less stagy, we become, the more insight comes from dialoguing. Our language becomes less calculated. We are less "fair" and more honest. We deliberately bare our faces, discarding our masks with the intention of changing for the better.

The dialogue with Patrick's picture *felt* as if I were talking to him. This sense of "making real" those people or objects with which we have business is important. The dialogue must wring feeling from us—must plumb our darkest depths, must flow as unguarded conversation can flow. Dialogue is a way of encountering parts of our experience hitherto hidden from us.

Creative projection is a tool to be used with art materials, dreams, sound, and movement. What we can imagine, we can use to our own ends. Dialoguing with the creations of our inner lives is a powerful way of discovering our unclaimed parts, exploring our darker sides, and working with our dreams.

Journal Work

The journal excerpts in this book were obviously not written with a reader other than myself in mind. My usual syntax and jumbled flow purposefully haven't been edited out of existence (a difficult task!). I do not share these excerpts as examples of literature or to be an emotional exhibitionist but to demonstrate the loose, personal form a journal can take.

Some journals are organized with dreams, plans, daily events, sub-personalities in neat, accessible categories. This can be useful. Ira Progoff is a pioneer in teaching people to use a personal journal, and I recommend reading his *At a Journal Workshop* for in-depth discussion.[7] My journal is like me, as yours will be like you. I mentally "change gears" very quickly and sometimes erratically. I learn primarily through my ears, and so my work *sounds* like me — at least to my ear it does. I am neither a timid nor a genteel person, and so my journal is written in the broad terms that characterize my life. Because I wasn't posing for an audience, my warts and crudity are apparent.

Poetry — that spare, evocative mystery of language that moves us beyond common prose — is a particularly fine expressive tool. In journal poetry, I have self-given permission to speak with intensity, economy, and emotion without the need to calculate the effect on a reader. The poetry in my journal was not written to share. It was written to express the essence of my feelings for the pure pleasure and relief of the process. I do not rhyme or adhere to any technical rules. I just write what I feel as cleanly as possible.

> I had a back-bending bellyful
> Before he was born.
> How he thrashed and made himself known
> Months before he appeared!
> That time is a trace memory in my womb.
>
> I had a bellyful of dirty diapers,
> Broken sleep, teething, PTA,
> Chicken pox on Christmas
> Though I've nearly forgotten it all.
>
> Now I've got a bellyful of fire.
> The coals burn my nipples and scorch my brain
> The heat chars my courage,
> Blisters my hope, incinerates belief.
> This bellyful is too much with me.

When I write, I talk to Maggie. That's my journal's name, Maggie. Somehow she — like a best friend — is always ready to listen, accept my complaints, absolve my wickedness, record my brags. She takes me as

I am and comes back for more. I keep no secrets back and conceal no reprehensible ideas. With her, I am baldly honest, sloppily sentimental, foolishly grandiose, and remarkably funny. She passes no judgments on me that I didn't think of first, and she is totally devoted to me—what a pal, what a comfort, and, strangely, what a teacher!

Maggie contains doodles, sketches, plans, and backsliding. When my life is intense, I use her frequently. I have carried her in my purse, ready to listen to a fleeting idea, record a friend's wisdom, mark an occasion of pain. I usually put my dreams into her for later work and contemplation. I like summing up my day in her pages. Sometimes I let her gather dust for days and usually regret it as I try to recall who I was day before yesterday.

She shows me, concretely, what my progress is, where I've fallen short, what my intensity was. This has been comforting. I discovered that I had most access to my anger and anxiety when I was premenstrual; that became a time of withdrawal from others and intense self-disclosure to Maggie. By studying Maggie, I learned how Patrick's Death Day Ritual (more later) evolved.

Maggie has listened longer than I could ever expect or hope another friend would tolerate my yammering "I, I, I." She is the history of my spiritual and practical evolution. Now she lives on a computer disk. Previously she's been a blank account book, a loose-leaf binder, and three-by-five cards. She's versatile and also fertile.

Thank you, Maggie.

Auditory Drawing

I balked at the notion of drawing or painting. The mystery of putting pencil to paper and producing a likeness seemed outside my capacity. "I couldn't draw a straight line," was my standing statement. Now, I look at drawing as an *expressive process* rather than a goal. I do not feel a need to draw a picture *of* something. A hard, jagged-edged scrawl expresses anger effectively; no need for a meticulous drawing. A puddle of yellow paint in the midst of feathered strokes of green may evoke spring; no need for carefully crafted daffodil portraits.

Auditory drawing is one way to evoke the images and emotions tied up in memory.[8] By *visualizing* grief being discharged in the drawing process, I was able to recall and release stagnant energy tied up in visual memory. A friend described a scene he recalled when Patrick and I were together. With eyes closed and a large paper pad before me, I allowed myself to draw with a medium-coarse marker pen. As my intuitive side took over and I concentrated on the memory as described by my friend, I made many strokes on the paper with the sole purpose of expressing my feelings. The following directions should help you start.

First, experiment with auditory drawing by working with your eyes *closed* while thinking of particular moments that you know are important for your grieving process. Keep your marker pen loosely grasped—don't overcontrol—and do make sweeping motions over the pad of large newsprint you use. Don't worry about boundaries or going off the page, it doesn't matter. A medium marker pen (color of your choice) is best because it doesn't gouge the page or lend itself to small, tightly controlled movements. Don't try to draw the objects or faces in your memory; rather, allow your intuitive process to direct your hand. Breathe deeply, and use a different page for each memory. You might have a friend read a letter to or from the person you are mourning, tell stories about him or her, or play music that you shared. Do not talk during your auditory drawing sessions.

Dream Work

The following discussion and journal examples represent my approach to working with dreams. Other therapists and theorists might differ with my understanding and procedures. Many approaches to dreams can be found. My own views are shaped largely by the ideas of Carl Jung and Fritz Perls.

Dreams are shadow visitors emerging from hidden parts of ourselves. They are projections of our unconscious and hold potent meaning. Dreams are feelings, experiences, ideas, sagas, instructions, and threats that appear to us in sleep, when we are most vulnerable, our ordinary waking reality suspended. Some rare dreams appear to be prophetic or clairvoyant, offering suggestion of events yet to occur or happening at a great distance.

Other dreams are problem-solving events. We go to sleep puzzled or blocked in our search for solutions and awaken with answers or seed ideas that can be developed productively. In a moment of madness, I once agreed to make six hundred sandwiches for a group to which I belonged. When the day of reckoning was approaching, I was in a near panic. A dream came to me of applying the egg salad and deviled ham to the bread with a clean paint roller. Desperately, I tried the idea, and it worked wonderfully well. Frivolous as this example may seem, it saved me from a dreary day, and it demonstrates the rich creative possibilities of dream time.

Other dreams hold what Freud called "day residue." We spend a day cleaning the garage or dealing with mechanics about the car, then find ourselves continuing these routine activities in sleep. It may well be that these everyday experiences are being "processed" for storage in the unconscious. Such dreams may have little significance for expressive grief work, or they may be remarkably productive. The only way to know is to try.

Some dreams are so garbled that we despair of understanding their significance, though experience has shown they may be laden with valuable teachings. What is needed are tools to decipher their messages. The discussion that follows will demonstrate some of the most useful ways I have found for dealing with such strange dreams.

With certain dreams we have a haunting and persistent feeling of importance. These dreams are "numinous." We know they connect us with a power and wisdom beyond our own. We may call this power God, the collective unconscious, or something else, but we *know* that something of significance has visited us in sleep. Again, we need tools to understand.

It appears that the third of our lives we spend in sleep may be critical to our sanity. It is certainly an enduring mystery, fraught with importance. People deprived of the opportunity to dream (not just deprived of sleep), often show symptoms of impaired psychological functioning. They sometimes become delusional and hallucinate; judgment is impaired, and behavior is unpredictable. Perhaps we must process our daily lives in dreams and store the material in our unconscious to avoid being cluttered by unassimilated material, which might make us act and feel crazy. Some cultures, such as the Native American Hopi, are guided in part by the dreams of the people, the teachings those dreams offer, and the ability to enter "dreamtime" to receive sacred instruction for waking life.

Even though some people claim they never dream, laboratory studies have established that apparently everyone dreams at frequent intervals each night. People who claim that they do not dream are probably blocking recall. Drugs, alcohol, extreme fatigue, and certain brain disturbances can suppress the capacity to dream. The irrational waking behavior associated with these conditions may be partly the consequence of dream deprivation.

It is possible to train yourself to recall dreams. There is a never-never land between sleep and waking where we float half in, half out of consciousness. This is a hypnogogic state and can be used to "plant" ideas in the unconscious. The techniques of creative visualization and self-suggestion may be utilized. Repeat over and over, as you fall asleep, "I will dream and remember tonight." Have your journal or other recording material nearby so you can record your dream as soon as you come into wakefulness. Persist. You will be touching into the most mysterious third of your life when you access your dreamtime.

For the grieving person, dreams are often vivid, frightening, evocative, and persistent. They may disrupt rest and haunt the waking hours. We know that some message is pounding on the gates of consciousness, yet we are blocked from understanding. We will do well to heed these visitors from our depths, for they may release us from misery and point a productive pathway to growth.

It is the nature of dreams to be *symbolic*. Dream images have a literal meaning—they are the boats and moonlight and bullies we have known—and they have a symbolic meaning—they also represent something else. In symbolism, one entity represents another. The flag is the symbol of the country; a wedding ring is a symbol of marriage; a dollar bill is a symbol of buying power. These ordinary symbols have consensual validation; that is, almost everyone agrees on their meaning.

There is no consensual validation on the meaning of dream symbols. Dreams cannot be properly deciphered through simplistic formulas based upon predetermined meanings for certain symbols. A black horse appearing in my dream might symbolize power and escape; in yours, it might mean misfortune and doom. Our unique personalities, experiences, and circumstances shape the personal meaning of the symbols that appear in our dreams.

No one else can interpret your dream; it is for you to decode. A skilled counselor or knowledgeable friend can offer method and perspective. Journal work and creative projection can be illuminating.

Courageously facing and learning from our dreams is one of the most effective ways to further our grief work and find direction for our lives. It is appropriate at every stage of life and in every emotional circumstance.

Earlier, I referred to Jung's concept of the "shadow" part of personality. The shadow is the powerful, dark aspect of oneself that holds all those characteristics we find unacceptable—violence, anger, revengefulness, immorality, slyness, deceit. Its messages to us are delivered directly from the unconscious and are laden with the seeds of creativity. But the aspects of the personality that are sheltered in the shadow, like my witch, can dominate our disposition and our decisions, albeit clandestinely. When we burst out with invective and rage, scarcely recognizing our own voice, our shadow is at the mike.

Once I threw a glass of cold water at a nasty child—something unthinkable when I am in my "right mind." This expression of my shadow was not my ordinary behavior. When we are weary or unguarded, as in grief, the shadow may shatter our reasonable, calm, and civilized way of behaving. Many women find their shadow bursting forth when they are premenstrual. This is an excellent time to work diligently to unlock the secrets of dreams, surprising impulses, and irrational feelings.

If we are to disarm the destructive parts of the shadow, thereby taking charge of our own energy, there is no better way than to begin to understand our dreams. It is in our dreams that the shadow stands revealed and vulnerable to the good sense and determination of the conscious mind.

Dreams instruct and warn us against our own impulses and self-sabotage. They point the way to our unfinished business—unexpressed, unintegrated anger, fear, confusion, and grief. They may, of course, be happy and confirming. Significantly, we speak of "emptying out" a dream of its symbols. With a combination of free association and creative projection, we convert the symbols to comprehensible messages.

Free association is one way to find the meaning behind dream symbols. What follows is a verbatim excerpt from my journal. I had a dream in which a spider appeared. I was puzzled—what did the spider mean to me?

> SPIDER: creepy—sinister—scary—poisonous—fangs—husband eater—murderer—suicide—Joe's suicide—husband death—fault—me—bad wife—destroyer—vengeful—unfair—not me—web weaver—beautiful—graceful—strong—productive—protective—motherly—me—bad mother—dead child—dead husband—tangled web we weave—no deceit—not mine—theirs—Joe and Pat—dead heroes—dead victims—live victims—the kids—me—all wrapped up in misery—poisoned—trapped—pointless.

Such stream of consciousness thinking, if allowed to flow verbally or on paper, can be immensely revealing, expressive, and cleansing. Any element of a dream may be used for free association. It is important to speak or write quickly without stopping to analyze, criticize, or explore. *Say or write whatever comes to mind.* We must move beyond our rehearsals. By injecting the pressure—"Keep writing!"—we give ourselves a useful structure. The time pressure also acts to suspend the critic that lives in each of us.

Dreams should be recorded immediately upon awakening. I keep a pad and felt-tip pen handy so I can grab a key image before the dream is lost to my waking consciousness. I write in considerable detail in order to have material for creative projection or free association. *Every element in a dream is a projection,* and they may all be explored. We can "become" a dust mop, an heiress, a sword, a bearded revolutionary, the sun, a dragon, a sailboat, or a Mozart sonata. If something appears in our dream, it reflects who we are. Each element has vitality of its own; even small items may be highly significant. The scarier an element is, the more energy it contains. Decoding such dreams holds great promise of self-understanding.

The following is an edited excerpt from my journal. It is not directly related to my bereavement. I chose it because it demonstrates the decoding of a very cryptic dream. It shows my use of creative projection and free association. I began by noting the date, describing the dream, and commenting upon my feelings on awakening, my main activities during the previous day, feelings I had about co-workers and a client, and my place in my menstrual cycle. *The dream was recorded first;* the detail added later. Note that most of this material is written in the first person (I, me, mine), in the present tense, and with the active voice—"I *am*." This is a convention that I use for recording dreams. It (I) feel more real and "here and now," which is important in expressive work. I clearly was not writing for an audience. I hope the dockside language does not give offense.

From My Journal—June 9

Wednesday, three days after my period, worked at Day Care Center/DS is a consummate jerk/DH has mental hemorrhoids/FI getting better—she laughed today!

Dream: I am on a tropical beach all alone. It's a picture postcard of paradise. I am dressed for work—pantyhose, heels, makeup, the works. There are no footprints on the sand except my own, and they are from these idiotic shoes I'm wearing. The heels make little wells in the sand where the seawater comes up. I look back and see a progression of little wells following me. I see something climb out of first one, then another, then all the wells—lots of things—sort of like something between a slug and a spider. Big, slimy, muscular things—they all grow or swell quickly to the size of a hen. They are everywhere behind me. Ahead the beach still looks like a "Visit Bermuda" poster.

I'm running faster and faster, leaving more and more holes behind me, from which come more and more of these horrible creatures. They don't seem interested in me, but I'm terrified that they'll want to eat me or something. I'm really afraid.

Suddenly I'm flying—I'm in a flock of Canadian geese, all honking at once. It's a wonderful sound with the wind in my ears and the whoosh of their huge wings soaring through the sky. I wonder how it is I'm with them and then discover that I'm a goose! Just as I realize this, I see hunters in a ditch, and I scream.

Woke up feeling interrupted—as if the dream had more to show me—glad to be awake—desperate to warn others—like there's something I *have* to do—lives depend on me sounding the warning. I'm scared—then disgusted thinking of those creatures. What in hell do the high heels have to do with anything? Pantyhose? I heard a guy hanged himself with his unfaithful girlfriend's pantyhose. That's the worst pantyhose story I know. Then there was the guy who got his wristwatch band caught in the crotch of—no, I'm getting silly—avoiding this dream. It (I) feels significant.

Will do a few CP's [creative projections] to see what's what:

I'm the hunter. I'm crouched in a cold pond, I've got my shotgun and ammunition, and I'm waiting in ambush for the geese. I like to kill birds. It feels good when I follow them with my barrel and then, leading a little, squeeze off a blast. If I do it right the bird and the shot get to the same place at the same time. Then that big bird just tumbles out of the sky like a bag of laundry down the cellar stairs. Yes, I'm a sportsman. I'm Death hidden in the rushes, holding a double-barreled shotgun, watching beautiful, free birds in my gun sight.

I'm a Canadian goose flying over a beautiful autumn countryside—there is a pond with room enough for our flock and the one down there near the rushes calling to us. I'm big and strong—I can beat my wings for hours, days, weeks. I'm one of many—it would be hard to tell us apart until attention is paid to our voices. I look like all the other geese, but my voice is different. We all have different voices—*I don't sound like anyone else!*

This idea was a revelation to me—I went on at length about my uniqueness. The symbol of the bird was clear—I was a unique being, even though I looked pretty undistinguished. I was part of a large flock, and we were all vulnerable to any bloodthirsty sociopath with a gun getting his sexual jollies or releasing his hostility by killing something free and beautiful.

I went on with feelings about my husband and son being wild geese too, singing special songs as they passed along. The same hunter, Depression, got them both. I reached other conclusions, but this gives an indication of the value of creative projection, at least to me.

Sometimes I find it enlightening to have two parts of my dream engage in dialogue—it's a no-holds-barred confrontation when I do. More often than not, the dream elements are antagonistic to each other at first. I "went back into" my dream to empty out the meaning of the high heels and the beach.

HIGH HEELS: I'm having a hard time doing my job. You're too mushy, Beach, I can't walk on you.

BEACH: You're making ugly marks on me, letting horrible stuff out. You hurt me. You disfigure me. Go back to the city where you belong—only bare feet should touch me. I'm Eden—unsullied, unexplained. You don't belong here.

HIGH HEELS: I wasn't meant for this! I was meant for smooth streets, carpeted rooms, elevators. If you were a ballroom, I'd be happy.

BEACH: Meanwhile, you mess me up. I was beautiful—peaceful—idyllic before you came galumping and marred me.

HIGH HEELS: If I can't use you, you're worthless.

BEACH: Typical—unless something is of immediate utility to you, you think it's worthless. You're silly—a twisted, self-defeating artifice, more an inhibition than useful.

> You're a monument to vanity. Leave me alone—you
> hurt me. I was natural, whole, graceful until you
> showed up. You're a show-off.
>
> HIGH HEELS: I make Peg's legs look long and slim. Is that so
> bad?
>
> BEACH: And torture her anatomy. *Now* look at me! Slug-
> spiders crawling out of their dens—ruining my peace
> all because you, you phony, stabbed me.
>
> HIGH HEELS: I didn't put the uglies in you, Beach, I just let them
> out.

Here I discovered that there was a conflict between my vanity, symbolized by the shoes, and the natural part of myself, symbolized by the
beach. Later I explored the uglies and found out painful but important
truths about myself. *All elements in a dream can be used for free association or creative projection.*

These demonstrations are pastel compared with the vivid experience
of engaging in dream work with a skilled therapist. Much of my most
significant work was done with my therapist's guidance; a set of objective
ears is very helpful. The journal is a refuge and a right place to keep
your dream records whether you decode them alone or with help.

Reframing

Another tool for expanding our awareness and shaping our responses
is reframing. Reframing is illustrated by the optimist who sees the glass
as half full or the pessimist who sees the hole rather than the doughnut.
One of the psychotherapist's most powerful devices when a client feels
trapped and hopeless is to reframe the situation to highlight opportunities
and foster empowerment. Like moving beyond a restrictive or outdated
personal myth, reframing breaks us out of narrow and self-limiting ways
of thinking and into a world of new possibilities. It serves particularly
well when we are in crisis.

Reframing is not denial of pain or anger; it is not a "Pollyanna"
attitude, nor is it "wallpapering over the cockroaches." It is, rather, a
technique for viewing adversity that creates an alchemical change of
energy—from despair to hope. It means seeking the best possible interpretation, searching each difficult situation for what it has to teach,
and exploring the range of conceivable options. Some people seem to
do this intuitively; for others, it is a learned skill. Joan Borysenko says,
"Using the energy that is tied up in resistance but channeling it in a
new direction is the mental equivalent of the martial arts, where subtle
shifts in balance allow the opponent's energy to be used to your own
advantage. In reframing, the opponent is often your own mind-set."[9]

In our opening section, "One Family's Experience," we saw that Rose and the senior Bennetts were emotionally and intellectually inflexible, holding on to their initial responses to the dreadful news of Dan's impending death. They were apparently unable to progress beyond their initial devastation. Rose's characteristic pattern of bewailing fate rather than demanding lessons from it, served her poorly. The elder Bennetts held to a rigid belief system that did not allow them to accommodate wisely to conditions they found intolerable. Dan did not share their vision of salvation; God had chosen to take their son unseasonably. Nothing had prepared them to open to new ideas, so as they faced this, their habitual mind-sets served to isolate them. Sadly, they froze into emotionally and intellectually rigid patterns just when the options were closing and when Dan had an urgent need for validation and intimacy.

The Bennett family (and I) were in a constant process of reframing our experiences throughout the intense period of Dan's dying. As he explained, "When I first got sick and found out how bad it was, my reaction was to be pissed off. There was so much . . . I wanted to do . . . I felt like I'd been tripped by a piano wire . . . I'd stumbled and fallen. I was really sorry for myself, sorry for Sylvia, sorry for the boys, sorry, sorry, sorry . . . So much has happened [since], that I'm sort of eager, to tell the truth, for what comes next." He compressed a lifetime of changes into four months. Necessity, in his case, was the mother of innovative reframing. Dan's transitions from matter-of-fact arrangements through bitter anger to serene acceptance of his impending death allowed him a dignified and sensitive passage from life.

Sylvia moved from anger at Dan's refusal of heroic medical intervention, to anger at the world for going on without him, to anger at God's merciless (it seemed at first) testing of the family, to a quality of acceptance that was neither resigned nor bitter. In the course of her growth, she found what was important to her: love and intimacy. In crystallizing her core values, she found an unexpected, unique purpose for her own life. She took longer than Dan to move from anguish to understanding, but then she *had* longer.

Today, Sylvia works as a pediatric nurse-practitioner and helps train volunteers for her local hospice. She speaks poignantly of the needs of the dying in terms of Dan's determined and dignified autonomy. She talks, too, of the creative possibilities of rituals for the bereaved. She has remarried, something she swore she'd never do; the pain of another loss had at one time seemed too great to risk. Brandon, the pediatrician she married, is vigorous and supportive. She says she cherishes every hour of their time together. Sylvia's life shows that creative growth is possible in passing through grief's fiery furnace.

Mike moved dramatically from his initial withdrawal and resentment to eventually approaching Dan for guidance. His reframing came hard; it took his father's heartfelt, skilled sharing and visible personal changes to open the way for him. Adolescence is a time of internal turmoil, irresolution, and questioning; when the exterior landmarks are disrupted, the youth particularly feels the reverberation internally. Dan understood this, and he directed a great deal of his effort to leaving a record that would support Mike in growing through the breach caused by his own death. Without Dan's foresight, Mike would have been in danger of feeling abandoned and unworthy, perhaps guilty, and certainly confused. In real ways, his life hung in the balance until he reframed his misery to creative ends. Today, Mike is a sports journalist featured in prestigious publications and, not accidentally, a competitive sailor of America's Cup status. He still rides for recreation and is married. He has two boys. The firstborn is named Daniel MacKenzie Bennett II.

Teddy, the youngest, is now nearly a man himself, though still living at home. He looks like a young Dan. His memory of his father is filmy, not quite reliable, but he cherishes the complete record, from which the opening section of this book was excerpted, and his rosewood bear. His work has been more in the nature of constructing a vision of the father he barely remembers; it is a good one. He had no difficulty accepting Brandon as stepdad. A picture of Dan, grinning from the deck of the *Good Times*, is prominent on his wall.

For me, the lessons were many: I enhanced my ability to value and encourage full expression, even of unlovely thoughts and feelings, and to *believe in* the transmutation of energy. Until the shadow is acknowledged, the conversion of its energy is slow and difficult. I no longer doubt human capacity to adapt, learn, and transcend. The prime teachings are to put the best possible interpretation on events, behavior, and people, as well as to search diligently for the lessons implicit in even the most devastating experiences. This does not imply that all questions can be answered or that pain is welcomed. This mind-set has served me well personally and professionally—and it is a good example of reframing.

The person who customarily finds gloom in change, challenge, or loss of control is handicapped. Often this way of structuring experience is an attempt to avoid disappointment or disillusion; the cost is living in perpetual darkness, hopelessly. The person may earlier in life have been wounded so sharply that all creative energy had to be marshaled simply to stay alive. Changing habitual negative patterns of thought and response takes work that is best learned in times of strength. The reward is parallel to that of the person who eats wholesomely, exercises regularly, laughs often, and sleeps deeply. Physical sickness comes less frequently and, when it does, is met with ready resources. When one has learned to habitually reframe potentially destructive experiences, the mechanisms are in place to grow through, rather than be crushed by, the losses in life.

To reframe is work requiring consciousness, will, and practice. The decision to change the internal focus involves becoming conscious of how one typically responds to stress, taking an unblinking look at assumptions about hope, comprehending myths that govern life choices, and knowing about characteristic ways of reacting. It also requires *will* to modify and to go beyond ordinary limits of behavior. This process takes *practice:* old habits yield reluctantly, and new ones are born of repetition. To view life's tests creatively is a decision.

Watch for the indicators—truth buttons—that reveal your way of reacting to stress. Some people tell themselves scary stories, mining events for every possible disaster. Others act tough or accepting without expressing their feelings, thereby internalizing or denying their misery. I have a tendency to "refer" my stress to my spine, stiffening it and being "brave." I carry on. Most people have some sort of physical response to emotional stress, characteristic ways of reflecting emotional disarray. When one learns what these are—brings them to consciousness—they become the signal for change. Without denying unhappiness, one can express it and empty it out. This is the first step of reframing, far from "making nice" or "putting on a good face." It is now that the mantra, affirmation, visualization, ritual, dream work, journaling, and movement have practical application. It is a time to use intellect, to search the landscape for all the possible views. One perception is not enough; creative thought is needed. *What is the best possible interpretation of the event?* Consider the players; consider the circumstances; consider the potential. Be kind (to yourself, most of all), be fanciful, if necessary, but crank consciousness from its rut and find a fresh path.

When the will to change is present, a backup plan—devised in a calm time—can be a powerful ally. It is difficult to be creative, to pull oneself out of the doldrums, when overwhelmed with stress. By planning a strategy for the inevitable hard times of life, one is prepared. The backup plan supports hope. It highlights resources and opportunities that may not be as visible in difficult circumstances. It is an exercise in reframing. Establishing a viable backup plan is seldom obvious or easy. That which awaits discovery is rarely anticipated. It must be sought diligently, the way a diamond miner burrows through tons of rubble for a single precious gem.

Recall how Sylvia came to awareness that "things are as they should be" during her vision quest, despite the pain, anger, and impotence she first felt. Her poem is worth repeating here, as an example of the possibilities implicit in unsolicited sorrow.

There is mercy in a drenching rain
Washing the dust and dog crap away,
Leaving trees and city freshly cleansed.
There is mercy in a raging storm
Ravaging the coast and removing all
The sailors' wine bottles and Twinkie wrappers.
There is mercy in the ripping, rending pain
In the agony of separation and unanswerable questions
Removing all the etiquette, false smiles, and
Untried, politic assumptions about reality,
Leaving truth and love and laughter and God in its wake.

To successfully reframe rending pain, as Sylvia so poignantly demonstrates, requires energy, determination, and practice. The alchemical change from common grief to precious creativity is accomplished not magically or mystically but through tenacious effort.

Rituals of Good-Bye

"Good-bye." How we pull back from the word, the reality! It signals the end: completion of a phase or cycle of life. Funerals, memorial services, monuments, grave markers, and condolence cards all point the way, yet most often the crucial word is left unspoken. We avoid finality. And in avoiding it, we block our alchemical changes and hobble our progress through our grief process. It is terribly hard to "go on alone," yet if we do not somehow make the break with our loved ones, then we have crippled our life without reviving them. We make a bleak testimony with our devotion.

How can we bear the pain? We must first understand the purpose of good-bye in order to reconcile ourselves to this final movement through our grief process. The use of ritual is particularly valuable in this context. Ritual is not only useful in recruiting support but in making the real passage of time and energy. The form of the ritual must be in harmony with the belief system, emotional vitality, and spiritual vision of the mourner. It often seeems that we approach the critical moment of release—we almost say the word good-bye—and then retreat with our work unfinished. I was afraid I'd forget Patrick, not understanding at first that to say good-bye is not to develop amnesia. Just as I can wave "so long" from an airport terminal to departing friends without forgetting them, so is it possible to break the bond with the one who has died without losing memory of the closeness of the relationship. Its importance in our life is not lost to fond memory. The influence of such loving ways always belongs to us.

We must affirm that the life coursing through us has purpose beyond sorrow. The alchemical changes possible in the grief process will imbue the events with meaning and confirm the preciousness of our own lives. We may become less profligate with our assets and more joyful in our experiences, difficult as it is to believe this in the beginning.

I was not a church member when Patrick died, and I felt confusion about "what to do." He had chosen to die in Carmel, California, by carbon monoxide poisoning in the car. I lived five hundred miles away in San Diego. I was at a stage in my own life when I found religious rites hollow. The following excerpts from my journal may seem harsh to those who have found comfort in conventional forms of funeral arrangements. I recognize and respect that each of us must find peace and meaning in our own characteristic style. I offer these journal excerpts as windows on my own evolution with the hope that they will provide you with useful glimpses as you manage yours.

From My Journal

I am afraid to examine the depths of my pain. . . . I am going to venture in a little further. Son-boy-man. I love you. You are memories and intellectual understanding. I won't hear any more stories about Russian countesses who speak of things as "giftedly drawn" or "splish-splash" being the sound of dripping water. Your dialect was magnificent. Your sense of the absurd and your kindness in characterizing others delights me. I remember doing dishes with you when you were small and we did intellectual games . . . "name five mountain ranges beginning with *A*." You named seven. I remember your agony at baseball season when you were humiliated by sadistic coaches and savage classmates for your inability to hit the ball. I remember your only fight . . . when you got even with the guy who punched your typhoid shot. I remember you in a coat of Brillo mail as the lead in a school play . . . *The Mouse That Roared*—you were so handsome!

I could fill pages with memories. And I want your hug. Son—son—I am weeping now—can't see the pages. I know you're gone. I don't want you gone. I don't know how many children I have—three or four? Three living—one dead. What does my eldest son do? Float as ash on the sea or make surfboards? Answer me, damn it, Pat! What limbo is this? You are, you aren't, you are. I could tear you out of me . . . I am strong enough, and I know this writing loosens our bonds. I don't want you gone. I cannot (read: will not) do the clean and beautiful thing Stan and Peter and Bulldog [a buddy] did.

Good ol' Bulldog—strong, virile, handsome, fighting hard to be a little kid and manhood coming on fast. He reminds me of a Scots chieftain—with humor. Bulldog went with Peter and Stan the night we learned of your death—your self-murder. They went surfing—the sea is a mighty ally to those wanting a fight and communion and competence and a sense of their own vitality.

And they went to Carmel. On a mountain all green like the Ireland you loved so much—with fingers of fog miles below—clear icy water hitting hard shore—in a field of grasses, rocks, and flowers they built you a cairn. Not the confining man-sized grave of ordinary men. No. A huge statement . . . in letters eight feet high of hauled stone . . .TO PAT. SUBLEJOS. *Sublejos*—a secret word. They put daisies in the hollows of the *P* and *A* of your name. In the picture that good Bulldog took, Peter is joyfully holding his dog, the wind ruffling his straw blond hair and an innocent smile on his sixteen-year-old face. The pictures are real and clear. I love my sons and Bulldog.

And I want Patrick to stride through the door, accuse me, in his inimitable way, of sentimentality and melodrama. God, how I felt his contempt for my storms and changes—how afraid I was of his evaluation . . .

Patrick is dead. Patrick Joseph-Elliott Pleskunas, twenty-three, Yale graduate, linguist, artist, teacher, writer, humorist, observer, is dead. His body, not even fit for organ donation, is ash on the sea. I resisted the memorializers, the ritualizers, the conventionalists, and did not have a "service." He would approve. I hate dead bodies propped up in satin coffins, wearing eyeglasses while sanctimonious people carry on with their minicatharsis, their mindless incantations, their pious sentiments that boil down to "Thank God it's not me." Not yet, it isn't. I feel superior. I feel honest and nauseated at traditional cant . . .

The ideas and sentiments reflected in this journal entry are as foreign to me now as if written by a stranger. There is a curious blend of denial (if I don't have a service, he can't be dead), defiance ("I feel superior"), honesty, smugness, self-indulgence, and struggle. It is an embarrassing and valuable record of who I was.

In the intervening years I have come to respect funeral ritual and ceremony as serving two vital purposes—closure and memorial. I went on for months torn between the hard-edged reality of Patrick's death and an irrational unwillingness to acknowledge it *emotionally*. Intellectually, I did all right. Closure came much later for me—when I had a ritual funeral that I will describe later. Though my journal remains my main memorial of my son, a more clearly ritualized and purposeful remembrance has grown from my later understanding of the need for wholesome acknowledgment of his central importance in my life.

Dropping handfuls of dirt on a coffin resting in a grave has a terrible finality. We will return to our warm, fragrant, noisy houses, eat meals, watch the seasons pass, buy clothes, take trips, laugh, and welcome new children into the world, while our loved one will rest in the grave, senses extinguished, knowing nothing, and no longer participating in our lives. The wrench of separation is a rending of spirit and agony beyond language. The wound, though, is clean. We can heal, given the right disposition, determination, and opportunity to do our grief work.

I now feel the wound of Patrick's death as clean, dry scar tissue. When I stretch it, as I am in this writing, or when I work with bereaved clients, I can feel the place on my psyche where I took the wound. In some ways, writing this piece hurts. But I am not obsessed—I do not think of Patrick hourly or even weekly. I am all right. By following my instincts and the teaching of wise healers, I have found my way through the same refining alchemical fire many people experience as part of their growth. I have closure at last on the misery. I do not want closure on the good parts of being Patrick's mother. It is through ritual that I am able to have memorial and release.

There are four stages I associate with the final phase of transmuting grief to creativity in expressive grief work.

First, we express the resentment and anger associated with the loss. I have discussed this in considerable length.

Second, we dredge our memories and recall the person we've lost and our associations about the person. Making a long list of "I remembers" is very useful and often primes the pump for the last two stages.

Third, we do well to express our appreciations. Speaking or listing these brings balance and gives a sense of legacy from our absent loved one.

Finally, and with much resolution, we give a benediction and say good-bye.

Saying good-bye has always been hard for me. I don't like to see a carload of friends pull away. I don't like lingering admonitions at airports or giving kisses on the forehead in hospitals. Yet good-bye is as inevitable in life as hello. When I had advanced in my grief work sufficiently, it became clear to my therapist and me that the time had come to say good-bye. I resisted, but eventually the inevitable was unavoidable.

We made a ritual of me recounting my good memories of Patrick from his conception to his death. It took a long, long time, and I felt spiritual power supporting the painful effort. Visualizing him in a chair before me, I told Patrick how much I had appreciated him—how glad I was he had been born to me. I spoke of my sadness and confusion, but my anger was spent. As I spoke, I saw him fade before me—becoming less and less substantial. I wept to lose his red-gold thatch, bright blue eyes, and rueful expression. I told him so. Still I permitted him to fade. At last, prompted by my friend-therapist, I said the momentous words:

"Good-bye, son. Goodbye, Patrick Joseph. Be good. I have to go on without you. Good-bye; I love you and will always love you—you will always be a source of pride. My heart hurts. I wish you well, wherever you go—good-bye. Good-bye. Good-bye. Go with my blessing, son—good-bye."

No words ever came harder or meant more. I had reached the final stage of grief—acceptance. I was facing an empty chair and a life with unknown potential. I was ready to live—I was nearly free of the fire. It only licks around my heels some now, mostly around anniversaries, which is why I have devised both a birth-day and death-day anniversary ritual.

My rituals are short, changeable, and informal. Other people may be more elaborate and ceremonial in their observations. For rituals to be meaningful, they must reflect the personality and needs of the people performing them. The marriage ritual of the Bantu tribal people of southern Africa would not meet the needs or match the personalities of Portland Presbyterians. Both, evolving out of vastly different cultures and beliefs, are authentic and beautiful, and both satisfy the human need to celebrate the coming together of a man and a woman.

It would be atypical of me to forget significant dates. I suppose I will always remember Patrick's birth and death dates and others from his growing up. Rather than repress these times, I have chosen to honor them and make a small ritual that satisfies a primitive need within me.

Patrick's death day, February 27, comes in a dark time of the year. I go by myself to a secluded place and light a big, fat red candle like the one he gave me for the last Christmas he lived. I remember "last" things—the last time I saw him, the last phone call, the last hug, the last letter. I weep. I sing "Let It Be" to the flickering flame, and I speak aloud of my love. This year I will add toning, which I have recently come to value, to my ritual. I will make the wordless sounds that reflect my love, regret, hope. Because I now live far from our old family home, I cannot go out and touch the bark of the loquat tree he planted. I cannot physically visit the Sunset Cliffs, where we walked and talked. I cannot gather his brothers and sister close around me and exult in their vitality. What I *can* do is visualize all this, letting the healing energy of positive remembrance flow through me. When I feel complete, I say good-bye again and blow out the candle.

December 22 was his birthday. The winter solstice—shortest day of the year. I was nineteen. He was born at home on a gray studio couch, delivered by a ruined old doctor who had sacrificed himself during the Second World War, but that's another story. Joe, his father, was twenty-one. He was there, though I can remember no comfort; instead of comfort

I got ether dripped on a gauze cone by a faceless nurse whom Dr. Eby had brought with him. I tried to be brave, like Melanie in *Gone with the Wind*. God! How young I was! How long ago! The very next December 21, Katie was born. Two untwinned babies in one year—how efficient of me.

One of my proudest motherly boasts is that neither of my Christmas-week children ever did without a birthday party or celebration. I was determined that "their" day (it alternated between the twenty-first and twenty-second in different years) be special for them.

It is my good fortune to have a precious friend, David Feinstein, who was also born on December 22—just two years before Patrick. I use the shining example of his maturation and goodness for hope. It is as if he is the living recipient and giver of the love I associate with that day. This is not to divide Katie out of my affection—she still has December 21 all to herself in my heart. David's sharing of birthdays with Patrick gives me a focus for my remembrance ritual for my son. I use David on this day, *not* as a surrogate for Patrick but as a friend who shares a memory. He is one of Nature's gifts into my life, and his birthday proves it.

I make every effort to call David on their birthday and tell him how much I love him. I tell him some of the good events of the day and past year. I feel a summing up and marking of progress. We joke and share the emerging issues in our lives. The trust between us is total—we do not pull back from hard truths or bitter choices. Mostly, we take stock of the year with a positive emphasis. After the call, I go out into the forest. Though I seldom walked in the woods with Patrick, the times I did were memorable. I spend the time going through the happy moments of his life. I rarely weep. I give thanks that he lived, that he had successes, pleasures, loves, and appreciation. I assure myself that his short life was meaningful, that he is remembered positively. This book is part of his memorial, making something that may be useful to others out of the unwanted experience of his death.

This year I will begin, at least, to give his things away. I have many boxes of old books—textbooks and art books, mostly. I have ceramic pieces he made and other precious things. It seems time to give Katie, Stan, and Peter part of this legacy. I will do it with a sense of ritual, honoring my son and honoring life. A birthday is meant to be happy, and I propose to keep it that way. Patrick will always be twenty-three—he will not change. I will remember the fat legs he had as a toddler, the practical jokes of his grade-school years, his singing "God Rest Ye Merry Gentlemen" outside the Unicorn Theater in San Diego, where he had treated us all to *The Wizard of Oz*. When I come in from the forest, I will feel satisfied that he still has a special day set aside for pleasure and marking growth. And I have planted a candle-red rhododendron at my new home in his memory. Beneath it are buried his books, feeding the roots.

Because ritual making is a deep, intuitive human impulse, it can be channeled to support expressive grief work, to give memorial and bring closure. It is a living link with the good energy for the dear departed. Give yourself a wholesome ritual of remembrance—you will feel confirmed in the value of life.

Chaos to Creativity: An Opportunity for Spiritual Awakening

Chaos is the confusion that precedes creation. It was out of chaos, we are told, that God created the cosmos. On the human scale, we experience chaos when our landmarks, traditions, beliefs are disrupted by the threat or reality of death—our own or another's. The raw materials for creation are present, but our disorganization is so terrible that we may lack the energy or the vision to direct the process. If we have nurtured worthwhile psychological habits—affirmation, meditation, integrity, expressiveness, finding the best possible interpretations, loving relationships, and spiritual openness—these tools will serve us well in creating a life deepened and enriched by our trials. Lacking those tools, we must either learn them in the crucible of our sorrow or risk living and dying chaotically.

I think of the creativity that is transmuted from sorrow as the capacity to use experience, talent, and opportunity in ways that bring satisfaction, learning, and vitality. It is a lively process that may produce a work of art, a change in career, or a quantum leap in compassion. In its finest form, it enlightens the spirit and manifests itself as resilience, purpose, and compassion.

We will be changed, but not necessarily reduced, by the death of an intimate or by other griefs. If we honor our sorrow, not pulling away, we may hope to find our talents and viewpoint enhanced when our grief process is resolved. Our innate capacity for understanding others may deepen into empathy that can be a guide and comfort for those still in the alchemical fire. We will grow in awareness of our empowerment as we recognize our progress from chaos to creative living through our own hard work. Our values will certainly undergo alteration. One seasoned woman said of her mastectomy, a year after her son's death, "It was nothing—not after losing my son—that was *real* loss. If I hadn't experienced Greg's death, the loss of a breast would have been the end of the world for me. Now I know better."

For myself, I have grown in my capacity to forgive myself my blemishes and inadequacies, to "play my strengths," and to savor everything good or stimulating that comes my way. What was precious has become more dear, and what is foolish has, to some extent, been dropped. This is part of my own ongoing refinement.

That I am incomplete, immature, and flawed is unmistakable, but I do not imagine my worst traits following me, unaltered, to my grave. During the past decade and a half, I have come to believe that change is inevitable and that I have the responsibility and opportunity to direct much of that change. I am, in Carl Rogers's memorable use of the term, "becoming."[10] I am becoming more complete, more mature, more in touch with the Infinite as I live. This is my self-defined purpose in life. It is my affirmation and my mantra.

Resurging vitality, desire to be of service, capacity to enjoy, willingness to commit to and receive from others, delight and fun, enjoyment of nature, ability to plan and persevere, and a clear sense of purpose in living—all these are the signs to watch for in charting your progress through the alchemical flames of grief. Each step in refining creative living from the chaos of misery is to be celebrated as it occurs. We are marvelously resilient organisms.

We have virtually unlimited avenues for our expressive work. We have our bodies with all our vital sensory gifts—movement, touch, sound, and vision. We have our innate intelligence and our ability to study, to gain understanding, and to seek wisdom. We have our emotions—ranging from apathy and alienation to excitement, love, and rapture. We have our deep connection with the infinite or divine, however we conceive it to be. We are equipped to live, learn, and evolve.

If we choose to break free of our stagnant energy, to cultivate hope rather than live with dreary images, we have passed a critical test for moving on in our lives to greater creativity, fulfillment, and spiritual awareness.

The choice is mine. And yours. Blessings.

Notes

Foreword

1. Herman Feifel, "Death," in *Taboo Topics*, ed. Norman L. Faberow (New York: Atherton Press, 1963), 8–21.
2. Elisabeth Kübler-Ross, *On Death and Dying* (New York: Macmillan, 1969).
3. Elisabeth Kübler-Ross, *Death: The Final Stage of Growth* (Englewood Cliffs, NJ: Prentice-Hall, 1975), 1.
4. Mary Chadwick, "Notes upon the Fear of Death," in *Death: Interpretations*, ed. H. M. Ruitenbeek (New York: Delta, 1969).
5. Stephen Levine, *Who Dies? An Investigation of Conscious Living and Dying* (Garden City, NY: Doubleday, 1982), 5.
6. Levine, 5.
7. Stanislav Grof and Christina Grof, *Beyond Death: The Gates of Consciousness* (New York: Thames & Hudson, 1980).
8. Timothy Leary, Ralph Metzner, and Richard Alpert, *The Psychedelic Experience: A Manual Based on the Tibetan Book of the Dead* (New Hyde Park, NY: University Books, 1964).
9. E. J. Gold, *American Book of the Dead*, rev. ed. (United States: Doneve Designs, 1978).

Preface

1. David Feinstein, "Personal Mythology as a Paradigm for a Holistic Public Psychology," *American Journal of Orthopsychiatry* 49 (1979): 188–217; David Feinstein and Stanley Krippner, *Personal Mythology: The Psychology of Your Evolving Self* (Los Angeles: J. P. Tarcher, 1988).
2. David Feinstein, "Conflict over Childbearing and Tumors of the Female Reproductive System: Symbolism in Disease," *Somatics* 4 (1982): 35–41; David Feinstein, "Psychological Interventions in the Treatment of Cancer," *Clinical Psychology Review* 3 (1983): 1–14.

Part Two

1. Edward Hoffman, *The Right to Be Human: A Biography of Abraham Maslow* (Los Angeles, J. P. Tarcher, 1988), 325.
2. from Nanci Shandera, "Midwifing Death: An Alternative Method of Working with Death and Dying," *Shaman's Drum* 14 (1988): 21.
3. Irvin D. Yalom, *Existential Psychotherapy* (New York: Basic Books, 1980).
4. Ernest Becker, *The Denial of Death* (New York: Free Press, 1973).
5. Marcel Proust, *Remembrance of Things Past* (New York: Random House, 1982).
6. after Joseph Campbell, *The Power of Myth* (New York: Doubleday, 1988).
7. Jules Henry, *Culture Against Man* (New York: Random House, 1963).
8. For further discussion of the mythological predicament of the contemporary individual, see the epilogue of Feinstein and Krippner's *Personal Mythology*.
9. Kübler-Ross, *Death*, 2.
10. Roger Woolger, *Other Lives, Other Selves: A Jungian Psychotherapist Discovers Past Lives* (New York: Doubleday, 1987), 12.
11. Stephen Levine's books *Who Dies, Meetings at the Edge*, and *Healing into Life* are heartily recommended.
12. Feinstein and Krippner, *Personal Mythology*.

13. Raymond A. Moody, *Life After Life* (New York: Bantam, 1976); Kenneth Ring, *Heading Toward Omega: In Search of the Meaning of the Near-Death Experience* (New York: Morrow, 1984).
14. Grof and Grof, *Beyond Death,* 6.
15. David Feinstein, "Mythologies of Death and Their Evolution," *What Survives? The Prospect of Life After Death,* ed. Gary Doore (Los Angeles: J. P. Tarcher, 1990).
16. Becker, *Denial of Death,* 19–20.
17. See Yalom, *Existential Psychotherapy,* for further discussion of these existential issues.
18. Yalom (*Existential Psychotherapy*) offers a brilliant synthesis of many of the most profound thinkers regarding death, illuminated by reports of his own innovative work in helping people face their mortality. His theoretical framework was a constant reference point in writing this section of the book.
19. Yalom, *Existential Psychotherapy,* 91.
20. Yalom, 111.
21. Yalom, 27.
22. Yalom, 163.
23. Yalom, 165.
24. Ken Wilber, *Up from Eden: A Transpersonal View of Human Evolution* (Garden City, NY: Doubleday, 1981), x.
25. Robert Jay Lifton, *The Broken Connection: On Death and the Continuity of Life* (New York: Basic Books, 1983), 35.
26. Lifton, 21.
27. Lifton, 20.
28. Lifton, 24–25.
29. William James, *Varieties of Religious Experience* (1902; reprint, New York: Crowell-Collier, 1961), 332.
30. Yalom, *Existential Psychotherapy,* 188.
31. Yalom, 196.
32. Yalom, 43.
33. Yalom, 189–90.
34. Yalom, 212.
35. Yalom, 212.
36. Yalom, 212.
37. Yalom, 159–87.
38. Here we are speaking of the atheistic form of existentialism represented by writers such as Jean-Paul Sartre.
39. Fritjof Capra, *The Turning Point: Science, Society and the Rising Culture* (New York: Bantam, 1982); Roger N. Walsh and Frances Vaughan, eds., *Beyond Ego: Transpersonal Dimensions in Psychology* (Los Angeles: J. P. Tarcher, 1980).
40. Ernest Becker, *Escape from Evil* (New York: Free Press, 1975), 31.
41. Wilber, *Up from Eden,* 99.
42. Wilber, 98.
43. Wilber, 13.
44. Aldous Huxley, *The Perennial Philosophy* (New York: Harper & Row, 1970), vii.
45. Huxley, viii.
46. Abraham H. Maslow, *Religions, Values, and Peak Experiences* (Columbus: Ohio State Univ. Press, 1964).
47. Grof and Grof, *Beyond Death,* 22.
48. Grof and Grof, 6–7 and 22–23.
49. Various "vision quest" experiences and workshops on shamanic practices are regularly announced in periodicals such as *Shaman's Drum: A Journal of Experiential Shamanism* (PO Box 16507, North Hollywood, CA 91615); *Yoga Journal: The Magazine for Conscious Living* (PO Box 6076, Syracuse, NY 13217); and *Magical Blend* (PO Box 11303, San Francisco, CA 94101). Organizations such as the School of Lost Borders (Box 55, Big Pine, CA 93515) and the Foun-

dation for Shamanic Studies (Box 670, Belden Station, Norwalk, CT 06852) may be contacted directly. Books that present powerful psychospiritual techniques for facilitating experiences that may resemble traditional death-rebirth rites include Michael Harner's *The Way of the Shaman* (San Francisco: Harper & Row, 1980) and Stanislav Grof's *The Adventure of Self-Discovery* (Albany: State Univ. of New York Press, 1988).

50. Ring, *Heading Toward Omega.*

51. Philip Shaver, "Consciousness Without the Body," review of *Flight of Mind: A Psychological Study of the Out-of-Body Experience* and *Heading Toward Omega: In Search of the Meaning of the Near-Death Experience, Contemporary Psychology* 31 (1986): 646.

52. Woleger, *Other Lives, Other Selves.*

53. Ian Stevenson, *Children Who Remember Past Lives* (Charlottesville: Univ. Press of Virginia, 1987).

54. Shaver, "Consciousness Without the Body," 647.

55. Levine, *Who Dies?* 200.

56. Levine, 27.

57. Levine, 26.

58. Levine, 26.

59. William Irwin Thompson, *Passages About Earth: An Exploration of the New Planetary Culture* (New York: Harper & Row, 1974), 174.

60. These practices were perceptively explained by Rabbi Aryeh Hirshfield of Ashland, Oregon, and his insights are gratefully acknowledged.

61. Many of these issues are raised in a valuable little book by Danielle Light called *Remembering Me: A Journal for You and Your Loved Ones* (available for $9.95 postpaid from Mt. Shasta Publications, PO Box 436, Mt. Shasta, CA 96067).

62. Sir Edwin Arnold, *The Light of Asia* (1879; reprint, Wheaton, IL: Quest Books, 1969).

Part Three

1. Shakti Gawain, *Creative Visualization* (New York: Bantam, 1982).

2. Joan Borysenko with Larry Rothstein, *Minding the Body, Mending the Mind* (New York: Bantam, 1988), 36.

3. Herbert Benson, *The Relaxation Response* (New York: Morrow, 1975).

4. Lawrence LeShan, *How to Meditate: A Guide to Self-Discovery* (New York: Bantam, 1984).

5. Joseph Goldstein and Jack Kornfield, *Seeking the Heart of Wisdom: The Path of Insight Meditation* (Boston: Shambhala, 1987).

6. Thich Nhat Hanh, *The Miracle of Mindfulness: A Manual on Meditation* (Boston: Beacon, 1976).

7. Ira Progoff, *At a Journal Workshop: The Basic Text and Guide for Using the Intensive Journal* (New York: Dialogue House Library, 1975).

8. Auditory drawing, in a slightly different form than described here, was developed by Sister Miriam Murphy of the Sisters of the Holy Names, Marylhurst, Oregon, and was taught to me by Dorothy Matthews of Philomath, Oregon.

9. Borysenko, *Minding the Body,* 141.

10. Carl R. Rogers, *On Becoming a Person* (Boston: Houghton Mifflin, 1961).

Suggested Reading

Adler, C. S., Stanford, G., and Adler, S. M., eds. *We Are But a Moment's Sunlight: Understanding Death*. New York: Pocket Books, 1976.

Becker. E. *The Denial of Death*. New York: Free Press, 1973.

Bugental, J. F. T. "Confronting the Existential Meaning of 'My Death' through Group Exercises." *Interpersonal Development* 4 (1974): 148–63.

Carlson, Lisa. *Caring for Your Own Dead*. Hinesburg, VT: Upper Access, 1987.

Cutter, F. *Coming to Terms with Death*. Chicago: Nelson-Hall, 1974.

Doore, G., ed., *What Survives? The Prospect of Life After Death*. Los Angeles: J. P. Tarcher, 1990.

Ettinger, R. W. C. *The Prospect of Immortality*. Garden City, NY: Doubleday, 1964.

Feifel, H. *New Meanings of Death*. New York: McGraw-Hill, 1977.

Feinstein, D. "Psychological Interventions in the Treatment of Cancer." *Clinical Psychology Review* 3 (1983): 1–14.

Feinstein, D., and Krippner, S. *Personal Mythology: The Psychology of Your Evolving Self*. Los Angeles: J. P. Tarcher, 1988.

Fortunato, J. E. *AIDS: The Spiritual Dilemma*. San Francisco: Harper & Row, 1987.

Gold, E. J. *American Book of the Dead*. Rev. ed. United States: Doneve Designs, 1978.

Goldstein, J., and Kornfield, J. *Seeking the Heart of Wisdom: The Path of Insight Meditation*. Boston: Shambhala, 1987.

Greyson, B. "Near-Death Experiences and Attempted Suicide." *Suicide and Life-Threatening Behavior* 11 (1981): 17–21.

Grof, S., and Grof, C. *Beyond Death*. New York: Thames & Hudson, 1980.

Grof, S., and Halifax, J. *The Human Encounter with Death*. New York, E. P. Dutton, 1977.

James, J. W. *Grief Recovery Handbook*. New York: Harper & Row, 1988.

Kapleau, P. *The Wheel of Life and Death: A Practical and Spiritual Guide*. Garden City, NY: Doubleday, 1989.

Kreis, B., and Pattie, A. *Up from Grief: Patterns of Recovery*. San Francisco: Harper & Row, 1969.

Kübler-Ross, E. *On Death and Dying*. New York: Macmillan, 1969.

——. *Death: The Final Stage of Growth*. Englewood Cliffs, NJ: Prentice-Hall, 1975.

——. *Working It Through: An Elisabeth Kübler-Ross Workshop on Life, Death and Transcendence*. New York: Macmillan, 1982.

LeShan, L. *Cancer as a Turning Point: A Handbook for People with Cancer*. New York: E. P. Dutton, 1989.

Levine, S. *Who Dies? An Investigation of Conscious Living and Conscious Dying*. Garden City, NY: Doubleday, 1982.

——. *Meetings at the Edge*. Garden City, NY: Doubleday, 1984.

——. *Healing into Life and Death*. Garden City, NY: Doubleday, 1987.

Lifton, R. J. *The Broken Connection: On Death and the Continuity of Life*. New York: Basic Books, 1983.

Light, D. *Remembering Me: A Journal for You and Your Loved Ones*. Mt. Shasta, CA: Mt. Shasta Publications, 1986.

Moody, R. A. *Life After Life*. New York: Bantam, 1976.

——. *The Light Beyond*. New York: Bantam, 1989.

Ring, K. *Heading Toward Omega: In Search of the Meaning of Near-Death Experiences*. New York: Morrow, 1984.

Rowe, D. *The Construction of Life and Death*. New York: John Wiley & Sons, 1982.

Ruitenbeek, H. M., ed. *Death: Interpretations.* New York: Delta, 1969.

Schneidman, E. *Voices of Death.* New York: Harper & Row, 1980.
Simpson, M. A. *The Facts of Death: A Complete Guide for Being Prepared.* Englewood Cliffs, NJ: Prentice-Hall, 1979.
Stevenson, I. *Children Who Remember Past Lives.* Charlottesville: Univ. Press of Virginia, 1987.

Tatelbaum, J. *The Courage to Grieve.* New York: Harper & Row, 1980.
Tilleraas, P. *The Color of Light: Meditations for All of Us Living with AIDS.* San Francisco: Harper & Row, 1988.

Viorst, J. *Necessary Losses.* New York: Fawcett Gold Medal, 1986.

van der Hart, O. *Rituals in Psychotherapy: Transition and Continuity.* New York: Irvington, 1983.
van der Hart, O., ed. *Coping with Loss: The Therapeutic Use of Leave-Taking Rituals.* New York: Irvington, 1988.

Wass, H., Berardo, F. M., and Neimeyer, R. A., eds. *Dying: Facing the Facts.* 2d ed. Washington, D.C.: Hemisphere/ Harper & Row, 1988.
White, J. *A Practical Guide to Death and Dying.* Wheaton, IL: Quest Books, 1988.
Woolger, R. *Other Lives, Other Selves: A Jungian Psychotherapist Discovers Past Lives.* New York: Doubleday, 1987.

Yalom, I. D. *Existential Psychotherapy.* New York: Basic Books, 1980.

Index